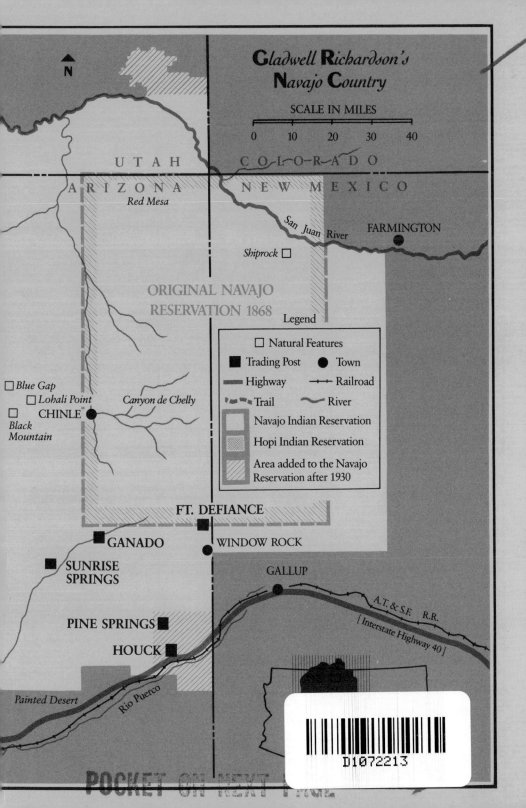

Gladwell Richardson's Navajo Country

SCALE IN MILES

0   10   20   30   40

UTAH   COLORADO

ARIZONA   NEW MEXICO

Red Mesa

San Juan River   FARMINGTON

Shiprock ☐

ORIGINAL NAVAJO
RESERVATION 1868

Legend

☐ Natural Features
■ Trading Post   ● Town
━━ Highway   ┽┽ Railroad
▸▸▸ Trail   ∿ River
☐ Navajo Indian Reservation
▦ Hopi Indian Reservation
▨ Area added to the Navajo
Reservation after 1930

☐ *Blue Gap*
☐ *Lohali Point*   *Canyon de Chelly*
☐ **CHINLE** ●
*Black
Mountain*

FT. DEFIANCE ■

■ **GANADO**   ● WINDOW ROCK

■ **SUNRISE
SPRINGS**

● GALLUP

PINE SPRINGS ■   A.T. & S.F. R.R.
[Interstate Highway 40]

HOUCK ■

Painted Desert   *Rio Puerco*

D1072213

POCKET ON NEXT PAGE

Navajo Trader

Gladwell "Toney" Richardson
c. 1939.

NAVAJO TRADER

by **G**ladwell **R**ichardson

Edited by Philip Reed Rulon

Foreword by Barry Goldwater

The **U**niversity of **A**rizona **P**ress
Tucson

Gladwell "Toney" Richardson

was a member of a prominent trading family in northern Arizona. His great-uncles came west and began trading with the Navajos in the late 1870s. Richardson arrived on the reservation in 1918 and spent the next forty years as a trader. Before his death in 1980, he also published hundreds of short stories, historical articles, and novels about the closing of the American frontier.

Philip Reed Rulon

Director of Research, Center for Excellence in Education at Northern Arizona University, has written on Southwestern biography for over twenty years and is noted for his work on L. B. Johnson and U.S. national and international education policy. He joined the history department at Northern Arizona University in 1967 and is a frequent contributor to scholarly journals.

All photographs in this book were taken by Gladwell Richardson and are used courtesy of Millicent Richardson and the Richardson Collection, Northern Arizona Pioneers' Historical Society, Northern Arizona University.

The University of Arizona Press
Tucson

This book was set in Linotron Sabon types and Cochin Italic with Peignot caps.
Manufactured in the U.S.A.

Library of Congress Cataloging in Publication Data

Richardson, Gladwell.
Navajo trader.

Bibliography: p.
Includes index.
1. Navajo Indians.   2. Richardson, Gladwell.
3. Arizona—Biography.   4. Navajo Indians—
Trading posts.   5. Indians of North America—
Arizona—Trading posts.   I. Rulon, Philip Reed.
II. Title.
E99.N3R53   1986   979.1'00497   [B]   86-11443
ISBN 0-8165-0963-8 (alk. paper)

To the memory of my mother
Susan **A**nnabelle **M**eador **R**ichardson
one of the first white women to pioneer
the Navajo Mountain country

Contents

Illustrations

Illustrations

MAP

Foreword

From as far back as 1878, when Lorenzo Hubbell, the first trader at Ganado, journeyed out from the East to that isolated post on the Navajo Reservation, traders and their trading posts have been the primary contact between Indians and whites. The traders exchanged merchandise and food that the Indians wanted for rugs, jewelry, and other handicrafts. The first trade items were coffee, salt, and sugar. Later on, the Indians became interested in vegetables, other food items, clothing, and kerosene. The trading posts themselves slowly changed from places with dirt floors to modern stores almost like supermarkets.

The Richardson family, important to me, was of major significance in the history of Arizona trading. The first time I met any of the Richardsons was in the early 1920s, when I drove to Cameron, on the way to Tuba City, and over to the Hopi villages to watch a snake dance. Hubert Richardson, an uncle of the author of this book, built the Cameron Trading Post in 1916. By 1986 that small post, with its handful of tents and huts, had become a substantial community serving the approaches to the Grand Canyon, Page, Lake Powell, the road to Tuba City, and on up to Monument Valley.

It was the Richardson family whose fortitude and perseverance made possible the establishment of Rainbow Lodge and Trading Post, in which I acquired a share in connection with Hubert's son, Jack Richardson, and brother-in-law, Bill Wilson. The fifth chapter in this book describes in wonderful, close detail the construction of the Rainbow Trail road. Certainly it is a challenge to convey in words the experience of driving that torturous trail as it was in those days. No one ever dared to drive it at night for fear of winding up in the bottom of a canyon.

The role of the Navajo trader in the lives of the Indians was, most of the time, fundamental and many times humane. Whether providing whiteman's medicine or an understanding ear, he tended to be there when needed. Traders developed the pawn to enable Indians to buy things they needed without cash by leaving their jewelry with the trader. This pawn had a very strong meaning for the trader—he would rarely sell any of it to anyone; in fact, I know of no trader in those early days who ever did that. Traders even buried the dead of the Navajos on many occasions. Because of belief in a malevolent spirit surrounding the dead during a four-day period, the Indians would often ask the traders to perform the burial. Several times in my life I participated—knocking out the west wall of a hogan, removing the body, and depositing it in a grave along with that person's earthly possessions, jewelry, fine saddles, and all.

The traders were often kind and generous people, and they are fun to remember. I will never forget one trader named McSparron who lived at Chinle. Every New Year's Eve, McSparron would shoot an arrow into the ceiling of his house so he could count the arrows and find out how many years he had lived there. Many traders were not only gracious and generous, but had an attitude toward living that enabled them and the Indian people to trust each other.

Being part of the trading-post life will stay with me always. I know that Gladwell Richardson's book, telling so much about the traders' lives, full of color and adventure, will be treasured by people who have known that life and by those who, until now, could only imagine it.

BARRY GOLDWATER

Preface

Americans never cease to be fascinated by the hold that stories of the Great West have on the European imagination. Not just a product of radio, films, and television, this phenomenon goes back to the tales of James Fenimore Cooper and to the appeal of the "noble savage" in eighteenth-century France. Gladwell Grady "Toney" Richardson,* the narrator of *Navajo Trader,* was one of the most prolific writers in the first half of the twentieth century about the American Southwest, range adventures, and Indians. His voluminous literary output, mostly published in magazines, achieved book production in England. Many novels were subsequently translated into Polish, Czechoslovakian, German, Spanish, Dutch, and Scandinavian languages for consumption on the continent. Ironically, Richardson had only one clothbound manuscript published in the United States—some forty years along in his writing career.

Although Toney was born in Texas, his ancestors were Arizonans—a veritable dynasty of traders to the Navajos with a history of succession from uncle to nephew for four generations until it came to Toney, who followed his father, S. I. Richardson, to the trading posts in northern Arizona in 1918. Fascinated with the closing of the frontier, Richardson is estimated to have published about three hundred novels and perhaps as many as a thousand short stories and historical articles during his lifetime. The short works were printed in a wide variety of local, state, and national journals and magazines in the U.S. Most of the books were published in London for marketing in the British Isles and eastern and western Europe.

Richardson, so as not to saturate the market for which he wrote, employed a number of *noms de plume,* including Maurice Kildare (his most famous pseudonym), John R. Winslowe, John Winslowe, Calico Jones, Ormand Clarkson, George Blacksnake, Cary James, Frank Warner, Laramie Colson, Warren O'Riley, Buck Coleman, Grant Maxwell, Charles

---

*Richardson was called "Toney" (high-toned or fashionable) by his friends because of the colorful garb he wore.

McAdams, I. M. Ford, Toney Richardson, Tony Richardson, and, probably, also John S. Haines, Pete Kent, Don Teton, Stuart Flagg, Jeff Corner,
Frank Parker, and Rocky Benton. Sometimes Toney selected these names
himself; on other occasions, a publisher bought manuscripts from a number of different authors and printed them under the anonymity of *one* fic-
titious identity—stock names, so to speak. The writers, including Richardson,
did not like this procedure; however, as a general rule they did not make
enough money to make demands on the houses they served.

The Robert Thomas Hardy Agency in New York City sold many of
Toney's short stories to magazine publishers, but Richardson was not able
to sell book manuscripts in the United States. Fortunately, however, Hardy
also represented an English publishing firm, Curtiss Brown Limited, and
the English-language foreign rights (except Canada) to his books were sold
in great quantities. On the average Toney received from two hundred fifty
to three hundred fifty dollars per book.

It is difficult to determine whether it was a mistake for Toney to get so
deeply involved with Curtiss Brown and, later, with Ward Lock. In selling
the books to English publishing houses, Richardson had to take a flat fee
as opposed to royalties, for the latter option would have meant that he
had to pay twenty-five percent of the royalties to the British government in
taxes. And, on the other hand, American publishers lost interest in publishing his books because they lost potential income by not being able to
sell the international rights themselves.

Paul Sweitzer, a lifelong friend, on Richardson's death on June 14, 1980,
estimated that Toney had published in the realm of sixty million words.
(He also left a number of unpublished manuscripts, such as "Navajo Trader,"
"Turquoise Woman," and "The Life Of Henry Plummer.") It is possible
that the ongoing research into the life of Richardson may one day reveal
that he was the most prolific author of his age. In preparing this book, and
in his other literary efforts as well, Toney was assisted by his wife, Millie,
who was his personal editor and typist.

Millicent Margaret Green, the daughter of George E. and Maryann Davis
Green, met her husband in Modesto, California; they were married in June
1925 and spent the next fifty-five years together. Their first daughter, Cecile, was born on March 1, 1926, and their second, Toni, on January 9,
1939. Millie survived her husband and lived in the family home in Flagstaff until 1983, when she moved to Augusta, Montana, to be near her
two children, Cecile and Toni, and their families.

Preface

Gladwell Richardson was born on September 4, 1903, in Alvarado, Texas. He divided his childhood between Oklahoma and Arizona. Largely self-taught, Richardson did attend two institutions of higher education. He entered Oklahoma Agricultural and Mechanical College (now Oklahoma State University in Stillwater) on September 5, 1919, enrolling in math, English, drawing, woodwork, physical education, and military science. He had better than an eighty average his first semester and did slightly better the second, but he did not return the next year, even though he had been offered a scholarship to come back. In 1924 he registered for classes at the Northern Arizona Normal School (now Northern Arizona University in Flagstaff), but he left shortly thereafter.

In the fall of 1918 Toney went to Houck Trading Post, south of Window Rock and near Gallup, New Mexico. He worked on the reservation until 1920, when he journeyed to San Francisco to join the Marines. He was in uniform only a few months when the chaplain of his unit discovered that Toney was only seventeen and recommended that the boy be discharged. (S. I. Richardson, Toney's father, had written to the chaplain to convey the information on his son's age.) The younger Richardson, however, liked the military (almost as much as he loved the West), and he walked across the street and enlisted in the Navy after receiving his Marine discharge papers. This time his parents did not interfere and their son stayed on active duty with their consent until 1924. In the Navy he traveled extensively—to Guam, to Japan (where he witnessed the great earthquake of 1923), to Russia (to retrieve the dead bodies of two Americans), and to other strange and forbidding ports of call.

During World War II Richardson was recalled into military service after Pearl Harbor; this time he served in Arizona, Indiana, and the South Pacific. While in the islands, he became reacquainted with some Navajo young men that he had met at Inscription House Trading Post. These individuals later achieved fame and recognition as the fabled Navajo Code Talkers, whose Marine Corps messages could not be deciphered by the Japanese in the Pacific theatre.

When the Korean War began, Chief Journalist Richardson was on a cruise for the naval reserve; he was dispatched after a short leave directly for Seoul. Completing his tour in Korea, he spent several months in San Diego (commuting to Flagstaff on every other weekend) prior to being discharged from the regular navy.

In the winter of 1926, the year in which Cecile was born, Toney and Millie put together the writing team that would entertain and inform millions of readers around the world. One of their first purchases was an old, black Underwood typewriter. Toney worked at a cannery in Modesto, California, during the day; in the evenings and on weekends he would compose while Millie would edit and type. Their first book-length publication was sold three years later to *Complete Novel Magazine* by agent Robert Thomas Hardy.

Toney returned to Inscription House Trading Post on the Navajo Reservation in 1928, and in 1930 an annual Indian Pow-Wow was started in Flagstaff. Gladwell Richardson managed the celebration from 1935 to 1939 and was responsible for separating the rodeo from the evening dances. By 1936 seven thousand Native Americans came to the Pow-Wow, representing the following tribes: Navajo, Hopi, Apache, Supai, Papago, Yaqui, Ute, Yuma, Mojave, Kiowa, Walapai, Maricopa, Blackfoot, Cherokee, Shoshone, and Choctaw. Ten to twelve thousand people were expected for the 1937 Pow-Wow. Toney convinced a New York radio station to give play-by-play coverage, with Howard Pyle of Phoenix doing the announcing. According to a 1937 article in *Every Week Magazine,* "Public-spirited citizens, and the leadership of Toney Richardson, made the Pow-Wow a major western celebration from the years the latter was associated with it."

In 1940 Toney served as a census taker on the reservation. His familiarity with the Navajos made it possible for him to compile the most accurate population statistics to that date, and some of the events that occurred during that time are recorded in this book. In later years, whenever Toney and Millie visited their children and grandchildren in Montana, they were always alert to documents and stories en route that could be written for magazine publication. A number of trips were taken, too, to New Mexico, where Toney visited many of the Pueblo Indians, sharing with them stories of his early days in Arizona as an Indian trader. In the 1950s and 1960s Toney's literary career, including the "treasure stories" he was writing at the time, brought hundreds of visitors, telephone calls, and letters to Two Guns Trading Post and then to the last home that he and Millie bought in Flagstaff.

The garage, converted to a library, in the Richardsons' Flagstaff home held a tremendous amount of important material. Not only were the shelves filled with Toney's articles and books and the top of the shelves stacked with documents, but there were also file drawer after file drawer and large, brown, paste-board boxes in the middle of the floor. These files and boxes contained thousands of rare photographs of life on the reservation and in the military, as well as newspaper clippings about the Southwest, research notes that Toney had kept on old manuscripts and notes that he had never rewritten in narrative form, programs of the Pow-Wows held in Flagstaff, huge folders of personal correspondence with his friends and fans—all mementos of a dedicated writer who had been both a part of the Old West and a part of a disappearing breed of men who kept the West alive through stories and novels.

It was from this material that I secured a copy of "Navajo Trader," one of the few manuscripts that Toney Richardson ever rewrote. He meant for the book to be just right, for the pages that follow not only cover his own journey through life, but they also tell the dramatic story of two divergent cultures—the Navajos and the men and women who traded with them—as they met in a strange and desolate land that others had shunned. *Navajo Trader*, then, is an eye-witness account of America's last real continental frontier.

Life on the Navajo Reservation was difficult for both the traders and the Indians. The lack of communication and the difficulty of transportation meant that two groups often had to develop their own means of handling financial matters, treatment of the sick and burial of the dead, sending and receiving messages, and observing religious ceremonies. Trading posts, then—as did monasteries in the Middle Ages—served as bank, hospital, post office, school, church, restaurant, inn, tavern, and community center. Because they played such an integral part in the lives of both Navajos and traders, probably no institution in America has had a more colorful history than the trading posts covered in this narrative.

Acknowledgments

Some of the descriptions and events narrated in this book appeared, in earlier versions, in popular American periodicals. Although all sections have been substantially revised, I would like to acknowledge the cooperation of the following individuals and sources: Paul Schott (*Arizona Days and Ways*); Mrs. Cecil Wells (*Science Southwest*); Ed Doherty (*Real West*); St. George Phil Cooke III (The Press of the Territorian, Santa Fe); Don Dedera and Richard Stahl (*Arizona Highways*); Marion Stevens (*The West*); Stanley Weston (*Golden West*); Joe Small (*True West* and *Frontier Times*); *Desert Magazine; Big West; Adventure;* and Jim Dullenty (*Old West* and *True West*).

Many people have assisted in beginning the process of obtaining some of the recognition Gladwell Grady Richardson so richly deserves, includ-

P*reface*

ing Platt Cline, Flagstaff newspaper man and friend of Toney's for more than forty years; friend and writer Paul Sweitzer; Bonnie Greer, who is cataloging much of the Richardson material for preservation by the Pioneer Historical Society; Pamela Mendoza, Vincent Biles, and Wanda Warner, valued research assistants to the editor; Mrs. Nancy Warden, who performed volunteer bibliographic work; June Koelker of the Arizona Research Information Center in Tucson; Katharine Bartlett and Mary Jansen of the Museum of Northern Arizona Research Center Library; Elma Peterson and Jean Lewis of the Flagstaff Public Library; and Luther Diehl and others from the Northern Arizona University libraries. Gayle Tyler and Marge Maston ably assisted with manuscript production. Martha Blue, a talented writer herself, advised the editor on several matters. Cynthia Leach, Julianne Lungren, and Yvonne Kudray each contributed vital bibliographic research. Finally, my heaviest debts are owed to two delightful ladies: first, to Millicent Richardson, who is a skilled counselor, editor, researcher, and writer; and second, to Becky Staples, a talented Tucson editor who lifted more burdens from my shoulders than I should publicly admit.

It is a pleasure to extend my gratitude to all of these co-workers.

PHILIP REED RULON

Navajo Trader

Old Houck Trading Post

It proved to be a regrettable error taking rubberneck tourists to the *yei-betchai* (a Navajo healing ceremony). They had bought several expensive blankets from the trader at Houck Trading Post, and when they asked about the Navajo ceremony, he felt obligingly generous enough to tell me to take them. The Navajo woman sat in the west end of the medicine hogan near the chanters. As was customary, she appeared for treatment naked to the waist. One of the white women tittered and spoke loudly to the man sitting on the ground next to her. The visitors continued their comments concerning the patient. Three times I politely cautioned them that this happened to be the Navajos' most devout healing ceremony, asking them please not to make rude remarks.

In a pause between chants one of the few Navajos who understood English addressed Windsinger, the medicine man conducting the *yeibetchai*. He repeated the whites' coarse remarks in Navajo loud enough for every Indian present to hear. In sudden and deep embarrassment the woman pulled a shawl about her upper body; the stupid tourists had made her ceremonial nakedness obscene. Windsinger said to me in his own tongue, "Will you take your friends away, my younger brother?"

Ashamed that *billakonas* (Anglos) had acted so atrociously, I apologized to him and the people present. They were not my friends, I explained, and were there because they had asked to attend. When I informed the tourists that we had been asked to leave, they objected. My friend Frank Walker, a Navajo-Mexican, interpreted our exchange in whispers to Windsinger. Since he would support my position, it wasn't necessary to say more, and I walked out of the hogan. As I had expected, Windsinger, without raising his voice, gave the order: "Remove them." From that night on I would never again sponsor strangers at any Navajo ceremony.

Outside I waited in night shadows under the cedar trees. The tourist women appeared, considerably alarmed, followed by three white men. One wheeled abruptly to poke his fist into the face of a Navajo in the gathering crowd behind them. The sorry fight didn't last long. The Indians clobbered the visitors street-gang style, and I set off, walking the three miles to the

Dancers preparing for a Navajo healing ceremony.

trading post. The March night was cold, especially at two o'clock in the morning, and late winter snow had crystallized in muddy patches under the cedar and piñon trees.

Houck Trading Post, called *maitoh* (coyote water) by the Navajos, was built by James D. Houck in the southeastern part of the Navajo Reservation. It was known as Houck's Tanks until the Atlantic and Pacific, forerunner of the Atchison, Topeka and Santa Fe Railroad, passed close by, just north of the Rio Puerco in 1881. Jim Houck had originally carried mail as an express rider between Fort Apache and Fort Whipple. In 1874 he built the main section of the Houck post, an oblong red sandstone building put together with mud and mortar. In 1885 he disposed of his business and moved south to the Mogollon Mountains. Various traders operated the Houck post until about 1910 when my great-uncle George McAdams bought it. He enlarged the store and built a square stone dwelling nearby.

4

The Rio Puerco separated the post from the railroad depot and steel water tanks on the north side. Old Trails Highway, which later became U.S. Highway 66, followed wagon roads across northern Arizona. Crossing to the south side of the railroad at Navajo, it came on east to Houck, recrossed the Rio Puerco over a dugway, and followed the river and railroad thirty-three miles to Gallup, New Mexico.

I arrived at Houck in the fall of 1918. I had been hired only to clerk by the man who had bought the post from my great-uncle George McAdams, but almost immediately the entire business was shoved onto me. The trader's numerous in-laws, including his wife's father and mother and her two brothers with their wives and children, lived off the trader. Periodically other people arrived to stay indefinitely without bothering to ask his leave.

My working hours began before dawn, and ended at ten o'clock at night or later, when necessary. In addition, during spare time, if I had any, my job included doing all rough work around the post. The trader's wife appeared every midmorning, remaining long enough only to sort the mail brought over from the depot by a Mexican baggageman. No one else came around until the trader came over from the house. He did a considerable mail-order business in Navajo blankets, or rugs. I have been connected with only two other trading posts that had more Indian business than Houck. Almost wholly barter, it came from the surrounding area, which was thickly populated by Navajos. The buying of wool, sheep, cattle, and piñon-nuts increased enormously in each of the seasons for these items. Blankets, skins, pelts, and pawn business continued steadily all year long. The tourist trade from the highway wasn't much in those days, but business from Mexican section hands from the railroad ran heavy and came from a distance. If these workers were caught buying merchandise that was not from the railroad supply company, they were fired; hence they slipped into Houck at night to make purchases

A young Navajo woman at a healing ceremony.

5

at cheaper prices than the company store charged. This trade accounted for most of the after-sundown business.

In addition to the regular items of merchandise and supplies found in any trading post, Houck in those days had old-type Indian goods. We sold for five dollars a yard bluish black and turkey-red *bayeta* (baize cloth), indigo and cochineal for dye, and bulk seashells for decorative purposes. Silver and turquoise jewelry and manufactured dyes for blanket weaving were also standard items. The baize cloth there was the last I ever saw sold in a trading post. It had been imported from England into Mexico since Spanish Colonial times, and I mention it because most Navajo authorities have claimed that none was sold after 1880.

Houck's enormous volume of business could not have been handled by only one man except for a device then in vogue at most Indian trading posts: metal tokens or "tin money." We used aluminum dollars, halves, and quarters—good any time the recipients wanted to spend them. When buying a blanket for twenty dollars, we handed the seller that many tokens, which were stamped with the firm's name. In a pile of refuse in the storeroom I came across several brass money tokens that had been used by George McAdams. One of the most ambitious handlers of tin money in the old trading days was the famous "Don" Lorenzo Hubbell. In addition to the "bit" pieces, he coined nickels and dimes which so closely resembled real money that the government made him quit issuing them. After that, all trading tokens were made of aluminum or some other cheap metal, and in as many different shapes as possible. Finally, the government banned all tokens on the reservation; only unlicensed posts off the reservation continued their use a little longer.

My first week at Houck revealed the astonishing fact that the trader's in-laws were bullheadedly determined to break him or take over the business. He had gotten rid of one unmarried brother-in-law earlier by building another post at Pine Springs, about ten miles north of Houck, and putting him to running it.

Sometimes the job of handling freight from the depot fell to me. For my first trip, I locked up the store, but when I returned the door stood wide open and most of the in-laws were snooping around inside. After their departure, the cash register contained no currency whatever. When this happened a second time, I removed all bills and hid them. My employer soon discovered the situation; fortunately, he backed me up and thereafter he instructed me to lock all bills and all silver dollars in his desk drawer.

Every few days his in-laws had contrived all manner of excuses to get me away from the store, even for a few minutes. Now since they could find no currency anywhere, they took small change from the cash drawer and

Old Houck Trading Post, established in 1874, where Gladwell "Toney" Richardson started as an Indian trader.

began telling tales to the trader. He never mentioned a thing, but, knowing what they were doing, he would laugh at them derisively. The matter developed into a crisis one hot night at the supper table (the family all ate meals at the main house). The trader said to the arguing brother-in-law, "The kid is doing exactly what I tell him to. Does that answer your question?"

"You don't trust any of us, that's it!" the brother-in-law shouted. "Are you accusing us of taking money? You told him to hide it?"

"I sure haven't missed any lately!"

The brother-in-law leaned from his chair to go for the trader. The trader, who had only to stand to meet the onslaught, punched the man smack into the wall with a single blow. An hour later the brother-in-law's old rattletrap touring car pulled away, loaded with his wife, kids, and their forty years' gatherings.

I didn't know anything about all this because I had not been to supper that night. The next morning at dawn I cut the day's wood to fill the stove box in the restaurant kitchen. This chore had become one of mine, despite all the loafers hanging around. The trader's mother-in-law, who ran the restaurant and rented rooms to tourists, had always clearly resented my presence at the post, but I treated her courteously at all times. The poor woman did more work at Houck than all the rest put together. This time when I greeted her, she gave me a stony stare of pure hatred. Then she said to me, "I suppose you think you're real smart by causing all this trouble!"

"What trouble, ma'am?"

"Don't lie about it! The fight last night and my son having to leave here on your sneaking account!" The trader himself never mentioned the incident to me at all, but my friend Frank Walker told me about it later.

One time I had to keep the store open until two o'clock in the morning. Consequently, I didn't awaken as usual at four-thirty. In fact, I got over so late for breakfast that the dishes had been washed and put away, so . . . no breakfast. That night when the trader showed up, he began, "You didn't cut wood for Mother this morning. Dad had to do it."

I explained what had happened the night before. I also told him about the endless hours I had been forced to put in. Apparently he knew nothing about this, believing his in-laws had regularly worked in the store. By now I was fed up. Wrangling conditions at Houck were not the best and the money was meager; if he would pay me off, I would go back to Winslow. In fact, I stated my intentions were to quit then and there. The trader started persuading me to stay, although I never really did understand why. But I liked the man, and I agreed to stay when he volunteered that all outside heavy work would thereafter be done by the spongers. This would leave me handling the store and the most important matters, although my hours would still be long. Somebody else *did* cut wood that day, but, when he goofed off in a day or so, the trader's father-in-law refused to touch the ax. Back to shelling wood I went, whenever the time could be found.

The trading post enjoyed its biggest volume of business during the summer of 1919, and with the business came many interesting characters. Johnny Moore and Charley Duesha—two men I had first met in Winslow before World War I—camped nearby while prospecting the area. Moore had come to Arizona with his parents in 1876, settling along Pinal Creek above Globe. Duesha, who was perhaps the West's toughest frontier fighter, had been a leader in the infamous Pleasant Valley War in the Tonto basin during the 1880s.* The hand he dealt was one of sudden death. Few people ever knew how many men he had killed while siding with Thomas H. Graham, leader of the cattlemen's faction, against the Tewksbury brothers. While Moore and Duesha were at Houck we became better acquainted. Each night when the store closed I visited their camp, and from their conversation I got the

---

*There seems to be little doubt that the Charles Duesha mentioned here is, in reality, the Charles Duchet described in Earle R. Forrest's *Arizona's Dark and Bloody Ground* (Caldwell, Idaho: Caxton Printing Limited, 1936; repr. Tucson: University of Arizona Press, 1984), pp. 228–290.

idea they were actually hunting the storied Lost Adams Diggings. They would continue to be mining and prospecting partners for twenty-five years, until Duesha died in 1925 at age eighty-seven.

The most colorful groups that came through that year were Hopi Indian salt bands from the stark mesas far to the north. Enroute to Zuni Lake, still far southeast of Houck, they packed corn, dried peaches, pottery, and basketry for sale or trade. These annual pilgrimages were necessary to supply the Hopi villages with salt, which could be cut out in hard chunks and in almost all colors—from yellow to coal black—from the old lake beds below Zuni Pueblo in northwestern New Mexico.

The short, chunky, sunburned Hopis wore brilliantly colored silk neckerchiefs around their cropped black hair. They walked behind strings of burros in single file; the leading animal was adorned with a tinkling neck bell. These picturesque, plodding salt gatherers of the Southwest have long been celebrated in romantic story and song—"Where the Salt Bands Go." Their journeys across an alien land intrigue the imagination. The desert was searing hot and its suddenly descending storms were a menace. Often the travelers were confronted with cloudbursts and roaring arroyos. In the mountains, traveling too early or late in the year, they might encounter snowstorms and low temperatures, and in summer there might be torrential rains. Nevertheless, theirs seemed to be a happy mode of existence.

The salt bands were strung out through the country like sinuous snakes a mile or more long. Frequently the leaders were out of sight on a timbered mesa, the slow-moving caravan gradually melting into oblivion in the dark forest. About three weeks later they reappeared in the same steady, tireless march on the ancient trail, every burro loaded with salt. Their goods had been sold or traded to Zunis, Navajos, other Indians, and whites.

A Hopi salt band would come through from some village perched on a mesa top about every six weeks. We bought their pottery and baskets, but never the dried peaches, which were dark and saturated with sand. They would pile their baskets and pottery on the counter and begin by quoting the highest price for each item. They had no expectation of obtaining anywhere near the asking figure, but set it only to bargain down to the best price possible. With me, it didn't work, because I knew exactly what the cost of the item should be. Naming a figure, I would let it go at that while I continued other business; I could outlast even the timeless Hopis.

Frequently the Zunis arrived from their pueblo, forty miles east of Houck, with a wagonload of pottery. The trader told me always to buy it. Zuni pottery, while not as durable as the harder-baked Hopi, sold readily to tourists because it was inexpensive. It was also more colorful and decorative—especially the large *ollas*. The Zunis would buy a load of provisions and dry goods from us, whereas the Hopis spent none of their money back. Instead, they leaned on the counter smoking free tobacco and starving. By gazing intently at the pictures on can labels they seemed to enjoy a full meal; they would tighten up their belts, and seem not hungry again until the next day.

That summer I became well acquainted with Big Woman, who lived deep in the old Navajo country. One day she came into the store and informed me that the deer were fattening in the White Mountains. She wanted just two cartridges for a .30-.30 Winchester carbine. "Going deer hunting with only two shells?" I queried.

"Two deer are all I can pack on one mule," she replied. A few days later, sure enough, she returned carrying the butchered carcasses of two deer tied on the pack mule. Of course, hunting deer that time of the year violated game laws,* but she hunted about every fifth week, stopping by the store to purchase exactly two cartridges. She went alone and always came back with two deer. Whether or not she had other cartridges, I never found out.

Along in August considerable excitement developed. Billy Burke, a small Irishman who always wore an ancient black derby hat, owned a fine little post five miles from Houck on a timbered mesa. Before Arizona went dry he had operated a saloon in a railroad town. Prohibition had caught him with twenty unsold barrels of whiskey, which he moved to the trading post. The Navajos knew it was concealed under some hides in his picket-post warehouse, and one night they surrounded the building, ordering him to come out and leave with his wife because they were going to burn the post down. The tough little man dared them to try, and, when the Navajos opened fire, he shot back at them all night long. They didn't even come close to scaring Burke away. After sunup, he began bringing them down by shooting them in the legs, and that finished the Indians, who wisely pulled out. Burke came to Houck to send a wire to the county sheriff, but the officers who arrived never ascertained the identity of the would-be hijackers.

Right about this time my employer faced considerable problems harbinging his future no good. State highway crews under engineer B. M. Atwood were surveying a new and shorter route north of the railroad for a paved road. With its construction, the trading post would be isolated

---

*According to David Brown, Supervisor, Game Branch, Arizona Game and Fish Department, U.S. game laws "have never been interpreted as applying to Indians." David E. Brown to editor, October 2, 1984.

and ruined. In addition, another store on the new highway had already been licensed by the Fort Defiance Indian Agent (later established by Joe Grubbs, it became White Mound).

The Hopi salt band that had come by earlier in the year appeared on its second journey to Zuni. During their leisurely halt at Houck, I came near to going along with them. I spent most nights in their camp in the timber listening to the rehearsal of chants and learning a little of the Hopi language. Two old men and a boy who should have been in school became my special friends. They taught me the only Hopi words I ever learned; indeed, the songs they sang were easier for me to memorize than conversation. The band remained for two extra days, but in the end I reluctantly decided against going. In fact, my plans, although somewhat unmatured, were to return to school. The trader's extreme financial difficulties worsened, despite the big money made during that summer and fall, and he took his family with him to Gallup, New Mexico, to discuss the situation with his banker and wholesaler.

During the trader's absence Billy Burke came in for his mail. Stalling around before leaving for home, he said, "If this feller ain't busted already, he surely will be when this new highway is built next year. Why don't you come to work for us? Me and the wife are getting along in years and we want to travel some to visit kinfolks. We could make a deal whereby you'd own part of the store."

His remarks came as my first factual knowledge that the Houck trader faced almost certain bankruptcy. Thanking Burke for his offer, which was, indeed, a generous one, I mentioned my desire to obtain an education of some kind, whereupon he entered into more detail, asking me to think it over very carefully. He figured that I had enough book learning and that a few years trading, with my nose to the grindstone, could make me wealthy while still a young man.

Business was slacking off, and I took a look at post correspondence. Little attention had been paid to it, and the number of warning letters from wholesalers surprised me. In those years traders seldom paid off their sources of supply except at the end of the wool- and stock-buying seasons. They didn't have much money regularly and hoped that, after suppliers had been paid, there would remain enough to carry their families through until the next time of settling up. Indeed, wholesalers, who never expected to be paid more than twice a year, also enjoyed the same kind of extended credit from manufacturers who supplied them. A few years later this easy-going method would change.

The trader returned from Gallup in high spirits. He told me to take a load of merchandise in the Ford truck to the Pine Springs post. He wanted me to remain there, running the new, small store, while his bachelor brother-in-law worked at Houck for the next few weeks. I inferred from his grandiose plans that the trader would handle his own business from now on. I was eager to leave anyway, and the very same night that the trader returned from Gallup I loaded the merchandise for Pine Springs. Very early in the morning, I headed north into what then was the back of nowhere.

Pine Springs

The trading post at Pine Springs stood at an elevation of more than six thousand feet. It was surrounded by dense forest in an area that had some of the most varied and weirdly beautiful canyons in the old Navajo country. The road was hardly better than a sheep trail, and the truck could barely keep up the steady climb to higher elevation. Since every spit of sand stuck it solid, shoveling the truck out took so much time that it was afternoon before I approached the post, hidden in heavy timber.

The front door was locked tight. Parking at the lean-to warehouse door, I walked around to the rear. The kitchen door stood wide open for air circulation. Against the wall, before a small logging campstove, sat the trader's brother-in-law, who lived there alone. I called loudly to him but received no reply. When I came closer, he jumped up and spun around, facing me behind a leveled .30-.30 Winchester carbine. I stood motionless, staring at him.

"Who are you and what do you want?" he demanded, sounding more scared than dangerous. When I told him, he relaxed slowly. Replacing the saddle gun against the wall, he jerked his head at the flat-topped stove, on which steamed a five-gallon copper distiller. Whiskey ran off through a coil in a wooden bucket filled with water, and dripped into a funneled jug resting on the floor beneath it. The man appeared about half drunk.

After reading the trader's letter, he shook his head. "I can't leave for several days yet. All them ripe barrels of mash have got to be run off." A dozen barrels in the brush behind the store were concealed under piles of goatskins and wormy sheep pelts. Starting with sprouting Navajo corn, he added raisins, prunes, and breakfast cereals. The raisins gave the whiskey an awful taste but brewed powerful stuff. By relays, and in order to get him away sooner, we ran off whiskey all night long. The little still just wasn't big enough to handle so much mash. The oblong store part of the building faced east. Behind it, forming a T, stood the south room, the kitchen, and a north room, finished except for the plastering of one wall. The next day, while he kept the still going, I completed the wall with mixed clay and sand. There being little business, we ran three more barrels of mash.

That night I found out he had another reason for remaining over at Pine Springs: a young Navajo girl appeared at ten o'clock. Taking her and a jug of whiskey into the store, he shut the connecting door. Around midnight the front door slammed; when I peeked in later, they were gone.

Running the still alone all night didn't bother me since the stuff had to be "tested" often. It was approaching daylight when the man appeared in the kitchen door in a great dither about something. "Grab a shovel and come help me!" he ordered in a ragged voice. Together we dug a deep hole in the sand, into which he emptied a full barrel of good mash. We dug other holes, burying all the remaining mash. Obviously he was doing this for good reasons. Did he expect a raid by Indian Service officers? While chunking the cookstove fire, I stashed a jug of whiskey for myself, correctly surmising what would happen. He took the still off the stove and went out to bury it somewhere in the timber. On his orders, I packed all the filled jugs and bottles in fiber boxes. He returned, half out of breath, to help load them on the truck. Then, without a bite of breakfast, he got behind the wheel and took off, roaring down the narrow mountain road.

The man had been badly scared; indeed, he must have lived at the post frightened all the time, for behind the store counters, within easy reaching distance, hung several .45 automatics and leaded wagon spokes on leather thongs. Odd, too, because he had been a tough cowboy most of his life, and the only one of the trader's four brothers-in-law who seemed halfway decent.

This time he had reason to worry: at noon came mounted Indians, packing guns. This district had many real mean ones, and they were in no easy mood, asking for the leather-eared man (meaning the deaf one). I said I didn't know, hadn't seen him, and they searched the building and went into the forest seeking tracks. Not once did it occur to them that fresh tire marks going down the road might mean anything.

The girl who had been there the night before, returning with the warlike party, related what happened. She told how the old cowboy (who spoke no Navajo and, therefore, shouldn't have been in the tough country in the first place) had got her drunk and taken her into the forest. She had passed out and awakened at midmorning, completely nude. She described everything in detail before all the men present. Now that things were at the talking stage, they began teasing her for being so gullible as to allow a mere white man to take advantage of her. By sundown, when they departed, all were in good humor again.

Three days later Johnny Moore and Charley Duesha rode in with a pack horse. Coming from the west, they knew nothing of events at Houck and didn't expect to see me at Pine Springs. Since the post had an extra bedroom, I invited them to throw in with me; a remote trading post could become a lonely place for a man alone. Moore and Duesha were investigating a story they had heard many years before. It concerned a party of white men who found gold somewhere near the springs in this area. On their way out, heading for New Mexico, most of them had been killed by Indians. Moore and Duesha, believing they had come into possession of a good clue, were hunting the lost mine.

Several aged Navajos were summoned and the situation was explained to them. These Indians admitted knowledge of the incident (it may be that as young men, some of them had helped murder the prospectors). I interpreted for Moore and Duesha during the hours spent questioning them. My friends then hired two of the old renegades to guide them to places where they thought the dead white men might have mined for gold. For more than a week they rode the country and brought back rock specimens, but they never found any color whatever, and at the end of ten days they departed.

Every night they had sat around in the Pine Springs kitchen, yarning of prospecting, the dead days of their youth, and gold-hunting plans for the future. The pair had located many claims in south-central Arizona, principally near Aguila. Not considering them worth much, they had sold all except one in Gold Canyon; this mine they worked profitably during winter months, when the heat was not so terrible.

Heavy piñon-nut buying began with the hard frosts of late fall, and the store enjoyed a rushing business. Piñons were dumped on the ground behind the building and covered with tarpaulins to protect them from blowing sand and dampness. Then they were placed in heavy sacks; very quickly the hundred sacks on hand were filled. The store shelves at Pine Springs were soon very nearly empty of trade items, and I had no way of getting word to Houck other than by walking.

It seemed every Navajo family for miles around did nothing but bring in a sack of piñons every day. I was unable to fill their merchandise orders, and the unpaid trade tickets piled up. Here we used no tin money, only figures on paper sacks which were hung on a wall nail. Desperate, I tried hiring Indians to ride to Houck with a message, but everyone swore he was too busy to go. The situation looked bad until the afternoon my friend Frank Walker showed up in a government pickup. Working for the Indian Service at Fort Defiance, he was hunting a bad Indian to take to jail. He had a bottle of booze with him, and, after killing it, he agreed to carry a letter to the trader.

The following day a Mexican section hand hired by my employer drove in with a load of merchandise and another hundred empty sacks for the little brown nuts. I took him, along with two Indians, to the outdoor pile and put them all to work. With fifty of the eighty-pound sacks on the truck, the driver returned to the trader with an emergency order for five hundred more sacks. Unable to believe his good fortune, the trader himself appeared on the scene to assess the situation. He reported to me that his brother-in-law, without any explanation, refused to drive the truck to Pine Springs on any trips; hence others were hired to do so. Two more big trucks were dispatched after his return to Houck. Unloading merchandise I had already sold, they went back loaded with piñons. By the time they caught up with my buying, more than eight hundred sacks had gone out to the main store.

On Sunday the trader again drove his car to the post. With the unexpected amount of piñons from Pine Springs, he estimated that, instead of a thousand sacks, he would be able to buy better than two thousand, and he had come to see how many were on hand for immediate shipping. The man grew most enthusiastic concerning the future and got so drunk that it was remarkable he managed to get his sedan over the return road without wrecking it.

One day the body of a young Navajo was found less than a mile from the Pine Springs post. Missing for a month, he had apparently been thrown from his horse and killed. A delegation of his family visited the post and asked me to bury the corpse. On being informed that too much business prevented my participation, they settled down to lengthy persuasion. Being a white man, they said, I didn't have to fear the *chindi* (evil spirit) that stayed near the body. If they buried the dead man, they must then spend four days in a hogan performing the cleansing rite, just like the unfortunate man who had discovered the body.

Eventually they talked me into it when some of them agreed to watch the locked store. They purchased a new robe to inter the deceased. Taking a shovel, I proceeded to where they directed me. Fortunately the body lay on easy digging ground, but it smelled worse than a dozen skunks. The corpse wore a valuable silver belt, three bracelets, and two rings, and a silver band adorned the hat lying nearby. The evidence seemed to show that the youth's neck had been broken the instant his head struck the ground.

After digging the grave as close as possible to the corpse, I rolled the body onto the new robe and tied the ends together. Proximity to the putrid flesh made me very sick, and I sought fresh air to one side in the wind. The Navajos were hiding in the distant brush; at least ten of them skulked around the scene. After euchering me into burying the body, they cynically watched to see that the valuable jewelry also went into the grave. I was put out with them and hurried the job. Dropping the body into the hole, I filled it as fast as the shovel would work. On my return from the woods, the Indians watching the storefront ran for their horses, and departed at a gallop. For the next four days, not one came near the trading post, just in case the *chindi* had followed me home.

By now the Pine Springs region had about been picked out of piñons. The Navajos were flush in goods, so rich they decided to celebrate. They built a new hogan, hauled wood and water, and started a fire dance. When I attended on the last, or ninth, night, there were no other whites present. As usual, when gawking outsiders were not on hand to belittle the tricks, the leading medicine man exhibited many of them. There were several different stunts of dancing magic feathers on baskets. The growing yucca also proved something remarkable to watch. The medicine man planted a mere sprig in the ground but, by his magic, it grew eight feet tall before the spectators' eyes. Rats, mice, and various small birds were caused to appear and disappear. One excellent piece of legerdemain involved a disappearing stone. After burying a stone about the size of a baseball in the sand, the medicine man told two men to dig it up. They, along with everyone else, saw it buried. Yet when they cleaned out the small hole, the stone was not there. Then the medicine man produced it from the pocket of a man well away from the stomp ground. Its discovery on him greatly confused the man, much to the amusement of the crowd.

A few days later an old woman named Grandma Redbird had a four-day healing ceremony performed over her. The shaman and her family believed her well on the road to recovery from her illness when, one morning, she informed them that she would be dead in three days. Her grandsons came to the store asking for tools and scrap lumber to make a burial box for her; between waiting on customers, I helped them nail it together in the warehouse. "She said on that day when the sun gets to there," one told me, measuring the lower western sky with his fingers, "she will go away."

White people still scoff at a long-accepted fact that Navajos can and do actually predict their time of transition. I never doubted Grandma Redbird would die when she said she would—and she did. Whether you believe them or not, I accepted such incidents because they happened.

A few years later Lorenzo Hubbell, Jr., told me of a similar experience. En route from Oraibi to Gallup, he stopped one noon at the hogan of longtime friends. While he was eating and drinking coffee with them, the mother of the family inquired conversationally what day he would return. "Exactly ten suns from now," Hubbell replied.

The woman then produced some money, giving it to Hubbell to bring back a white man's casket. "For when you reach here in the afternoon," she explained in a casual manner, "I will have gone away that morning and wish to be buried in a box. My sons will have the hole dug to put me down there when you arrive with it." She wasn't ill, hadn't been in years, and appeared to be in perfect health, but when Hubbell finished his business in Gallup and returned, it happened exactly that way. For many years afterward, despite all that he knew about the Navajo, he still spoke of it in a puzzled way.

No trading post had been established at Pine Springs before 1921 because it had long been a hideout for Indians who were wanted by the law or who were just plain renegade. Even before that, the region had afforded concealment for raiders being pursued from New Mexico during the time of Spanish control of the Southwest. The evil reputation of the area discouraged Navajo herdsmen from moving in until the slow approach of white men from the south began to change the denizens thereof. After the first few families ventured in, settlement began to be extensive. White outlaws used the Pine Springs area to go back and forth from New Mexico to Arizona. Over the common border of these two states their trails cut dimly through sparsely settled country. The trails were remote from white settlements, and, if Navajos encountered the outlaws, they were not likely to be sufficiently interested to mention it.

One sunny morning in the fall, as I sat in the doorway, a suspicious rider appeared through the pine timber. Nearing the open, he reined to a halt, acting as if the store being there now came as a surprise. He was a skinny, tall man of uncertain age, riding a black horse. His face showed the effects of wind and sunburn and the hair below his floppy, brown hat was a faded, rusty color. He advanced, halting before me. The right patch pocket of his worn leather chaps outlined a six-gun. Dismounting to the tune of many saddle creaks, he range-tied his horse, then strolled closer in apparent unconcern. "Reckon I could buy a sack of smoking in the store?" he began. "I been out a spell."

His horse showed evidence of weariness, indicating that the man traveled fast. One gray blanket tied behind the saddle probably contained a few items of eating grub, but it couldn't have been much. Rising cautiously, never turning my back on him, I stepped down, permitting him to enter first. A hunch warned me that this lone rider could be dangerous.

A Navajo medicine man in
front of an earth hogan.

A lidless cigar box on the store counter contained loose tobacco, cigarette papers, and matches—free for Navajo customers. Spotting it, he dived in, rolling a thick smoke. Saying nothing immediately about buying the makings, he looked over the interior without moving his head. He also listened intently, eventually determining that no one was present in the rear living quarters.

With the first smoke finished quickly, he rolled another like a man real hungry for tobacco. Then, grinning amiably, he nodded his head. "I'll take two of them Bull Durhams," he announced. His right hand dropped as though reaching for money in his pants pocket. The carton of tobacco reposed on the shelf directly behind me, which meant I had to turn my back to reach it. Instead, I turned all the way around and slid the muzzle of a fast-drawn .45 automatic at him over the counter edge. His right hand, which had lifted part way from the chaps pocket, froze there. Ten seconds later, with a twisted smile, he let his hand fall and said, "You win."

"Get on your horse," I replied. "And it might be your best idea to be headed south. In case you aim to sneak back here tonight, don't try it. My Indian helper, who'll be around outside, won't think much before he blasts you down with a greener [a long-barreled rifle]." There was no such helper, but the stranger didn't slip back to find out. A few days later, officers picked him up near St. Johns and held him for bank robbery in New Mexico. The loot, not grub, was found in the rolled blanket I had seen on his saddle, but it, too, wasn't much.

The trader hired a man in Gallup and sent him to relieve me at Pine Springs when business slacked off in 1920. Instead of waiting until the next day, I started south at sundown. My future plans were now figured out. I left my trunk at the depot before driving the truck across the river. I told the trader it was necessary for me to go to Gallup at once; the next day I caught the train in Gallup for California and joined the Navy. The trader's fourth brother-in-law, from New Mexico, took over Pine Springs early the following year.

Even the heavy piñon season the next fall didn't save old Houck trading post: it passed into other hands and went completely under. Creditors did not close the trader out; growing very weary trying to hold on by his teeth, he just gave up. Locking the trading post, he loaded his family into the car and departed for California. One of my uncles, C. D. Richardson, who knew him well, stopped at Houck soon after to see the trader about buying some rugs. To his surprise, two cowboys lived in the building that once housed the restaurant and tourist rooms. They had also broken into the store and were selling the remnants of merchandise for whatever they could get to anyone who came along.

On the cookstove C. D. saw an old still that had been dug up and brought down to Houck from Pine Springs. The two men were making whiskey while holding down what amounted to a line camp, since their outfit ran cattle in the area. Although old Houck has long been abandoned, Pine Springs kept improving and growing. In later times a good road reached it from Interstate 40, and it became one of the better known posts on the Navajo Reservation.

Dynasty of Traders

My ancestors traded with and lived among Navajo Indians in their incomparable Turquoise Empire from about the 1840s. Curiously, the trading line passed from uncle to nephew, rather than from father to son—although in later times the latter has been the case. The first of the traders was Frederick Smith from Tennessee. He left home about 1830, while still a youth, joining the mountain men during the halcyon days of prime beaver. After 1838, when high silk hats ruined the beaver trade, apparently he roved the Far West like most footloose old trappers, seeking some other worthwhile pursuit to compensate for the one gone under.

About all we know of him derives from a few communications, scattered intermittently over the years, to his half-sister in Tennessee, my great-grandmother Mildred Ann, two decades later. The trade goods he dealt in were principally powder, lead, bullet molds, dyes, robes, flints, Green River knives, manufactured silver jewelry, iron bridle bits, and cloth; all these items were packed on mules or horses. Traders proceeded to common meeting places, not unlike the old rendezvous of the mountain men, although on a very minor scale. In trade they received furs, some money and other valuables taken in raids, and livestock—when they were not too far west to drive animals into New Mexico for disposal.

Smith often ventured through Navajo country all the way to the big Colorado River near sacred Navajo Mountain. Sometimes he entered Navajo Canyon, then known as West Canyon. On one such trading expedition he was accompanied by two former mountain men of note, W. E. (Billy) Mitchell and W. C. Siewert, the latter an Englishman. Two miles upstream from junction with the Colorado River they made camp on a side canyon of Navajo Canyon in August 1861. Their horses were placed that night under an overhanging cliff, their meager camp pitched before it. When Indians attacked at daylight, Smith was killed. All three of their names are chiseled at the base of a salmon-pink sandstone wall, where Mitchell and Siewert buried Smith after fighting the Indians off.

The two survivors continued up the canyon for thirty miles, where they were attacked again in their second-night camp; their names and the date

Genealogy Chart of the Richardson Family

by Julianne Lungren

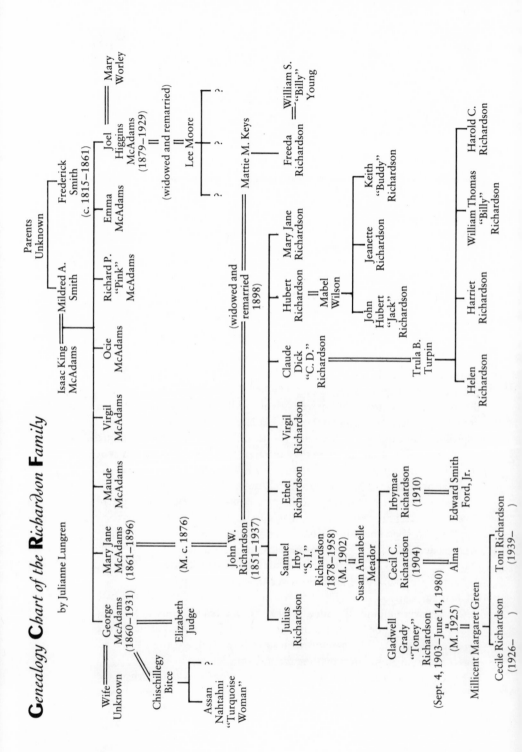

were cut into the cliff face there, too. The site where they made their stand is on a low bench. There was an aboriginal ruin on it (the walls were probably standing at that time) behind which they forted up. According to Navajo versions of the incident, the two men were under siege for three days, and several Indians were killed in charges against their strong position. Then the two men broke through, escaped into friendly territory, and made their way back to Santa Fe. All their goods had been lost in the fighting, and they were lucky to get out alive. It could be true that their attackers were Utes, as Navajos claimed, and there were also Paiutes and Havasupais in the country at that time; more likely, though, Navajos participated in the surprise attacks.

The Civil War had put an end to Smith's widely spaced letters home—or so his family presumed. They did not wonder about him until long after it ended. Mildred Ann Smith had married Isaac McAdams, who moved his family to Texas from Tennessee in 1875. In 1877 their oldest son, my great-uncle George W. McAdams, came west looking for Frederick Smith. The uncle whom he had never seen had assumed a glamorous, adventurous role in young George's mind. In Taos and Santa Fe, McAdams could obtain no information about his uncle. He went to live with the Navajos on the reservation where they had been placed in 1868, and he traded there for a while, but it proved unprofitable because the Indians were too poor.

Back in Santa Fe again McAdams had better luck: he found Billy Mitchell's family. Although Smith's companion had died some years after the Civil War, his widow and her oldest sons had known Smith well, for he had often stayed at their home. They told McAdams all about his uncle and that his Navajo name meant "The-white-man-who-moves-camp-after-dark." (Moving secretly from a visible camp into hiding was an old mountain-man ruse to remain alive just in case local Indians decided to attack.)

McAdams now went over to Las Vegas, throwing in with the Bowers brothers, George, Dave, and Fred, and the four of them cut hay for the U.S. Cavalry. After they were paid for hay cutting, they all went into town on a Saturday night. During the course of the evening, a gang of seventeen rowdies jumped them in a saloon (this gang had recently come down from the north and had been running riot over the local citizens). Not being armed, the Bowers brothers and McAdams seized chairs to defend themselves. McAdams happened to get the only iron-framed one in the place. A powerful man, six feet four inches tall, he laid the attackers down in rows. When the dust settled and officers arrived on the scene, three lay dead among the bleeding and unconscious, and McAdams was credited with killing them. In later years George Bowers told my father about the ruckus—McAdams had never mentioned it. The bloody fight being a clear case of self-defense, McAdams and the Bowers brothers were not held.

The next time he went to Las Vegas, McAdams carried a gun. Alone this time, he started gambling in the same saloon and cleaned out a poker game for big money. The heaviest loser drew a gun, but McAdams shot him dead across the table and escaped to the Bowers brothers' camp. They warned him that a posse, from whom he could expect no justice, would be coming for him. While he saddled a fresh horse, intending to streak for the Arizona Territory, the brothers decided to go with him, saying they had had enough of New Mexico themselves. They loaded their wagon to hit the trail, while McAdams raced on far ahead to wait for them.

The four men traveled all the way to Flagstaff. The Bowers brothers occupied farming land east of the small settlement (in a section later in the city limits, known as the Greenlaw Addition). The rich, volcanic soil produced bounteous crops of anything planted; unfortunately, there wasn't anybody to sell it to. With the approach of the railroad in 1882, the four men cut cross-ties for contractors. After a few years (during which a wild horse dragged Fred Bowers to death), they disposed of their improved land to a man named Greenlaw.

McAdams then went north into the wild country that was uninhabited except for renegade Navajos who had eluded capture by the Army during the campaigns of 1864. His first trading post was a small pole cabin on Rabbit Mesa, five miles north of Tuba City, which had been settled by Mormon colonists in 1876. Two years later he moved farther north to Redlake (later known as Tonalea).

His permanent post at Redlake was a stockade occupying a salt-and-sagebrush-covered hummock in what appeared to be an always dry lake bed. A year after he set up, heavy spring runoff filled it completely with water, leaving the post marooned on an island. Making a raft, McAdams ferried his goods south to high ground under the hill where Redlake Trading Post now stands. Hiring Indian help, he brought in more logs and erected a larger, longer, flat-roofed stockade of four rooms. Shortly thereafter, a son of Lot Smith put in a one-room trading post, roofed with canvas, upstream under a canyon wall; this place lasted almost two years.

In the 1880s George McAdams branched out with other small trading posts at Tuba City and Willow Springs on the Mormon Immigrant Trail below Lee's Ferry. Almost all remote posts of those days, until about the mid-1880s, had a small bull pen in which only a few Indians were permitted at one time. Usually the counters were enclosed by heavy wire mesh from the outer edge up to the overhead roof logs. In the center of the mesh was a hole too small for even a baby to crawl through. All trading of articles was done via this opening because, if they were able to seize anything, outlaw Indians would do so and run.

It wasn't until 1882 that George McAdams pieced together the story of Frederick Smith's last trading expedition and his death in 1861. One suspects the information came to him piecemeal, probably almost by accident, but he did take time to locate the grave and inscriptions on the cliff wall where Indians told him they were. Smith had made a lasting impression on the Navajos and many decades later he was still remembered by some clan historians.

In 1895 George McAdams got young Joe Lee and his father from Tuba City to run his Redlake store for him while he went to Texas to visit his sister Jane (my grandmother). None of his family had known where he was for nearly twenty years; in fact, they had believed him dead. His tales of adventures in colorful Arizona Indian country thrilled Jane's sons—my father and his brothers.

In 1899 McAdams bought Wolf Trading Post on the Little Colorado River. In the early 1900s he sold the place to a man from Detroit, went up-river to Benton Mesa, and put in another old-fashioned stockade post with a dirt roof. Selling this post in 1904 to R. M. Bruchman, he traded next at Chinle until 1910; that year he bought Houck and operated the post until 1919. For a brief period he lived in Gallup, New Mexico, where he bought considerable investment property. Finally, he went back to Chinle, opening another trading post in 1921. Two years later he moved to Farmington, New Mexico, where he was involved in trading and banking until his death in 1931.

My ancestors were a singular group, with an odd characteristic—almost a mania—for not keeping track of each other. This was true of them even in my generation: there has never been a detailed history handed down about any group and any one of them. What little I know about the McAdams family came from my great-uncles George and J. H. McAdams, but most of what they told me concerned their Navajo Indian trading days, not their brothers and sisters, of whom there were several. My father and my uncles also remember very little about the brothers and sisters of their mother

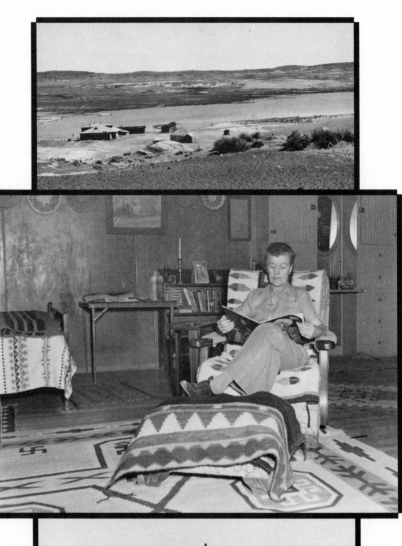

Redlake (near Tonalea), where George McAdams established a trading post in the early 1880s: (top) the lake; (middle) a friend of the Richardson family in the living quarters above the store; (bottom) entrance to the trading post.

and have referred to them only vaguely. One of the McAdams nephews, however, was named for the old mountain man, Fred Smith.

My grandmother Jane McAdams was born and raised near Memphis, Tennessee. Her father and his two brothers were in business there long before the Civil War. She and my grandfather Richardson were married in the mid-1870s, and they migrated to Texas almost at once. Her parents, with their many younger children, followed them, settling near Alvarado, where both parents died in less than a year. My grandmother wrote poetry. She never tried for publication—which probably wouldn't have been possible anyway on the frontier—but she filled a huge, leather-bound ledger with her work. In this book she also kept a few old letters as mementos. Once, when Grandfather Richardson was showing me her poetry at Winslow, we found four of Frederick Smith's faded letters pasted in the back. A man of some education for those times, he wrote well, describing places he had been with dramatic vividness.

My grandfather John W. Richardson was born in 1851 in Mississippi; his family later moved near Memphis, Tennessee, where he met and married Jane McAdams. Grandfather Richardson held rigidly to an old, established custom that the father was supreme ruler of his household. As fast as his sons reached working age, around twelve or thirteen in those days, he put them out to labor and collected their wages. The first to rebel over this foolishness was my uncle Julius C. Richardson. He ran away from home, wandered afar, and became a fireman and then an engineer on the Santa Fe Railroad in Arizona. He never had the slightest ambition to become an Indian trader, whereas all his brothers and uncles engaged in the business.

My grandmother died when my father, Samuel Irby (S. I.) Richardson, was fifteen. S. I. then worked to help take care of the rest of the children, although Grandfather hardly needed the money—he simply insisted on his imposed right to his son's earnings. The day Father reached eighteen in 1896 he headed west for Arizona. The first eighteen months he clerked in the Redlake Trading Post for his uncle George McAdams. For a short period he worked as timekeeper and bookkeeper for a company installing the first water and sewer lines in Flagstaff. On finishing the project, the company sent him to Prescott on a contract job there. When that work ended, S. I. started cowboying, an occupation he had learned in southwest Texas.

In 1899 Herman Wolf, a former mountain trapper who had established a trading post on the Little Colorado River before 1870, died suddenly. George McAdams sent for his nephew S. I., and they bought Wolf Post from the estate as partners. At that time the store occupied a stockade down under a small mesa before Wolf Crossing; S. I. and McAdams built the stone post on the mesa directly against the canyon rim, where it boxes. McAdams maintained his other posts some time longer, so S. I. ran Wolf Post by himself until 1901. Disposing of his other stores, McAdams went to California, married another of his numerous times, and brought his bride to live at Wolf Post.

During the time that S. I. ran the store alone, a hunting party of Navajos and county officers engaged in a gun battle in Elliot Canyon, south of the post. An Indian and a cowboy were killed, and two of the three surviving officers were badly wounded, although they escaped afoot to the railroad. The Navajos prepared to raid Flagstaff, convinced that the Army was en route to round them up. They claimed the white officers had tried to murder them. One night three hundred well-armed Indians crossed the river at Wolf Post. Several of their leaders entered the store to talk to S. I. After arguing their case for some time, the head chief asked S. I. outright for advice, as they didn't really want to engage in a big war.

S. I. advised that only a few ride in and return the horses and saddles taken from the scene of the fight. There would be a hearing, but he didn't believe the evidence justified holding any of them for trial in the white man's court. The leaders decided to follow S. I.'s advice, and all the rest went along. The Indians hid in the pine forest above Flagstaff while the headmen presented themselves for a parley; if the leaders were jailed, the war party would raid and burn the small town to the ground. Fortunately, the case turned out the way S. I. had thought it would. Two nights later the returning war party stopped at Wolf Post to tell him about it.

Late in 1901 S. I. returned to Texas where he married my mother, Susan Annabelle Meador. For a while he engaged in the cattle business in Oklahoma before returning to Arizona as an Indian trader. After retiring from Inscription House Trading Post in 1951, S. I. invested in the Two Guns Trading Post on Interstate 40, which he still had when he passed on at eighty years of age.

Another of my great-uncles, Joel Higgins (J. H.) McAdams, came to Arizona when his brother George returned to Redlake in 1895. J. H. worked at Redlake until George put in a store for him at Tuba City, which he ran until the Spanish-American War broke out in 1898. Shortly before it did, a twenty-year-old brother, Richard P. (Pink) McAdams, joined J. H. After taking back the Tuba City post, George McAdams sold all his stores and headed north for the Klondike gold rush.

J. H. and Pink McAdams then went to Albuquerque, where they enlisted in the Rough Riders, Company H, 1st U.S. Volunteer Cavalry. They had both been born in Mt. Pilia, Tennessee, but the Rough Rider monument in the square at Prescott lists their Texas homes. After service in Cuba, Pink McAdams became an ephemeral figure. He was here and he was there, following no particular trade or profession that any of the family knew about. He was rumored to have died in Gallup, but I finally traced him to Albuquerque, where he was buried in 1928.

J. H. returned to the Southwest; from 1902 to 1904 he owned a trading post at Chaves, New Mexico. He then bought another post at Cuba, New Mexico, which he sold to one of John Wetherill's brothers. In 1907, in partnership with E. J. Marty, he built a new post at Sunrise Springs, Arizona, and subsequently bought Indian Wells and another post at Keams Canyon. Hardly did J. H. and Marty open Sunrise Springs for business when Don Lorenzo Hubbell stormed in there in a great huff. Informing them all that the Indian trading area belonged to him exclusively, he gave them until the next sundown to leave.

Marty did go back to Gallup, but J. H., his Scottish temper aroused, told Hubbell that he and all his Navajo cronies were not big enough to run him one foot in any direction. He bought Marty's share, taking two wagonloads of fine blankets to Gallup to pay him off the next spring.

While other traders gave attention to promoting the sale of Navajo blankets, J. H. turned to silver and turquoise jewelry. He sold Sunrise Springs in 1909 to my uncle Hubert Richardson, while he stayed at his Indian Wells post. That year he went to Texas to marry my great-aunt Lee. Returning to the big Indian country, he proceeded to enter the business of buying and marketing Indian jewelry exclusively. Selling Indian Wells to Hubert, he went to Gallup in 1910 and opened a trading post north of the railroad tracks.

S. I. Richardson, Toney's father, was a Navajo trader from 1896 until the early 1950s.

Navajo blankets and turquoise jewelry were promoted by Indian
traders in the early 1900s.

Here he handled general trade goods and also trained a number of
silversmiths in making fancy, light-weight jewelry. He then placed these
artisans on contract, buying their output by the piece. Advertising widely,
mailing thousands of brochures, and developing more skilled silversmiths,
he soon promoted a silver jewelry business that gave employment to almost
four thousand native craftsmen.

The business became so remunerative that several companies started man-
ufacturing phony Indian "handmade" jewelry with machines. In disgust,
and very unhappy about it, J. H. sold his company to John Kirk in 1918.
He bought two other trading posts and also invested in the Winslow Indian goods wholesale house of his two nephews—my uncles C. D. and Hu-

bert Richardson. Ordered to leave the high altitude for his health, J. H. sold everything once more and went to Texas. Still unable to remain out of the great Indian country, he returned to Gallup and in 1921 (the year I worked at old Houck Trading Post) established his second J. H. McAdams Trading Company.

J. H., alone and with keen business foresight, promoted the Indian jewelry business into a million-dollar turnover annually for the tribesmen. He not only trained them, but provided the best in modern smithing equipment. Most of the designs, types, and styles used decades later were originated by him. In 1928 J. H. retired permanently and sold his trading company to my uncle Hubert. He went to California and passed on the following year; Great-Aunt Lee buried him in Gallup beside their fifteen-year-old son, who had died some time before.

My uncle C. D. Richardson joined his brother Julius in Arizona in 1903–1904. After working several months at Grand Canyon, on the construction of the Grandview Hotel, he returned to Texas. As soon as he turned eighteen, my uncle Hubert Richardson also hurried to Arizona, where he went to work for J. H. McAdams at Sunrise Springs in 1908. Two years later, when J. H. departed from Indian Wells, Hubert took over that store.

C. D. came back to Arizona and, with Hubert, opened a trading post in leased government school buildings that had been the J. P. Williams homestead at Blue Canyon in 1913. Prior to World War I, both moved to Winslow where they opened a trader's wholesale house, first with J. H. as a member of the firm, then with E. J. Marty. Before the war ended they were sole owners. Additionally, they each operated several reservation trading posts. C. D. had The Gap, Shonto, Kaibito, and later a store in Tuba City. Hubert owned Leupp and Cameron. Next he bought Kaibito, then sold Leupp to Stanton K. Borum. In 1966 he disposed of Cameron and Kaibito. C. D.'s last trading post was Sunrise, near Leupp. After leaving the reservation, he owned various stores and curio businesses in Arizona until he retired in the early 1960s.

A host of Richardson family in-laws also engaged in Navajo trade for short or long periods subsequent to 1915. Most notable among them was William S. (Billy) Young, who clerked at Leupp Trading Post after he and my Aunt Freeda (Grandfather Richardson's daughter [my age] by his second marriage) were married in 1918. He managed Leupp, Cameron, and Bellemont stores over the years, but owned and traded longest at Redlake, across the Little Colorado River north of Leupp. This Redlake—there are several on the reservation—was once known as Cornfields.

In 1913 Hubert and C. D. Richardson opened Blue Canyon Trading Post in leased government school buildings that had been the former homestead (1882) of J. P. Williams.

Like me, my brother Cecil C. Richardson, for eighteen years Coconino County Sheriff at Flagstaff, operated several family-owned trading posts at different periods. We were the first to break the line of succession from uncle to nephew—the first of the family trader's sons to become Navajo country storekeepers. In turn, my cousins John (Jack) Hubert and Keith (Buddy), the sons of Hubert Richardson, also became traders. Only one other Richardson—the son of my uncle C. D., William Thomas (Billy) Richardson—took to Navajo trading and opened his own store in Gallup, New Mexico.

The pioneering McAdams and Richardsons established permanent trading posts at new places, opening up the biggest Indian country in the United States. They developed water and laid down the roads necessary to freight merchandise into the back of beyond. Their roads were the usual ones of those times, threads wandering off seemingly into nowhere. Later, some were improved for automobiles and trucks, but some of the wagon roads were abandoned.

Frederick Smith apparently created no new trails, using those of Indians or none at all, merely passing his pack stock over negotiable terrain.

George McAdams instituted the route off Mormon trails, north of Winslow on the Little Colorado, across the wide Denebetoh Valley, via Blue Canyon, to Redlake (Tonalea). C. D. and Hubert Richardson rebuilt part of this route for their Navajo freighters to get long wagon trains over to Blue Canyon, Shonto, and Kaibito. By that time the old McAdams road had worn out itself and three different names. McAdams also laid out the short way from Tuba City to Redlake directly over Rabbit Mesa. The old Mormon road ran far to the west, circling the mesa. Still another route followed under the east rim around to the lake. McAdams also stretched traces from Redlake into remote country for summer trading—Cowsprings Canyon, Red Valley, Tseghi, and another deep in the unknown fastnesses of Black Mountain where only gold hunters had ventured before. After his final summer and fall encampment there in the mid-1920s, no trading stock of goods ever went in again.

My uncle C. D. Richardson is responsible for the direct route from Tuba City to Kaibito through the sand hills, a route which was not used after 1925. He established other roads from Kaibito to The Gap and from Kaibito to Redlake (over a shorter stretch that was still used decades later). Also, he first made a road over the mesa down the canyon rim into Shonto. When sand piled over it in great dunes, he opened up a way down the canyon to the Kayenta road past a series of small lakes.

The last family road building was from Redlake to Willow Springs on Navajo Mountain—by my father, S. I., my uncle Hubert, and my brother Cecil. From the end of this road S. I. and his hired Indians marked trails and built pack-train passages from Rainbow Lodge to Rainbow Natural Bridge via Redbud Pass, from Little Navajo Valley to Surprise Valley (off the ancient Ute War Trail) and to the San Juan River, from the Wetherill Trail near War God Spring onto the top of Navajo Mountain, from Rainbow Lodge across the country into Navajo Canyon, to Kaibito and Tower Butte. A cabin or a hogan was constructed at the end of each of these trails, or somewhere conveniently along them, to maintain holdover supplies for dude packers.

At the end of these offshoot roads and trails there were trading posts, Navajo Indian schools, missions, and other establishments. Some trails were long ago abandoned, except those in the Navajo mountain country which were improved by the government to become main arteries of travel in the undeveloped wilderness. The longest stretch of road laid out by George McAdams, from north of Winslow to Redlake, was abandoned soon after World War I, and the old ruts and dugways became washes and arroyos. Outlying roads to those places used by Indians became entirely the industry of others. The rest of the Richardson routes became highways and improved roads over all or most of the expanse they originally laid out to further their business enterprises.

After these first road builders came government agents, explorers, scientists, missionaries, a few traders, and—always—the tourists. It can truly be said that the newcomers camped by the cold ashes of their pioneers' dead fires and used their watering places as they passed safely through once-forbidding country.

Many of the early pioneers' undertakings were total financial losses. Instead of being credited with any development or with doing any good for the Indians and those who followed, the old trail blazers have been too often derided, belittled, and accused of being cold-hearted commercialists. Yet, what they accomplished at their own expense opened up this magnificent country for others. It is certain they accomplished many firsts in this last frontier of the West. But "firsts" were of doubtful importance, even in the days of old. There exists nowhere a chronicle of what they actually did or when. The men who were with them, who knew, are dead and gone. No historians were around to write their exploits for posterity. Others gained the credit in later decades. As for that, not a McAdams or a Richardson cared then or now for accolades or for being mentioned in history. To them the one and only important fact is that, by choice, they became part of The People, the Navajo. They did this during the decades when the valiant tribesmen most needed a forward boost economically and politically. Their Navajo friends have been numberless.

Many of these old Navajo friends traveled long distances to attend the funerals of members of my family. For a Navajo, especially a "long hair" [one who keeps to the old ways], to appear at a white man's burying is most unusual, regardless of the high esteem in which they might have held that individual. At both my mother's and my father's funerals, more than half the crowd in attendance were Navajo and Hopi Indians; some had come from as far as two hundred miles off the reservation.

Down through the years I have been asked numerous times, "Didn't the old boy [naming one of my relatives] once have a Navajo [or Paiute] wife?" A tiresome question, even if one of mere curiosity occasioned by rumor. From the time of the earliest trader through 1890, or even later, how did a lone white man survive in the renegade, fighting, western Navajo country? Simply, he had to have close ties with the most important, leading family of the region in which he had located. Certainly some of my people at one time had Indian wives. In those days a tribal basket-marriage could be as binding as any other.* Let it be said, too, that as far as these white men were concerned, the liaison was for keeps. That it didn't turn out so wasn't due to their decision: most often the wife and her family broke the ties. Nor can the Indian women be censured for reluctance to leave their own people.

For years I heard rumors of this and that Navajo family being my kinfolk, but not until 1925 did I actually meet a Navajo relative. While I was standing in Redlake Trading Post one afternoon a very distinguished-looking Navajo woman entered the store. Tall, as were all the old western Navajo people, she was also handsome, with great dignity in her bearing. She wore well-made clothes and expensive silver and turquoise jewelry. The ten or fifteen Indians in the store fell silent; they even quit dickering with clerks. The stately woman glanced around, her eyes coming to rest on me. Smiling slightly, she came over to where I leaned on the counter in conversation with trader Johnny O'Farrell. Holding out a hand in greeting, she said in Navajo, "I am happy to meet a relative. How is your family doing?"

Hiding my puzzlement, I replied politely, as I knew Navajos meeting each other would. I courteously inquired concerning the welfare of her own family. She reported small items connected with a son, a daughter, and one of several spoiled grandchildren. No names whatever were mentioned and nothing of where she lived. I had never seen her before, to my

---

*"The wedding ceremony employs the [Navajo wedding] basket in the following way: the bride cooks cornmeal in three colors: red for health, blue for happiness, and white for wealth. During the ceremony the basket with the cornmeal is placed between the couple. The white meal lines the bottom of the basket, with the red and blue meal forming a cross on the white. One axis is north-south; the other east-west. The bride eats a pinch of the meal from the east side, the groom repeats the action; then she takes a pinch from the south, west, and north. The groom repeats each action after the bride. Both together take meal from the center of the basket. The basket is then passed around to all guests, who also take a pinch of meal. This continues until all the meal is gone. The last person to eat from the basket usually receives the basket as a gift" (Laura Graves Allen to Editor, Jan. 8, 1985).

"So many taboos surrounded the making of the wedding basket that Navajo women stopped making them by the 1930s. The basket had to be started on its eastern side and finished on the east; no one could watch the weaving; it must be woven away from the hogan and not in a high wind; the weaver could not be menstruating or have sex; she could eat little meat and no salt; she must be sung over before and after the project. No wonder the Ute and Paiute women living at Navajo Mountain, Tuba City, or in other northern parts of the reservation, took over the craft. These non-Navajo women found a constant market for their baskets, even though they were not ritually cleansed" (William H. Lyon, "Navajo Culture and History," unpublished manuscript, pp. 139–149).

knowledge, but she seemed to know me by sight, or to have deduced who I was in some way, so she naturally assumed I knew all about her and her family.

After half an hour of this sort of conversation, she asked in a gentle voice, "And my father, is there news of him?" I wasn't certain which of my relatives could possibly be her father. But I still made my answers sound reasonably accurate by saying he had recently visited me in Flagstaff and he looked well but was, of course, getting along in years. Finally, turning to the trader, she made several purchases—articles undoubtedly intended as gifts to a family she planned to visit. Before leaving the store, she shook my hand, saying she hoped we would meet again soon and that I would visit her. Outside the store she tied the purchases on her saddle, mounted, and rode off toward Black Mountain.

Trading resumed in the post. The Navajos talked and laughed loudly again. The first one that I asked what they called the dignified woman stared at me in great surprise. He shook his head negatively, as did the next three or four, when the same question was put to them. None of them knew who she was, but they all instantly recognized a V.I.P. The query put to O'Farrell produced another astonished head shake. "You mean to say you don't know her?" he asked incredulously. "From the way you both talked, I sure believed you knew each other well. In fact, I intended to ask you who she was!" He remembered that she had been to Redlake a year or so before and that she lived on a remote part of Black Mountain. He had overheard an aged Navajo man talking to her in the store, but now he couldn't recall who the Indian was.

Why didn't I ask the woman who she was? That question would have been deemed improper according to Navajo social customs. In the first place, to honored friends of the family, one is a "relative." Therefore, until the conversation between us progressed, the actual truth wasn't fully apparent. Also I had felt then that she would soon drop a clue as to her identity, but it just didn't happen.

The following week Joe Lee—a friend who had been present when George McAdams, by tribal ceremony, married Chischillegy Bitce in 1882— identified her as McAdams's daughter. On upper Black Mountain, Navajos called her Assan Nahtahni (Woman Captain/Woman Chief), and also sometimes by a more important title—Turquoise Woman. Her grandfather, Hosteen Chischillegy, was a noted Navajo fighting man who had been killed in battle with the Ute Indians in Utah in the year of her birth.

At our next meeting, at Inscription House Trading Post, she related considerable family history: her mother had died in 1923; she had had one brother, who had passed on when he was twenty years old. Born in 1884, she and her mother had returned to live at Redlake when McAdams was there in the 1890s. When he left for the second time, to establish a new trading post, her mother had again declined to go with him, as she had before.

Assan Nahtahni never saw her father again, although McAdams stayed at Redlake briefly after returning from the Yukon in 1899. When Assan Nahtahni married at eighteen, her mother gave her half the sheep, cattle, and horses that George McAdams had settled on his Navajo family at the time of their first separation. The man she married was rich by Indian standards, and together they were considered a very upper-bracket family.

Another relative of mine owned a large trading post, employing from twelve to fifteen people. One of his workers was a handsome Navajo youth with a good education, who worked hard and competently most of the time. But every couple of months or so, he would get well soused and stay that way for a week. His abilities earned him a high income, but he blew money faster than he made it. When he was drunk or sobering up, broke, he would return to the store. Without saying a word to anyone he would pick up a blanket, a piece of expensive jewelry, or anything else he was able to sell or pawn immediately. The trader never said a word about this filching and never charged an item to him. Other employees, including the Navajos, were puzzled over these incidents. Anyone else acting as the young man did would have been fired or, perhaps, even sent to jail.

The trader merely smiled, making no comment. When he finally sold the business, the Navajo youth continued as a department head for the new owner. But now he didn't have it so easy, and he swiped nothing from the store. The trader's death found the young man worse than flat broke: everything he owned had been sold for whiskey, and by then he was also out of a job. After trying to borrow money and failing, he sold his one-hundred-dollar pocket watch to a store clerk for ten dollars. He spent it all for flowers to go on the trader's casket. "A Navajo doing that for a white man's funeral is the most astonishing thing I ever ran across!" the store manager said to me while relating the circumstances. "How come he didn't buy more rotgut whiskey with the money? Instead he bought flowers—which proves you can't ever figure what an Indian will do. Sure must have thought a hell of a lot of that white man!" He did. The trader had educated and taken care of him until he could make his own living. Why shouldn't he have? The handsome Navajo was his son.

Navajo Mountain

Discharged in 1924 after a four-year hitch in the Navy, I went immediately to Winslow and Leupp. My uncle Billy Young drove me to Cameron on the Little Colorado River, the jumping-off place for Navajo Mountain. Stanton Borum managed the Cameron post for my uncle Hubert Richardson. I spent the night there, and we started loading the truck early the next morning. Borum considerately dispatched it a few days early in order to get me home sooner to Navajo Mountain, far to the north; my parents, S. I. and Susie, had established Rainbow Lodge Trading Post there while I was in the Navy.

But "Sleepy," the sullen driver, stalled all the time, actively resenting any hurry. As a consequence, I loaded most of the merchandise on the truck myself. It was late when we started, and, aware that it took a long day's drive to reach Rainbow Lodge, Sleepy made an extensive, unnecessary stop in the Indian agency village at Tuba City. The next halt was Redlake (for the mail), and here he goofed away much more time. Obviously, he planned not to reach Navajo Mountain that night, just to prove he could do as he pleased. Eventually we got started once more and, off the Kayenta Road, entered the final seventy-four-mile rough and dim trace to Navajo Mountain. Five miles later, as we came up out of a deep wash at Eagle Nest Rock, the rear truck wheels dug deep into soft dirt.

Sleepy got out slowly, gazing around cursorily before announcing we would camp there the balance of the day and overnight. His voice sounded like a challenge, as if he were daring me to make an issue of it. It was then about three o'clock in the afternoon. According to him, after unloading in the morning we would get the truck out, reload, and proceed. I blew my top and drew my gun on him. Moving to the side of the truck, he studied the load, saying there were two thousand pounds of flour alone on it. When I didn't argue about that he climbed up the side, starting to unfasten the tarpaulin cover, only to halt. "Maybe I'd better try rocking it out," he spoke in a conciliatory voice. "Sure be hard work unloading and loading again."

Getting into the cab he started the cooled motor, gently easing the clutch in. The Reo Speedwagon moved upward a foot before it stalled and slid

"Eventually we left the myriad canyons for a plateau, with the mole-hill shape of Navajo Mountain bulking against the sky."

back into the holes. The second time brought it forward nearly two feet before the stall, but it wouldn't come out. Moving into the cab quickly, I slid the gun into my right hip pocket, away from his reach. The third try sent the heavily loaded truck forward in a lurch and we were free.

The road ahead passed through Red Valley for twenty-two miles before entering rocky and dangerous canyon country. Soon after we got out of the valley, night fell. It was a compliment to the trace to call it a road, as it was very uncertain where it passed over eroded stretches of solid sandstone. Several times it became necessary to get out and relocate the road by painted lines and stakes in the glare of headlights. This I let Sleepy do, lest he suddenly drive off and leave me stranded in a lonely, uninhabited place. Eventually we left the myriad canyons for a plateau, with the mole-hill shape of Navajo Mountain bulking against the sky.

At Haystack Rock we began a two-and-a-half-mile climb onto the mountainside. Truck lights and the motor roar warned those at the trading post of our approach. Presently yellow light came through the timber as we drove in at eleven o'clock. Sleepy departed—wordless—at once for a bunk in the guides' rock house higher on the slope. Restoring the gun to the glove compartment, I climbed out to greet Mother and Father, who were waiting in the store door.

My arrival came as a surprise, for they hadn't known exactly what day I would get out of the Navy. No such convenience as telephones then existed so far back in the wilderness of Navajoland. We talked until the beginning day announced it was time to cook again. After breakfast Mother read letters from my sister Irbymae, who was away at school in Winslow, and from my brother, Cecil, who was working for R. M. Bruchman near Winslow. We unloaded the merchandise from the truck and reloaded it with sacked wool and bales of hides. The sullen Sleepy departed immediately. He never came back, for Stanton Borum let him go on his return to Cameron.

S. I. had built a good post on Navajo Mountain. The main building contained the store, a huge living room, a dining room, and a kitchen with an attached porch on the sloped side overlooking a great valley. The roof was of packed clay over peeled poles. Visible from underneath, the frontier-type ceiling added to the red stone building's rustic attractiveness. The sleeping cabins for dudes were higher up on a leveled path, running northwest toward the nearest canyon and the guide house. The two permanent guides, rehired for the following season, were gone to care for stock during the winter in Jim Black Basin on the Colorado River, so my parents would be alone in the lodge all winter long.

A log barn and pole corrals were situated down the slope in timber far enough to keep flies away from the lodge. Water had been piped into the buildings from Willow Springs higher on the mountain at the base of some white sandstone cliffs. The spring's overflow passed before the store door as a small creek. Inside the lodge, walls were plastered with the usual mixed clay and sand. The only wood in the building, besides door and window frames, formed the floors and porch roof. (When this wood burned out in 1951 and destroyed the building for use, the lodge was owned by W. W. [Billy] Wilson, my uncle Hubert's brother-in-law, and Senator Barry Goldwater.)

Mother was one of the first white women to live at Navajo Mountain in western Indian country. She explored Cummings Mesa, adjacent canyons, and Navajo Mountain. During the three years Mother lived there, she went outside the area only once, when she accompanied S. I. to Winslow one June to bring my sister home from school. During the winter months, my parents were completely snowed in; no traffic was possible until late March or early April. They obtained mail around Christmas time by wagon, or, if the snow was deep, by pack mule. The mail came to Redlake on the Kayenta road, and they didn't get it again until spring thaw.

All winter long they saw no one except the Navajos and Paiutes who lived in the region. No matter how deep the snow, some of the Indians managed to get out of the warm canyons (into which they moved in November) to the store every week or ten days, depending on brewing storms. The store, the adjacent lean-to warehouse constructed of Arbuckle Brothers' Coffee packing-box boards, and every other available space had to be crammed with merchandise in order for supplies to last until spring. The lodge overflowed with goods in October, for any day snow might lay down deep. But this season S. I. hoped to get in two more truckloads before snow fly.

When the first customers arrived, he measured out bulk sugar for them in a baking-powder can instead of weighing it on the counter scales. He chuckled over my inquisitiveness. "Had no scales when we first came here," he explained. "Had to use a can and guesswork. When we did get a pair of scales, no Indians would let me weigh their sugar—they claimed the scales robbed them. This can actually beats them out of a couple of ounces of sweet salt!" (The Navajos called sugar "sweet salt.")

S. I.'s trade during the winter months was the usual: blankets, goat skins, sheep pelts, and furs—like coyote, badger, fox, lynx, or an occasional timberwolf skin from Utah. The coyotes were the mountain type, huge for the dog family. The lynx cats, called bobcats by the unknowing, frequently measured five feet in length.*

I think that, despite the long, harsh winters, Mother lived happier at Navajo Mountain than anywhere else on the reservation. After they moved away, she never ceased talking about the lodge, often recalling treasured incidents. Every morning while good weather lasted, she walked down the road to Haystack Rock and back. Sometimes I accompanied her. One morning on the return she halted to point along a purple-sage-lined wash. "Two graves are there," she said; "nothing to indicate whether of white men or Indians."

Thinking it over, I decided white prospectors were buried on the wash. The great rocks and cliff faces on that side of the mountain were cut with the names of prospectors who had been in the area as early as the 1870s. Many had been killed there—especially during the 1880s, when the lost Merrick-Mitchell mine attracted gold hunters from all over the West. S. I. carried two nuggets, found where the lodge now stood, taken from a small, round vein of white sandstone emerging horizontally from the mountainside.

On a cloudy afternoon I shoveled out one of the graves after locating it in the sagebrush by punching a steel rod into the ground. In the bottom, short pieces of ax-cut cedar covered the body pit. They rested on a six-inch bench of hardpan left all around the sides of the grave to a height of about fourteen inches. The skeleton of the man in this grave had a bullet hole through the skull. All fabric, leather, and paper (in a tin can) had rotted completely. Metal buttons and a belt buckle lay scattered among the remains. A cartridge belt and gun, probably carried by the deceased in life, had been thrown into the head of the grave. The .50-caliber cartridges were covered with verdigris, the revolver with an unidentifiable chunk of rust. Beneath the gun and the cartridges rested two twenty-dollar gold pieces which, upon cleaning, revealed the date 1874. Only white men would have buried murdered dead. But placement of the gold and the once-valuable gun in the grave (a Navajo custom) seemed most unusual. I did not touch the second grave; before leaving, I mounded both graves with rocks.

Working in the store with S. I., I began to take notice of his customers— some of them were definitely unusual characters. A Paiute, appropriately called Paiute Dick, when asking for potatoes always said in English, "You savvy spuds?" He thought all three words were the English name for them.

---

*Pioneer traders did refer to lynx cats as bobcats; however, cased skins extending to five feet in length seem to be a bit of an exaggeration. David E. Brown to Editor, October 2, 1984.

Living in Paiute Canyon, far to the northeast, he made the long trip to
Navajo Mountain rather than trade at Oljeto or Kayenta. The Paiutes lived
in groups, whereas the Navajos did not establish anything resembling a
community.

Hosteen* Indischee, the Navajo district chief, came into the world under a
cliff on Navajo Mountain. His family, with twelve others, had hidden in deep
canyons with their flocks when soldiers searched the country for Indians. The
troops had set up headquarters on top of Navajo Mountain in 1864. None of
the brave Navajos in this area had been captured and removed to the prison
reservation at Bosque Redondo, New Mexico. Very independent, they were
a bold, tough lot and brooked no interference from anyone. In the years
ahead they successfully resisted the government's stock-reduction policy and
gave government officials trouble until after World War II.

Although the Navajos and Paiutes around Navajo Mountain were dangerous at all times, they never once gave S. I. so much as an argument.
Traders that came later were beaten up, robbed, and tied to trees. The
Indians would invade pack-trip trail camps of whites, demand that a special meal be cooked for them, and get it. The Paiutes were members of a
band, led by a warrior named Old Posey, that fought deputy U.S. mar-
shals, Utah officers, and soldiers in southern Utah as late as 1923 (about
the same time that S. I. and Hubert were building Rainbow Lodge). The
local leader, the meanest of them all, had raped his own sister. As punish-
ment the other Paiutes had burned off one of his feet. At other trading posts
he continuously acted mean, yet at Rainbow Lodge he never once got out
of line until after S. I. left there.

The Navajo sheep were full of lice that winter. Anticipating the danger,
S. I. had trucked in several barrels of Blackleaf 40, a medication used to treat
the sheep. There were no dipping vats in the country, for agency government had not yet penetrated to Navajo Mountain. The Navajos bought
the poison by the gallon, mixed it with hot water in a wash tub, and swabbed
it on the undersides of their sheep. Those who didn't lost sheep all winter—
the lice literally ate them alive. The wool from these animals was used to
make blankets. The thickest woven blankets on the reservation, containing the poorest designs, were fabricated at Navajo Mountain. For many
years they sold only by the pound, never by the weave or pattern. The best
blankets came from as far away as Kayenta, where fine pine-tree and storm
patterns predominated.

* A Navajo term of respect.

Although I had heard about them before, I saw my first sandreader in action at Navajo Mountain. When he departed after trading, S. I. swore he was the real thing, citing as proof an incident that had happened the past spring, when S. I. had taken Homer Arhn (the head guide for packing dudes in to see Rainbow Natural Bridge) to Flagstaff to buy more horses and mules. Leaving Homer there, S. I. returned to the lodge. Shortly thereafter, Arhn wrote that he would leave Flagstaff on a certain date with a helper, driving across country on the nearest route to the mountain (which meant away from all roads, regular trails, and means of further communication). The date of Homer's estimated arrival passed, then

Navajo girls with lambs.

several more days. S. I. began to worry, afraid that Arhn had sustained an accident on some remote trail. Perhaps he had even been robbed and killed by some of the renegade Indians still around, especially the bad Paiutes at Willow Springs on Highway 89.

When the sandreader next came to the post, S. I. put the matter to him in all seriousness. The man, as is a fast rule with sandreaders, had to be promised that no matter what revelation he obtained, he would not be held responsible. Sandreading did not always turn out favorably or even answer the petitioner's question.

After being shown an old boot of Arhn's, the sandreader took a weaving batten to a pile of wind-blown sand. Smoothing and raking one spot continuously with the batten, he concentrated for more than an hour. Finally he spoke. "Your two men have crossed Navajo Canyon this way from Kaibito. Tonight, when the big star stands there in the sky," he reported, indicating its position, "they will be camped beside the road to Redlake near Red Mesa."

Interested, but somewhat cynical, S. I. asked for details about the stock that Arhn had purchased. The sandreader not only obliged, but described every animal, stating the age and the price paid for each one. Very carefully S. I. jotted this information down in a pocket notebook. Incredible as it may seem, the reader's statements proved to be the exact truth.

Thinking the matter over during the day, S. I. could scarcely credit it at all. Sure, he had known about sandreaders since his first days among the Navajos, but the wealth of details given him in this case was astounding. None of the information could possibly have been supplied to the man who read the sands of time. After supper, S. I. got out his Dodge sedan and drove across the canyons to the place where the sandreader claimed Arhn and his helper would camp for the night. On his approach, a flicker of firelight showed above the cedar-tree tops. Sitting at the fire, resting and drinking coffee, were the two men. They were well, nothing untowards having occurred during the trip; Arhn just hadn't gotten started on the date he had planned.

Beside the firelight with them, S. I. got out his notebook as Arhn began describing horses and mules, giving their ages and what he had paid for them. While marking them off in the book, S. I. would casually remark, "Yes, that's right," until, near the end of the list, Arhn stopped, staring at him suspiciously.

"What do you mean, 'That's right'? Somebody come up here and tell you what I bought and how much they cost? I can't imagine anyone knowing about these deals."

"A sandreader told me everything," S. I. explained. Arhn refused to believe any such stuff, even when S. I. called off the list that matched his statements. Finally Arhn began to smirk confidently.

"We're to that last little pony," he announced. "The *rocío* (roan) that ain't much to look at. We'll see how smart your sandreader is. How much does he say I paid for the critter?"

"It's already written down here. How much did you pay for it?"

"Twenty dollars."

"Like hell," replied S. I. amiably. "Since when did a gallon of corn whiskey cost twenty dollars? The whiskey's what you gave for the roan horse."

Arhn leaped to his feet, very angry, demanding, "What son of a bitch drove all the way up here just to squeal on me about the roan?"

"I told you—the sandreader; I asked him when I got worried about you."

"That's impossible! I'll figure out who told you and then I'll work him over until he can't see good!" Arhn absolutely refused to place any credence in the sandreader story, and for years afterward, whenever they met again, he would ask S. I. who had really given him all that information.

S. I. made it plain he wanted me to stay at Rainbow Lodge for the winter, but the next mail trip out of the area brought a letter from my aunt and uncle, Trula and C. D. Richardson. In addition to reservation trading posts, they owned a curio store in Flagstaff and another one in Phoenix. Since they planned on spending the winter in Phoenix, they wanted me to run their Flagstaff store. When the last truck headed south, I piled on it, barely getting out before the winter of 1924–1925 laid down the worst storm in years.

The Rainbow Trail

In the summer of 1923 (when I was still in the Navy), my uncle Hubert Richardson, accompanied by two friends, Billy Borum and J. J. Dunn, left his Kaibito Trading Post for Navajo Mountain. With a pack outfit the party plunged straight across the canyon country onto Rainbow Plateau, around Glass Mountain, and down Bridge Canyon to Rainbow Natural Bridge. Since the prospectors' invasion of the 1880s this area had remained almost unexplored. Some of the most magnificent scenery in the world abounded in the deep, spectacular, massed canyons. The wilderness represented the last known frontier in the United States: no roads entered here. The nearest Indian trading posts were at Kaibito and Shonto, both sixty-five to seventy air miles distant. The Colorado River on the west and the San Juan on the north blocked effective entrance from those directions, and the deep canyons south and east had, so far, proven barriers to ingress. The Navajo inhabitants lived in complete isolation, making annual pilgrimages on horseback to trade for supplies.

After this trip Hubert could not get the wild, glorious beauty of these magic lands out of his mind. He believed there was a great opportunity to open up its vastness and unmatchable scenery and that such progress would benefit not only himself, but also the Navajos living therein. To open the area would require a road for automobiles and trucks to supply a trading post in the heart of the wonderland. From his wholesale house in Winslow he began to consult old prospectors and others who had once been in the region; everyone assured him that constructing even the mere trace of a wagon road would be absolutely impossible. Had not Mormon colonists attempted it in the 1870s and failed? Penetrating that wilderness for trading and for tourists to have a jumping-off place to Rainbow Natural Bridge could only be a fantastic dream. Government agents, however, assured him of their complete cooperation if he dared make the attempt. The Indian Bureau, which wanted entrance made in this area in order to aid the Indians, would issue a trading license and the necessary permits.

The more people who ridiculed the idea and tried to discourage it, the stronger grew Hubert's determination to try. Furthermore, he felt confident

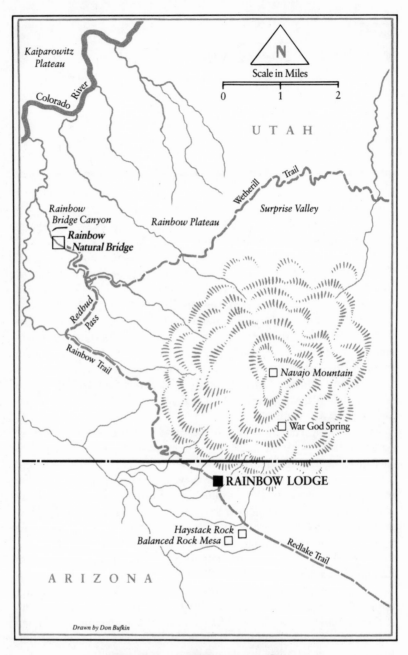

Kaiparowitz
Plateau

Colorado River

UTAH

N

Scale in Miles

0   1   2

Rainbow
Bridge Canyon

Rainbow
Natural Bridge

Rainbow Plateau

Wetherill Trail

Surprise Valley

Redbud Pass

Rainbow Trail

Navajo Mountain

War God Spring

RAINBOW LODGE

Haystack Rock
Balanced Rock Mesa

Redlake Trail

ARIZONA

Drawn by Don Bufkin

The Navajo Mountain Area

that he knew exactly the man who could accomplish the allegedly impossible. If anyone possessed the skill and know-how to get through into the Navajo Mountain country it would be his oldest brother—my father, S. I., the early-day Indian trader who then lived at Winslow. Hubert approached him with the proposition. They would be partners in the venture—S. I. would manage the lodge and trading post while Hubert would attend to outside business. This arrangement was necessary because the post would be two hundred miles from the railhead at Flagstaff, from which supplies must come via Cameron. A maintained road of sorts existed from Flagstaff to Redlake (Tonalea), the last outpost of civilization. Once leaving there they must cross sand dunes, valleys, and assertedly impassable canyons for seventy-four miles, making a road over which motor vehicles could move at slow speed.

Agreeing to explore the matter more, Hubert and S. I. went to Redlake to consult a long-time friend, Navajo patriarch John Daw. In early frontier times Daw had served as scout for the Army at Fort Defiance and Fort Wingate. On discharge, he moved west and he knew the Navajo Mountain country like the palm of his hand. They explained their proposal in detail to the old scout. At first he seemed dubious, but suddenly his brown face broke into smiles and his eyes flashed eagerly. "The Ute War Trail!" he exclaimed excitedly. "It is the only way to go. Others have forgotten it, but I remember. I can take you over it!"

This ancient trail, older than the memory of the Navajo, began from the confluence of four other trails: one, over which Father Escalante had come in 1776, crossed the Colorado River; a second moved directly down out of the Utah badlands; a third appeared from the junction of the Colorado and San Juan rivers; and the fourth came from the south, off the Hopi Salt Trail, to the joining place of the Colorado and the Little Colorado rivers. From where these paths became one, the joined trail passed southeastward through the canyon country, continued down through Red Valley, and then dwindled into tendrils that disappeared into the Painted Desert. Navajo raiding parties had used the upper trail from 1850 until the 1880s on their forays against Utah Mormon settlements. Their depredations had been so great during the years of the Civil War that frontier companies had been organized to guard the Arizona-Utah border.

Enthused over this precise information, the Richardsons returned home to begin assembling equipment and supplies for the expedition. Once put through, the road could be improved at leisure. They obtained a trading license and a permit from the Indian Bureau and posted bond. My brother,

Cecil, then nineteen years old, decided to go along, but not until March of 1924 did the expedition shape up.

The assembly at Cameron Trading Post included Hopi Walter Lewis, with his truck and several tribesmen, and Frank Mahan of Flagstaff, who would drive the Cameron truck. A stripped-down Dodge touring car and the three Richardsons completed the force. They expected to hire Navajo workmen along the route. The expedition left on March 17, driving straight through to Redlake, where John Daw awaited them.

Until the actual start, there had been discouragement and advice that the project couldn't be accomplished. But now, suddenly, hot opposition developed in many quarters. Telegraph messages burned the wires to important people in the national capital requesting immediate action to halt those enroute to Navajo Mountain. Hurried attempts were made to persuade first the Indian agent at Tuba City, then the Indian Bureau, and, finally, the U.S. Department of Interior to cancel the Richardson permits. They must be removed from the canyon country forthwith. All the attempts failed, however, because official attitude sponsored the opening up of the unknown area for the welfare of the tribe.

The main objection stemmed from the firm of Wetherill & Colville at Kayenta. John Wetherill had settled at Oljeto in 1906 and moved to Kayenta in 1910 in partnership with Clyde Colville. Wetherill had led the discovery party (in 1909) to Rainbow Natural Bridge, and thereafter he packed famous people there over a distance of more than seventy miles. Only rich people—like Theodore Roosevelt, Zane Grey, and Charles L. Bernheimer—could afford so expensive a trip. Wetherill and Colville were failures as Indian traders, going bankrupt four times;* they also suffered reverses by branching out elsewhere too fast. Their only livelihood accrued from costly pack trips into the wilderness which the McAdams-Richardson party now proposed to open to others. Their opposition to road building into the remote country was, therefore, understandable, but their attitude attempted to bar the progress of civilization, certain to come anyway.

John Daw joined my brother, Cecil, in the stripped-down Dodge—the spearhead for the explorers, which was destined to be the first motor vehicle to enter the Navajo Mountain country. Indians were easily engaged to work part of the way, and the first project on what became known as Rainbow Trail got under way five miles out along the Kayenta road.

---

*For a somewhat different interpretation of John Wetherill, see Frank McNitt, *The Indian Traders* (Norman: University of Oklahoma Press, 1962), pp. 271–272.

The party ripped out sagebrush all the way to Eagle Nest Rock. Here a dugway had to be cut through dirt banks over the rocky crossing of a wide wash that flooded often and unexpectedly. Sand beds were fixed for crossing, and then a switchback was cut up a rocky ridge. Emerging into Red Valley, the original road followed the eastern rim of the valley through low sand hills for twenty-two miles to the uppermost end of Red Mesa. The route then pitched suddenly into defiles over a narrow bench between two huge canyons. The pot-holed rock, leveled off a little, was lined with poles crossways, and clay mixed with bark was packed over them to form a corduroy road. The next twelve miles consisted of cutting brush and timber, grubbing out sagebrush, digging away hillside slopes to level passages, and making fills into and out of arroyos and washes.

In Zondelki Valley the party ran smack into Black Wash, and here the expedition very nearly came to an end. Navajo workmen hired along the way departed mysteriously in the middle of the night. Walter Lewis unloaded supplies carried in his truck and went back to Moenkopi Village with the other Hopis, and Hubert left on urgent business with his truck for Cameron. Abandoned on the side of the wash were S. I., Cecil, and John Daw. These three tore and blasted a hundred and fifty yards along a solid stone wall to create a narrow width of road. Fifteen miles of nothing but canyons faced them next—descent and ascent over the walls required heavy labor and hundreds of pounds of dynamite. Two Navajos living nearby appeared wanting work; they were hired and sent home for others. The following morning a large crew began road construction into a knifed-down canyon.

One afternoon a lone Indian rode up; he spoke briefly, and suddenly all the workers dropped their tools and disappeared quickly into the timber. Coming up to John Daw, the rider warned him to flee for his life—many strange Navajos had gathered at a hogan a few miles away, intending to raid the road camp. All found here would be killed.

Daw reported this to the Richardsons and dug out a six-gun that was kept handy in case of serious trouble. Hiding it in his clothing, he left at sundown. Walking to where the Navajos had collected, he found forty Indians who did not live in the area. They were armed and well supplied with grub. Their leaders were district headmen—Hosteen Little Salt (Wolf-Killer) and Hoskinni Begay—from Kayenta. None of them would talk to Daw and arrogantly ordered him to leave immediately, since he came from the camp of enemies.

Unable to obtain any information concerning their plans of offense, he had started to leave when he encountered an old woman waiting for him in the brushy timber. She informed him that the party planned to surround the road camp the following morning, to kill them if they refused to leave, and to destroy all equipment and supplies. Suspicious about the distant Indians' presence in the area, Daw asked her if white men had been around recently. She replied that three had departed just prior to his arrival. According to the old woman, the *billakonas* (Anglos) had spent the entire day haranguing the Navajos to proceed without further delay to run the Richardsons out.

Not the following morning, but that afternoon, twenty mounted Navajos appeared suddenly on one side of the road workers and twenty more on the other. The headmen talked in turn, screaming that the Richardsons must go immediately if they wished to live. John Daw remained alone on the new stretch of road—S. I. and Cecil, by prearrangement, had dropped down behind cover, wide apart, where rifles and six-guns were hidden for emergency use. The leaders eventually expended their wild talk, whereupon Daw picked up a long cudgel, informing them, "If you have come to fight, get down off your horses and let us get to it. If you have not come to fight, then go, for we have this road to build!"

Dark, inflamed eyes studied the tough old fighter, roving carefully over the two white men. Undoubtedly the Indians guessed that each one held firearms ready, although none were provocatively exposed to view. Daw now shouted at the bunch, telling them how stupid they were to engage in a fight at white men's behest. He warned that if anything serious occurred here, the Navajos who engaged in it would be the ones sent to prison, not

Navajo patriarch John Daw,
a long-time friend, acted as guide
and defended the Richardsons
in confrontations with hostile
Indians during construction of
the Rainbow Trail.

those who paid them to cause trouble. His angry words affected a few on the outside of each group. By twos and threes they began to slip away into the forest. Before long, the leaders sat in their saddles alone, and then they, too, wheeled their ponies off into the surrounding timber.

That night the road party hid out, armed and ready to beat off any sudden attack, but they agreed not to open fire unless absolutely necessary. A light snow fell before daylight. While the others cooked breakfast, Daw scouted the perimeter of the encampment. He reported that Indians had watched the spot all night long; at least ten had lurked around in the brush. "This looks very bad," he declared ominously. "The foolish ones may strike at any time, when we least expect them to jump on us."

S. I. suggested that Daw might not wish to fight against his own people. The old man looked indignant. "I finish what I start. Besides, these people aren't so tough!"

After completing the road across the deep canyon onto land between it and another canyon, they began blasting down the wall. But the trucks did not return on the stipulated date, and the Dodge could not move the equipment, provisions, and dynamite in a single day. Although an unguarded pile might be stolen, the men decided not to separate and thereby weaken each group enough to be more easily overcome. Every night Navajos surrounded the camp, their tracks being revealed in the next daylight. Then, one cold and snowy midnight, their scouts located S. I. in concealment and piled down on him in a mass. Before they could throttle him, he managed to create sufficient noise to alarm the others, who rushed to his aid. An unknown number of Indians engaged the men at close quarters. Clubs, rocks, and fists were thrown wildly in the melee. John Daw charged in yelling and swinging his cedar club. Amid all the noise of the struggle, the few attackers broke suddenly, fleeing into the night. Fortunately, no shots were fired. But the Indians were not gone for good; within the hour they could be heard crawling near the brush. The road builders were prepared now: sticks of dynamite had been fused to use as "bombs," and a few of these thrown about dispersed the attackers.

Rations were short and, in an attempt to get meat, John Daw went over into Paiute Canyon. While unsuccessful, he did manage to hire a Navajo with a wagon to come help move supplies. One load in it and one in the Dodge were taken across, but on the next trip, a dozen riders swooped out of the timber. Their anger frightened the wagon owner who unhooked his team on the spot and departed hurriedly. When challenged, these riders also pulled out. Since the next camp offered better defense, the Dodge was driven there with load after load as fast as it could be bounced over rocks and chuckholes. The men also carried equipment and supplies afoot. Daw didn't think they were being watched during the day, but they certainly would be after sundown, when Kayenta Navajos could slip in close unseen. By nightfall, however, the desperately working men had shifted camp.

A short time later two Navajos appeared from the south asking for work, and they proved to be of considerable help. One dark night a kinsman of John Daw's slipped in to warn him that the white men had been back demanding that the renegade Navajos from Kayenta make good their promise to get rid of the daredevil road builders. They had been paid to do so, and now they must produce results. The following day the attackers surrounded the new camp, the riders remaining at a stone's throw, while the leaders walked in. They came prepared with a new kind of argument—persuasion. They claimed that if the road was finished, many white men would come to steal all the Navajos' land. Water would be usurped and soon the Indians' sheep and cattle must starve for lack of it. Therefore, why didn't these white men go away and leave them in peace?

When they were talked out, S. I. stood up and explained that water for the new trading post would be developed. No water now claimed by Navajos would be taken from them. Exhibiting the trading license and entry permit, he informed them that Washington, the magic place of power to Navajos, stood behind the road to Navajo Mountain. Furthermore, on the way were truckloads of men necessary to complete the road and build Rainbow Lodge. He asked the Indians pointedly what their interest was in the security of the Navajo Mountain country, since they themselves didn't live anywhere near the area.

At this moment a party of Navajo riders, including headman Hosteen Indischee, White Hat, Sagney Yazzie, Red Shirt, and Little Man rode up. A huge man, Hosteen Indischee climbed off his horse, making no greeting to the white men. Instead, he addressed himself angrily to the Kayenta Indians. The previous night, he said, two white men had been to his hogan, asking that he arouse all Indians for miles around to attack the road camp. Only then had Hosteen Indischee learned what the renegade Indians were up to, or he would have come to the Richardsons' camp sooner. As chief of the district, he—and all his people—wanted the road put through and a trading post established for their benefit. No more interference from the Kayenta Indians would be tolerated; his men were on their way to the camp now to help work on the road. His speech drew short as he laid down the law. Without a word of rebuttal, the Kayenta Navajos rode away.

For breakfast the next morning there remained only one small box of Cream of Wheat; there being no other food, the road party ate it. Indians began arriving from the north to go to work, and the workmen must be fed, so John Daw started off, riding one of the newcomers' horses, hoping to buy meat and cornmeal at some isolated hogan. He didn't get far before he heard the grinding of approaching trucks. Hastening back to camp, he delivered the good news: after more than two weeks' absence, Hubert had returned with an abundance of supplies in two trucks and more workmen.

The road building now went forward quickly. Soon they were out of the canyons and on the open plateau, just below the slope of Navajo Mountain. At this point Daw was out of his element; the Ute War Trail split apart, and he didn't know how to reach Willow Springs on the mountainside—nor did any of the other Indians. Beyond the camp, pitched at Haystack Rock, stretched nearly three miles of ascending terrain filled with rocks and timber. The area was cut by many small canyons and washes and appeared impassable.

No water could be located anywhere, much less the fabled Willow Springs. Although renegade Indians and whites and hardships had failed to stop them, it looked as though the Richardsons were defeated at last. So discouraged did everyone in camp become that they took a vote whether to attempt going on or to abandon the project so near success. The majority vote favored immediate withdrawal. Consensus of opinion held that the road must end with water, which they couldn't find. Stunned, Cecil jumped to his feet and talked fast. They had stood off Indians and crossed all the dangerous canyons which they had been told couldn't be crossed; within sight of their goal, did they intend to submit to despair? His speech encouraged them to try once more.

With daylight the entire party spread out in a mile-long line, searching up the great slope toward whitish sandstone cliffs visible on a distant shoulder of the mountain. But they found no water. Where had they failed to look for the springs? At this point, through the thick cedars from the direction of Cummings Mesa rode Indischee Begay and Slim Fingers, both Navajos known to S. I. from his Kaibito trading days.

Following the exchange of greetings, the two Navajos inquired what all the men were doing walking around in the timber. S. I. told them and asked if they knew the location of the springs. Slim Fingers motioned him to split his saddle (mount up). Back up the slope they all went, closer in against the mountain cliffs, and there they found the wall containing the inscription "George Emmerson Ap. 1, 1882." Several springs flowed out at this spot to form a small stream that ran off a short distance before sinking into the ground again. Five days later the final section of Rainbow Trail became a fact, and camp was pitched on the side of the mountain below the spring where Rainbow Lodge and Trading Post would be built.

Redbud Pass
and Rainbow Lodge

Mother, whom we always called by her first name, Susie, came to Navajo Mountain behind the first truckload of freight over the completed Rainbow Trail in 1924. Hopi Indians were put to hauling steadily, and Mexican workmen from Flagstaff built the lodge. Before a dollar in trade passed over the store counter, the Richardsons had spent $50,000; soon they were to be confronted with an additional expense not anticipated.

Trader John Wetherill had taken Charles L. Bernheimer, a New York shirt manufacturer, to the west side of Navajo Mountain during the summers of 1921 and 1922. Supposedly they had spent months each year constructing a trail from there through what became known as Redbud Pass to Bridge Canyon, which afforded the nearest access to the giant natural bridge. If this information were true, then from newly built Rainbow Lodge it would mean only eighteen miles by horse to the national monument—a fraction of the distance via the long-used east trail. (The eastern passage formed a spur of the ancient Ute War Trail, over which Paiute Indians had entered Bridge Canyon to winter their stock for the past century.) But now the Richardsons discovered that the newer trail existed only in someone's fertile imagination. Homer Arhn, who worked for my father, drove in stock for the dude-packing end of the business. He and S. I. rode the canyons and slopes seeking evidence of the Bernheimer Trail. Finally Indians took them to scattered places where they said the Wetherill-Bernheimer party had camped at various times during those summer months. If these were actual sites, then the alleged trail—of which no evidence existed—approached through a distant flat valley to enter any one of several canyons. Even if the Richardsons had been able to use the supposed route, it would have meant an unnecessary thirty miles of trail travel.

Instead of even attempting to use the almost nonexistent passage, S. I. and Homer Arhn lined a twelve-mile trail direct from Rainbow Lodge, straight across precipitous canyons. Indians were employed to blast the rock and dig it out to negotiate the several narrow defiles. On Cliff Canyon, which had to be descended in a steep drop of two thousand feet, flat turnouts were made for the stock to rest on the ascent. The balance of the trail

Left: Redbud Pass, on the trail to Rainbow Natural Bridge.
Below: Entrance to the trading post at Rainbow Lodge on Navajo Mountain, near Redbud Pass.

into Redbud Pass came easily enough, but now they found that no such pass existed.

Two great masses of stone joined together to block the way, with only a mere crack between them. Apparently the Wetherill-Bernheimer party did no more than build up a saddle, with rubble in the lowest places in order to cross to the other side. Torrents of water running off the masses of solid stone had washed everything out to a depth of twenty feet in the crack, which was less than a foot wide. Drills and dynamite were packed in to tear stone asunder and widen the crack enough to get unladen stock through. This job required ten thousand dollars worth of explosives to create the first, very narrow Redbud Pass. In later years, several government agencies spent at least fifty thousand dollars more on the pass. By stretching facts a little, this one spot might be said to have once constituted part of the Bernheimer Trail—it was fifty feet higher on the wall than where the Richardsons made passage.

Trail building progressed rapidly on into Bridge Canyon and to Rainbow Natural Bridge. There improvements were made and a supply box set up. The first men who arrived at the bridge discovered that the free base of the stone arch had been chiseled and disfigured: a score of carved names left by visitors before 1909 had only recently been destroyed. Somebody must have hurried in ahead of them by the east trail to remove the dates, for those inscriptions disproved the claim that no white man had seen Rainbow Natural Bridge prior to its "official" discovery in 1909.

The arch spanning Bridge Canyon Creek—309 feet high, 278 across, and 40 feet thick at the top—had first been visited by beaver trappers. Then came prospectors seeking a lost gold mine. Scores of men saw the bridge long before 1909. Some of their names (once on the bridge and in Bridge Canyon) and the dates they were there include J. P. Williams, 1883; Ben and Bill Williams, 1884; George Emmerson, 1882; Ed Randolph, 1880; Jim Black, 1881; Alf Dickinson, 1888; George McCormick, 1894; C. M. Wright, 1892; A. G. Turner, 1896; G. E. Choistilan, 1888; W. Brockway, 1883; W. D. Young, 1882; J. E. H., 1880; John Hadley, 1885; and C. M. Cade, 1869 or 1889. These names had been cut with a chisel or marked with charcoal in many protected places on the bridge, in Bridge Canyon, and in canyons throughout the area around it. Probably for each one of those who left his name and date behind, fifty others didn't bother.

What I know of these men is the following: J. P. Williams took up a homestead in Blue Canyon in 1882, east of Redlake—Ben and Bill were his sons; Ed Randolph lived at Flagstaff until his death; Jim Black spent a lifetime in and out of Navajo Mountain country, and Jim Black Basin, not far from the bridge, is named for him; Alf Dickinson and George McCormick spent their lives at Flagstaff also; C. M. Wright and A. G. Turner found gold on Ashley Bar in the Colorado River; John Hadley was an early-day Indian trader, and some Navajos around Tuba City bear his name.

Joe Lee, who left his name cut nowhere, spent the winter of 1879–1880 in Bridge Canyon with the family of Paiute chief Nasja, wintering horses. Joe Lee and Nasja's nephew, Nasja Begay (son of Nasja Soney), who led white men there in 1909, played under the arch as youngsters.

Down through the years, a question has often been asked by the unthinking. If all these people actually saw Rainbow Bridge, why didn't they report such an astounding, wonderful object? They did, in fact, talk about it to others who were about to enter that far country. Then consider that there are a thousand square miles of southern Utah and northern Arizona containing natural bridges galore. Of what special interest to them was one more, when they were a dime a dozen?

The 1909 discoverers—the Byron Cummings–John Wetherill party—were joined by the party of government surveyor William Boone Douglass. Charges, claims, and countercharges arose among them before they even examined the natural bridge. The controversy over who had accomplished what grew in volume and exploded in furious anger on their return to civilization. There was no resolution to the claims of either side, and the bitter arguments lasted all their lives. Stories concerning discovery and personal claims of individuals were raised anew when the Richardsons entered the canyon country, making access easy for the ordinary traveler. Their printed brochures and the publicity produced by auto clubs, travel agencies, Fred Harvey tour cars, and travel caravans brought considerable response. Harry Carr, then travel editor of the *Los Angeles Times,* wrote extensively about the road and trails to Rainbow Bridge. Every time a major article appeared, members of the 1909 parties or their supporters wrote fiery letters insisting that their "true" statements on the controversy be recognized as valid. The Richardsons engaged in no quarrel with anyone. They acceded to no demands from either side to publicize one over the other—it became the policy to let the scrappers settle their own differences.

The Richardsons gave no name to their expensive trail through Redbud Pass, but they did sign and call the road north from Redlake "Rainbow Trail." For years they continued working the road, shortening it and improving passages through deep canyons around hairpin turns. Finally, the Indian Service took over. After S. I. withdrew from Navajo Mountain, various government agencies rebuilt and shortened more sections of the road. One important and scenic elevation on it became known as "Christmas

Tree Hill," so named by the first school teacher at Navajo Mountain, Elizabeth Eubanks.

Charles Bernheimer became very much incensed that this seventy-four-mile road, as well as the trail through Redbud Pass, was not named for him (he brought the matter up to Homer Arhn a year after Rainbow Lodge came into being). Influential people contacted Hubert and S. I. in an endeavor to name the road and several trails for various individuals among the 1909 discoverers. These people grew angry when their demands were ignored, but the Richardsons had no authority, not even by eminent domain, to name anything in the region. The land belonged to the Navajo tribe and was controlled by the Bureau of Indian Affairs under the Department of Interior. In the Richardsons' opinion, and correctly so, any titling of geographical features was solely within the jurisdiction of the federal government.

Over the new road, after the Richardsons, came others bent on exploiting the advantages it offered. A trading post was built at Cottonwood Springs (next to the east base of the mountain later called Dunn's, across the Utah line). The inevitable missionaries and hunters of clay pots were next to appear on the scene. However, because of the route built into their vast wilderness, the Navajos reaped formerly undreamed-of benefits. The government drilled water wells and put in dipping vats to rid their stock of lice and certain diseases. More important, the Indian medical service stretched forth a helping hand all the way from the hospital at Tuba City. Day schools were built (one of them later became a boarding school), better roads and trails were constructed, and a telephone line went in. Once hopelessly remote from the seat of their tribal government, more than three hundred miles away, the Navajos were placed almost next door to it by modern lines of communication.

Rich tourists, then better known as "dudes," began arriving on Navajo Mountain even before Rainbow Lodge was finished. Guides and packers were taking them to the natural bridge, up on the mountain, and through the vividly colored gorges in the area before the barest accommodations were ready.

Fixed rates to the bridge were never high, but private exploring pack trips were necessarily expensive. In those days one or two dudes didn't mind spending as much as twenty-five hundred dollars for a single trip into the canyon hinterland. There was far more to see and enjoy in the region than just the natural bridge—Surprise Valley, Poverty Butte, the Three War Peaks, Navajo Canyon, and cliff ruins of dead cities like Inscription House, Tsegi (Keet Seel), and Betatakin. These ruins, in turn, were minor attractions compared to the high cave homes of some long-vanished peoples, some never seen before by white men. The longest trip most dudes took by pack train wound through the vast wonderland of southern Utah to Escalante, one of the most remote villages in the United States.

Every year that S. I. managed Rainbow Lodge, advance reservations kept the post filled with guests. Despite this, the expense of traveling in a land of great distances prohibited any profit. The dude business, greater during his tenure than at any other period, hardly broke even; under other managers and owners it sustained a steady loss. The Indian business, however, made money at Rainbow Lodge: the first year a total of fifty-seven hundred dollars was collected. This amount, with twelve thousand dollars more, was paid back to the Indians for road and trail work. Despite the high cost of merchandise delivered at the lodge, the store continued to show a book profit. The freight rate both ways was exactly five dollars per one hundred pounds. The Richardsons tried to cut this cost by operating their own trucks, but they lost money; only Hopi Indians were able to freight profitably over the rough roads.

Life was hard on Navajo Mountain—few comforts, no telephone, infrequent mail—and the nearest medical aid in the mid-1920s was the government hospital at Tuba City, one hundred thirty miles and fifteen hours away. When people took sick, they had to make do with whatever was handy. The year after the lodge opened, my sister, Irbymae, returned home from school at Winslow. A few days later she came down with the measles, and then developed pneumonia. Home remedies and patent medicines failed to do much good: she was literally burning with fever. Homer Arhn rode onto the mountain, up by War God Spring, and returned with a sack of crystallized snow. It did the trick, killing her fever; the next day she could sit up in bed.

One worry was always in the background, although everyone carefully avoided mentioning it: during a harsh winter someone might become seriously ill or injured in an accident. There would be no possibility of getting the victim out to medical aid or of bringing it in—not with upper canyon heads filled with snow and snow lying five or six feet deep on the levels. In case of death there was the grim prospect of keeping the body frozen until spring for burial.

The ruined city of Betatakin in the western Navajo country.

When spring did arrive it beautified the country, which slowly turned green in the warm air. Then flowers bloomed and songbirds livened the trees. The roads were broken open, winter damage was repaired, and people came and went constantly. A cook and other help became necessary to care for the wants of the dudes, and all these people created a busy, close-knit community at Rainbow Lodge. Then, when the season ended and winter closed down, the trading post lapsed into silence and monotonous loneliness. The Navajos and Paiutes were still around, but finally their appearances at the trading post also slacked off because of ice and snow. Perhaps knowing the feeling of aloneness, the main Indian families around the mountain tried to get through to visit the people imprisoned at the trading post. When they did, they remained only a few days, returning to the warmth of deep canyons when the weather broke briefly.

Sometimes in the summer hikers showed up to camp in the timber below the corrals. When they shouldered packs and started walking the trail for Rainbow Bridge, S. I. and his guides regarded them in grave sadness. The trail for walking was a pure man-killer. Going downhill was one thing;

ascending the wall out of Cliff Canyon was quite another, requiring supreme physical exertion. Only the unusually fit could make it. Often, in
the middle of the night, a distraught man might awaken the entire lodge in
desperate urgency: far down the trail a party of hikers would be lying prone
on the trail, exhausted and unable to crawl another foot. So the guides
would have to saddle up and pull them out on horseback—gratis—in the
interest of humanity.

As was true elsewhere in isolated country beyond the law, the trader became a "judge" whether he wanted to or not, and his advice and counsel
were sought often. In case of a dispute, what was more logical for the liti-
gants than to take their argument to the nearby wise man, their friend, for
a decision? S. I. thoroughly detested the "judge" business, and always
avoided it if possible. The first case that reached him at Rainbow Lodge
concerned his old friend Slim Fingers, who had shown the way to the springs.
Another Navajo had recently taken Slim Fingers's current wife away from
him. What should he do to gain revenge and maintain his self-respect? When
pressed for counsel, S. I. began, "It seems to me that this man bought a
brand new wagon a few months ago."

"He did," agreed Slim Fingers. "You sold him a very good one."

"Tell you what," said S. I. "Why don't you slip over to his hogan some
dark night and unscrew all the taps from the wheels?"

Slim Fingers departed. S. I. had no idea he would dare venture so near
the tough wife-stealer's hogan, but the very next afternoon Slim Fingers
entered the store grinning from ear to ear. He dropped a grain sack containing all four wagon-wheel taps onto the counter. Having had his revenge, he felt his honor was avenged, and shortly after this he married
another woman to herd his sheep.

Another case of S. I.'s kept the countryside laughing for months. A
certain man who had two wives didn't care much for the older one. An
old friend arrived to spend the night. Because it was cold, the husband
told him to go sleep with his older wife, but the friend slept with the
younger one instead. Discovering this in the morning, the husband brought
the friend and the guilty young wife to the post. The facts were stated,
and the husband claimed damages; what did S. I. think the husband should
be paid?

The friend was wealthy in stock and owned far too many burros that were good for nothing but moving sheep camp. Since the burros were cheap, S. I. presumed he could easily stand the loss of one. He so rendered his decision: one burro for the night spent with the young wife. The judgment was satisfactory all around, and the group departed together in a friendly mood.

Unfortunately, S. I. had established a precedent and a price. That fall the burro owner showed up at Rainbow Lodge again. "You remember all those burros I used to own?" he asked, laughing.

"You *used* to own?"

"You remember I paid one burro for sleeping one night with my friend's wife? Well, I don't own even a single burro anymore. He has them all!"

After a few seasons S. I. sold his half share of Rainbow Lodge to his brother Hubert and moved down onto Red Mesa, where he established Inscription House Trading Post. Stanton Borum then managed Rainbow Lodge for a while before Hubert turned the running of it over to his brother-in-law, W. W. (Billy) Wilson. Later, when Rainbow Lodge had become a dude-catering business for the natural bridge and pack trips into the wilds, Hubert sold it to Billy Wilson and Barry Goldwater.

Tuba City

In the winter of 1924–1925 I ran a curio store in Flagstaff for my Aunt Trula and Uncle C. D. Richardson. That winter hurled down with a vengeance, and, in those days, about all you could do was den up and try to keep warm. People who could afford it garaged their cars, closed their businesses, and moved to Phoenix or California. I managed to stick it out until March of 1925, when I went visiting in California. In Modesto I ran across a blue-eyed Irish girl, Millicent Margaret Green. I persuaded her to marry me, and we motored back to Arizona in a Chevrolet touring car.

During my brief absence, C. D. and Trula had started building a trading post at Tuba City, where three other posts already did business. The people Aunt Trula had employed didn't know much about barter trading, and she wanted me to take over, at least until they could make arrangements for a resident manager. Because I was not very interested, Millie and I continued north to Navajo Mountain, visiting there with my parents at Rainbow Lodge for three or four weeks. Aunt Trula continued to ask me to work, and finally we went to Tuba City in the spring of 1925. The government had bought out the Mormon settlers long ago—the last of them had moved away in 1904. The Western Navajo Indian agency had been established there in 1902, and to it was added a vocational school at Blue Canyon; the agency then became a general boarding school.

The new Richardson trading post stood at the west end of Main Street in Tuba City, against a mass of sand hills through which the old road to Kaibito ran. Second-story living quarters of the stone building were not yet completed, so we moved into a shack of boxing plank. Consisting of a kitchen and a bedroom, it stood on a narrow lane directly south of the post under Lombardy poplars planted by Mormon colonists.

Khaki, a Pima Indian, and Buster Prochnow, from Flagstaff, worked in the store when I arrived. The business ran very heavy for a new post; in addition, sheep-buying season was about to start. After inventory, the stock orders were sent in. Supplies had to be built up to accommodate the expected extra rush of customers that would arrive when sheep dipping began in the wash three miles away. Navajos in the district dipped their flocks on government orders, and during that period we would buy lambs and old ewes. This year the Indian agent wanted traders to purchase, and, thus, remove from eroded ranges, as many sheep as possible. The area was over-stocked far beyond capacity, and there wasn't enough grass to carry the Navajo sheep through the winter.

Every night after sundown a group of Navajos would hang around the Tuba City post. One of them was blind old Charley Day. A small boy would lead him in just at sunset. He lived a short distance away at a spring named after him. Charley had been raised in England by a wealthy couple, who had brought him there when he was a small child. After their deaths, he had returned to the United States, but had forgotten his own language and the tribe he belonged to. After eight years of wandering around, he stopped in Flagstaff. On the street he heard Navajos talking in their dialect, and a few words came back to him. He then went to Tuba City to work at the boarding school. He learned Navajo and really turned "native." So much did he take to the tribal religion that it had probably caused his blindness: some minor illness had inflamed his eyes, and instead of going to the agency doctor, he had called in the Navajo medicine man. The native belladonna used to treat him destroyed both pupils. By the time the agency doctor got him to a specialist at Fort Defiance hospital, nothing could be done to save his sight.

Once he said wistfully to me, "I wish that one more time I could watch the *Kisani* use their throwing sticks." He was referring to the Hopis' boo-merang. At certain times of the year they gathered in a large group on Rab-bit Mesa northeast of Tuba City. Attired in moccasins and g-strings, they carried these throwing sticks in a hunt for rabbits. Forming a big circle in the area, they closed in, pushing cottontail rabbits to the center. When nar-rowed into such a small space, the rabbits tried to dart between running Hopis, who then threw their curved sticks, knocking them over one by one. This was tops among Indian sports, and it also served the purpose of ob-taining a winter's supply of meat and rabbit skins for making robes.

Another of our night gossipers was Saginitso, a Navajo cowman who lived down Moenkopi Canyon. He sold cattle by the hundreds and kept his money in the post safe. In those days Indians often left funds with the trader for safekeeping, and at that time, Saginitso had about eight thousand dollars in a sealed envelope. When his store bill reached several hundred dollars, he would take it out, pay us, take another hundred dollars to spend elsewhere, and reseal the envelope. Saginitso wanted to own and drive a car like the white men, so he got an Indian who knew how to drive to teach him. That winter they went to Flagstaff and purchased a Dodge sedan. The lessons were progressing well until one night when the radiator was not drained of water; the motor froze up and busted the block. Instead of buying and installing a new motor, Saginitso bought another new sedan in a hurry. Before long he dismissed his teacher, deciding he could drive his car anywhere. En route to Flagstaff on a weekend he missed a highway bridge and completely wrecked the second new car. He never tried driving another car; the one with the busted block sat for years beside his canyon hogan, rusting away. He talked about it constantly, always mentioning "my car" as if he were using it every day.

Big Jim Maloney was a Navajo in charge of the apple orchard which had been set out by Mormons in 1880. He packed and stored fruit every fall to feed school children during the winter. He also juiced the culls and wormy apples, making an excellent hard cider on the quiet. Occasionally he gave us a gallon at the store. Somehow a missionary found out about the hard-cider business and griped to a special Indian Service officer, who jailed Big Jim before seizing any evidence. While the officer was occupied trying to make Big Jim reveal the whereabouts of the cache, I decided to act quickly. Taking Buster Prochnow along, I drove to the far orchard fence. We slipped unseen behind a packing shed and located the hole in the ground where Big Jim kept his stuff. We removed a ten-gallon oak keg, about half full, and hid it in the post warehouse.

By sundown, sans evidence, the federal officer had to release Big Jim. The Navajo did just what the officer reasoned he would: he hastened to get rid of the evidence. No sooner did Big Jim open the cache than the officer and an agency policeman grabbed him, but when they looked into the hole, they found it empty. A week later, we told Big Jim to come and get what remained of his cider. Because we had saved his hide, Big Jim could never do enough to return the favor. He kept us in boxes of apples and bottles of cider until supplies ran out.

The missionary who had tried to get Big Jim was a sly character. Every September, when truckloads of children arrived at the boarding school, he had them marched to his church on Main Street. He issued the boys a pocket knife and the girls a string of colored glass beads for permitting themselves to be dunked into a tank of water. They didn't know they were actually being baptized into his religion. Each fall the childrens' names were sent to the headquarters of the church as new converts, so for ten years the missionary had an outstanding record with his home office. Then one day a preacher from his own group found him out, and the sneaky preacher was transferred hastily to a distant post.

T*uba* C*ity*

In 1925 Bill O'Brien ran Babbitt Brothers Trading Post in Tuba City; the post was down at the village entrance on Main Street. John Kerley, who had managed the Babbitt store for fourteen years, had finally quit and had put in his own store, Kerley's Trading Post, which was down in the canyon beside the road out to the highway. The James brothers, two Hopi Indians, operated a store in nearby Moenkopi village. Although I soon had C. D. and Aunt Trula's store doing more business than any of the long-established ones, none of them ever gave me any trouble. In fact, we got along fine, doing favors for each other—which happened to be unusual in a sometimes cutthroat business. Neither the James brothers' nor the Babbitts' post bought sheep; Kerley started in buying but, since I got about ninety percent of them, he made a deal for me to take the few he had off his hands at cost.

After we began buying sheep, a man named Max—with his wife and three children—arrived at the post, bringing a letter from C. D. telling me to put him to work. This came as a big surprise because two years before, while running The Gap post for C. D., Max had been fired for stealing: a considerable sum of money in government checks, received in the course of post business, had been converted by him into cash, which he had pocketed. I didn't want any part of Max, but these were orders from the boss.

Max considered himself better qualified to manage the business than I was, and he tried ordering everyone around. He also considered himself something of a slugger: obviously, before long Max would have to be put in his place. When the time came, I decided I would not argue, but would knock him down first. Knowing him to be crooked, I warned the clerks, Buster and Khaki, to watch him all the time; if he started fooling with the cash drawer, they were to let me know.

When we started buying sheep, I took Buster to the dipping pens. I taught him how to tooth the sheep, and how to guess reasonably closely the weight of lambs (this was before we used scales). Buyers wouldn't accept any animal under forty pounds, and gummer ewes (old ewes that had lost most of their teeth) could never make the long drive to railroad shipping pens, so these sheep were not to be selected. Buster caught on to the business fast and the buying was turned over to him. We used silver to pay for sheep— dollar, fifty-cent, and two-bit pieces; this cash, carried loose in flour sacks, was thrown onto the back seat of a car. At the time of payment, sales tickets were made out to keep records and to certify to the Indian agent how many animals and what types were purchased. The post brand was painted on the sheep, and they were then turned over to our Navajo herder.

Ten o'clock one morning after Max's arrival, Buster returned to the store very angry. He wanted to know why I had taken him off buying. Max had shown up, sworn that I had sent him there to do it, and had taken over. We tore back down to the dipping pens, where I took charge of the sacked silver and the sales book. A check against balances revealed a shortage of twenty-five dollars. When I demanded the money, Max sneered at me. Within a moment, however, he must have decided not to tackle me, for he sought to make light of the situation: "I did put some money in a coat pocket before going over to buy those last lambs. No use packing it all around. Clean forgot!" Digging into a pocket, he produced the exact amount in silver.

After he left the buying area, I remained with Buster for about half an hour. When I returned to the store, Khaki reported that Max had taken some money from the cash drawer—a quick count showed seventy-five dollars gone. Going to the door, I saw Max loading his family into their car. When I called him to come over, he surprised me by doing so. "Let's have the money from the drawer," I said. He said that they were going to town and that he had drawn some money against his wages. He had worked less than a week, however, and had already charged a hundred and five dollars in merchandise on the books against his one-hundred-fifty-dollar salary.

"You owe the store several times what your wages amount to," I told him. "Fork up the money you stole and then get out of here. You're fired."

"You can't fire me!"

Without another word I hit him in the jaw. He fell against one side of the front door frame, sliding down on his haunches. The money had been wadded into a side coat pocket, where I found it. Only addled, he got up, slowly shaking himself. Instead of going for me, he hurried to his car and drove away to Flagstaff.

But I wasn't rid of Max by any means. Two days later my uncle C. D. drove up and entered the store. Behind him appeared Max, unloading his family at the cabin again. When I gave C. D. the story in brief, he nodded glumly. "The man is a natural-born thief, but right now I've got to keep him a little longer for old times' sake. He and I went to school together in Texas. The family is hard up, and his wife cried half the night on Trula's shoulder about his losing his job. We'll try to keep him from stealing too much."

Before I could tell him that maybe, under the circumstances, he also needed to replace me, C. D. announced that he was taking personal charge of the post. This relieved me of any responsibility, no matter what the crook stole. Of course, Max kept right on swiping anything not nailed down. Later that fall, when C. D.'s son-in-law, Harold Wheeler, worked at the post, he caught Max red-handed. Harold put a sudden end to Max's employment by tossing him through the front door into the road.

It is my belief that old-time traders made thieves of their employees. When teaching a new clerk the business, they explained in detail the necessary tricks of beating Navajo customers before they robbed you. Many of the old Navajos were sharp as diamond dust. As trader Joe Lee said, they had nothing else to do but sit around their hogans for days, thinking up a shrewd scheme to take the trader. When a Navajo managed to pull off such a scheme, fellow tribesmen looked on him with great respect, and he could also brag for weeks of being cunning like *mai* (the coyote).

Traders used to short-weigh wool because it often had a few rocks, sand, or ten pounds of sheep excrement in it. There were a thousand and one ways wily Navajo customers could beat the trader sight unseen. This was the reason that the inexperienced, investing in a trading post, soon went broke. But a new clerk, trained into being a shrewd trader, would sit down at night and total how much he had beaten customers out of during the day. It didn't occur to him how much the customers had cheated the store with their combined small swindles. What he seemingly crooked them of would grow larger and larger in his mind: since he was making his boss incredibly rich by his own smartness, why shouldn't he be entitled to part of it—along with the niggardly salary he was drawing? Very soon the embryo thief would convince himself he had something coming, and he'd start to pocket it. As a result, the trading post would soon start to show a loss instead of a profit.

Fortunately, in later days Navajo trading was considerably different, with packaged goods and set prices. Indian products bought over the counter for cash could be sold for cash, and this change for the better made for square dealing between customer and trader. Unfortunately, there were no longer any real traders in the Navajo country. A post manager became a merchant's clerk, keeping regular hours, as in town stores. He worked for a corporation or an absentee owner who was seen perhaps once or twice a year. Nor, in these later days, did he need to speak the Navajo language as we did; for his customers spoke, read, and wrote English almost as well as he.

Shonto

In 1925 the resident trader at Shonto Trading Post for my uncle C. D. Richardson was John Howell, a Texan who had come to Arizona trying to arrest a case of tuberculosis. He appeared to be recovering slowly; then one night he nearly bled to death. Indians hauled him in a wagon to Redlake, where he caught a ride by truck to the hospital in Tuba City. "You will have to go to Shonto now," C. D. told me. "I had planned on sending you there anyway, to buy piñons. You and Millie drive up there and open up again."

Shonto was twenty-five miles from Redlake in a canyon. In those days the road branched off the Kayenta highway through Rock House Valley, thence into and up the canyon, between and around a series of lakes, to the post, which was located under the east rim. Joe Lee had originally built a one-room store there in 1914, running it in partnership with Wetherill and Colville. That same year, since they had not been able to keep him stocked with trade goods, Lee had persuaded them to sell the post to C. D. Abandoning the very small cabin at a spring, C. D. had put in a long, stone store building. Living quarters on the east end formed the post into an L shape.

Piñon season had just started when Millie and I arrived at the locked store in the fall of 1925. At least fifty Indians had arrived also, and the post mailman was there watching the place until we reached it. Someone had named this man Calamity because his frozen face had never shown a smile once during his sixty years. There were sheep waiting, also, watched over by the post's herder, Hosteen Senijeni. His niece, an educated girl named Edith, worked in the living quarters and occasionally helped in the store.

It took me until late that night to buy piñons and some sheep, and then trade them out. After missing supper at the regular mealtime, I sat alone, eating in the kitchen. Edith had gone to her hogan and Millie to bed. Unexpectedly, the side door leading to the rear yard opened slowly, and in stepped a small, aged Navajo wearing a purple neckerchief around done-up, long hair. Barely inside the door, he halted and studied me at some length in the lamplight glow. When I asked him what he wanted, he replied, "I must talk to you about your father. Will you allow it?"

Inviting him to the table, I offered him an extra cup of coffee. He gazed at me appraisingly before accepting it; then tears beaded his eyes. "What the devil," I thought. "Is this *hosteen* nuts?" He probably supposed C. D. was my father, or maybe Hubert, for, according to the Navajo system of kinship, your uncles were also considered your fathers, and your aunts your mothers. Then, in one of the few times I ever heard a Navajo break the ancient custom never to speak his own name, he announced quietly, "I am Hosteen Ushe Yazzie."

Here sat Little Salt, one of the Navajo renegade headmen who had caused the Richardsons so much trouble when they were building the Navajo mountain road. Curious, I waited for him to proceed. Little Salt meant my real father. He related in a sorrowful voice how he had been misled by once-trusted white men. The deed he greatly regretted, and it preyed on his mind, for he said men could have been slain on that road. Of course, he minimized his part in it. Talking at length, he revealed much more evidence of the white men's part in instigating the Navajos to surround the road-builders' camp than John Daw had learned at the time.

Eventually my visitor arose to leave. At the door, shaking hands, he said, "Tell your father all I have spoken. You can plead my cause, for surely you can see I am not a bad man. I wish to be friends." Believing that I had, in fact, spoken to my father, he walked two weeks later into Rainbow Lodge trading post. Smiling and shaking hands, he called S. I. "friend," and, until Little Salt died many years later, he proved to be just that.

Old traders were unwholesomely tricky. Even best friends, if competitors, took business away from each other. Sometimes they pulled fast tricks just for kicks, and to amuse the remote countryside. I remember a trader from Redlake, who went into business after World War I. His post was the nearest to Shonto, and was a good friend except that, since I was a Richardson, he considered me the worst kind of competitor.

C. D. had stocked the Shonto store with twenty-five-dozen Army O. D. woolen trousers, bought cheap. He could retail them at a low price, and this hurt all the neighboring traders, since it lured trade from their district to Shonto. One day a Redlake Navajo, while examining the trousers at Shonto, remarked to a store full of Indians, "These pants came from the bodies of dead soldiers who fought the *Bish ba'Chi* (Germans)." My regular customers went silent instantly. No Navajo dared touch anything remotely connected with the dead, for fear of evil spirits. If this statement were allowed to stand, these O. D. trousers would rot on the shelves. Worse, the devout Navajos—and maybe all of them—would refuse to trade at Shonto for fear that maybe the *chindi* of dead soldiers hovered unhappily about.

How did the Indian know the trousers were from dead men? Because the Redlake trader had told him so! His statement furnished me all the necessary information to realize he had been deliberately sent to Shonto. Throwing my head back, I laughed in derision, while I frantically sought some counter-measure story. One Navajo inquired, in all seriousness, what could be funny about a dead soldier's pants. Producing the wholesaler's bill, I exhibited it saying that this paper proved no white man had ever worn the trousers—much less died in them. Since no one present was able to read, they didn't know the bill listed the pants as *reconditioned*.

The man from Redlake asked why his friend the trader would tell him a big lie. "Because during the war he lived on a ship in the big ocean," I replied. "There is no grass for cattle, sheep, or horses on deep water. What did they eat on the ships? Nothing but fish caught out of the ocean. The Redlake trader likes to eat fish!" The trader had, indeed, often talked about serving on a Navy ship, and my customers now looked worse than unhappy. According to Navajo mythology, most of their tribe had perished during a great flood, and they believed that monsters of the water—fish—had eaten drowned Navajos. For that reason, the Indians refused to consume fish under any circumstances: anyone who did, fed a *chindi* on the flesh of dead people. Convinced, the Redlake Navajo returned to his district to tell my story about the fish-eating trader, who for weeks couldn't understand why his usual customers took their sheep, piñons, and blankets from Redlake to Shonto or Tuba City to sell.

At Shonto the pants business boomed, and the warehouse soon bulged with little brown piñon nuts. A former trader at the post had carefully drawn nails from the boards of hundred-pound packing boxes that Arbuckle Brothers coffee came in. He had made some furniture with the boards, but he couldn't possibly use them all, even for other projects, so he had stacked them flat in square piles from the warehouse floor to the ceiling. At that time Navajos used the wood from these boxes to make hogan doors, crude furniture, grub boxes, baby cradles, and cradleboards, so I sold the stacks for twenty-five cents a bundle, and the whole countryside hurried to buy.

Our mail came once a week to a locked box on the Kayenta road, near mailman Calamity's hogan. One day a letter came from C. D., telling me to move the sheep band to Redlake for another herder to pick up. Hosteen Senijeni trailed out thirty-five hundred head, and Edith went along to help him; they would be pulling into Redlake on Sunday afternoon. Locking the post, Millie and I drove out to make a delivery, and, nearing Redlake, we found the band still five miles away. Going on, we gained three more miles before getting stuck in slick clay from a brief rain shower on the flats. For the only time in my life I had traveled without chains or a shovel. Hoofing two miles to Redlake, I tried to borrow an old rope so Senijeni could pull me out with his horse.

The sly Redlake trader blandly assured me he had no rope. On the wall hung lariats cut to length, so I bought one of them. Customarily, traders charged each other wholesale price. The rope actually cost seventy-five cents, but he soaked me for the regular retail price, a dollar and a half. Having heard about the fish story, he was pulling this stunt in retaliation. The deal made me mad. After Senijeni helped me out, I tossed the rope back at the trader; I did not want it. After delivering the sheep, we drove back to Shonto. Sensing my anger, Millie asked the cause, and I told her, as I kept mulling over possible schemes to get back at the trader.

When I had just about abandoned the idea, the means fell into my hands unexpectedly. One of the trader's regular customers laid a valuable string of turquoise and shell beads on my post counter. He wanted to pawn them for a few days while visiting friends in the neighborhood. I knew that the previous year the Redlake trader had helped two brothers bury a very rich and influential Navajo named Yellow Horse in a secret grave. The body had been adorned with all the personal jewelry possible, and a seamless sack filled with the balance of his valuable jewelry had also gone into the

A Navajo baby on a cradleboard. Sometimes rough boards pulled from the packing crates of Arbuckle Brothers Coffee were substituted for traditional cradleboard materials.

grave. Staring at the beads, I shuddered visibly. "Take them out of here! You bought those beads at Redlake!"

When the Navajo admitted it, I added, "They are exactly like the ones Yellow Horse often pawned here!"

The man knew the story of the secret burial, and, gaping at me in stricken horror, he fled the post, leaving the beads behind. Immediately he spread the word that the jewelry had once belonged to Yellow Horse. The Redlake trader knew the location of the grave; ergo, he got them there. No Navajo would thereafter buy a piece of jewelry at Redlake, regardless of how new it looked. The whispered story caused Indians to "recognize" pieces of Yellow Horse's jewelry for sale in the store for weeks.

The trader was hurting badly for business when the story finally reached Tuba City Indian police. They decided to take some of Yellow Horse's kin out to the Redlake post, but the relatives failed to identify any of the jewelry. Now cognizant of the trouble, the trader sent for the brothers who had helped him bury Yellow Horse; after visiting the secret site, they reported the grave undisturbed. Never again, however, did that trader pull any tricks on me.

All the traders thoroughly hated the Anglo stockman at Tuba City. Indians, too, took a few distant rifle shots at him. A thoroughly unlikable man, he often had the water in the sheep-dipping vats heated too hot. Standing at the head of the vat, he would shove sheep under, holding them down too long with an iron rod. The sheep were so weak that year that few of them could swim through to the wooden steps out, and not many reached the dripping pen unaided. The stockman deliberately held them under to drown. When the vat end filled up with carcasses, they were grappled out. In this way he killed many sheep.*

---

*The slaughter of the sheep by this unidentified stockman is probably not related to the problem of stock reduction on the Navajo Reservation. Nevertheless, the reader of *Navajo Trader* should know something about this thorny situation, as the reduction program was in operation during the period that Gladwell Richardson traded with the Navajos in the early twentieth century.

According to William H. Lyon (personal communication, September 1984), the problem of overgrazing on the Navajo ranges was first identified in the early 1880s by Indian Agent Denis M. Riordan. In the 1920s the first attempts were made, by government mandate, to reduce the number of both horses and sheep on the reservation. By 1932

One afternoon this stockman and his wife visited Shonto. His wife joined Millie in the living quarters while he remained in the store, talking in a very friendly fashion. At this point Hugh Dickson ("Shine") Smith‡ showed up, reporting that the canyon lakes were covered with ducks and that we should get some for supper. The stockman fell in with the idea, and in a few minutes we set forth with guns. Letting me off at the first large lake, they went on to another. In a very short time I had knocked off a dozen mallards. At the distant lake beyond sight, however, the stockman kept blasting away like mad for an hour. When they drove back to me, he had a gunny sack filled with birds—certainly several times the limit—which I didn't appreciate. Back at the store, when the sack was emptied, every bird proved to be a mudhen: the stockman didn't know the difference between them and ducks. Shine Smith didn't either, but upon finding out what had happened, he kidded the stockman unmercifully. The man got so mad he ran outside to his car and tore off for Tuba City alone, and after supper Shine had to drive the man's wife home.

Near the end of that week Millie and I went to Tuba City, and, on our return across Rabbit Mesa, we came up behind the stockman in a blue coupe. The road in this area dropped into one-way deep cuts through sand-hill banks for several miles, and turn-outs had been made at regular intervals for vehicles to get around each other. Approaching one, I pulled into it, having spotted rising dust from an approaching, but invisible, car. The stockman should have stopped also—he knew we had raised no dust to warn any approaching drivers. Instead he plowed right on through. When the oncoming car appeared suddenly before him, both drivers barely managed to stop.

Jumping from his car in a terrible rage, the stockman began to bawl out the woman driver. Recognizing the Riordans from Flagstaff, and their son-in-law Bob Chambers, I also walked forward. Bob's wife, who had been

---

it was recognized that the Navajos needed horses for transportation, but President F. D. Roosevelt's administration took the program of sheep reduction very seriously. John Collier, the Commissioner of Indian Affairs at that time, inaugurated mandatory, flat-rate reductions on a yearly basis for all herds. The Navajos opposed what they perceived as a threat to their livelihood and resented this outside interference in their affairs. As the Indian Service encouraged more Navajo participation in the governmental process, the Tribal Council and local committees voiced such strong opposition that the program was discontinued. As a result, the ranges bacame vastly overgrazed, and by the 1980s there was a definite decline in sheep-raising as a means of livelihood and a corresponding switch to wage work as a major means of earning a living.

‡A one-time missionary at Kayenta, "Shine" Smith later drifted around the reservation working at odd jobs.

driving, sat badly shaken up over the near accident. The stockman ordered them to back up the crooked sand road half a mile to a turn-out; it was very doubtful they could have done this, even if the request had been made reasonably. Behind the unruly stockman's coupe were flat stones onto which he could have moved in seconds, and he should have done so in the first place. Refusing to budge, he swore loudly, informing them what a big-shot government official he happened to be.

Bob Chambers walked close to the stockman. "You could see our dust when we couldn't see yours," he began quietly. "We can't back that distance without trouble. Why don't you back those few feet into the turn-out here?"

"Because I can kick hell out of you if you don't move! I am an officer. Do as you're told or I'll arrest you!"

The unreasonable man then got what he had coming. "Feel this?" Bob shoved the muzzle of a small gun against the stockman's protruding belly. Still threatening all manner of arrests and prosecution, the man backed the few necessary feet so that the heavy sedan could drive past and on down the road. The stockman then set off at high speed for Redlake. When we pulled in there, he stood beside his coupe swearing steadily into the wind.

A few days later a wire came from Washington discharging the stock-man. The Chambers family owned a hunk of the transcontinental Santa Fe Railroad, and their power had done the job. Although not many trad-ers in western Navajoland knew Bob Chambers, they all wanted to give him a key to the country, for he had rid them of an obnoxious man who had caused much grief in the area through his cruel personal whims.

During the time we were at Shonto, an abused, unpaid Navajo who worked for a turnip-raising missionary set his boss's wooden house on fire in the night. A terrible tragedy resulted: the house burned to the ground, and the missionary's wife and two of his children died in the holocaust. Immediately, he raised a great to-do about having sacrificed most of his life to church work, and now he and his three surviving children were completely destitute. He made speeches and begged for help. Flagstaff and some other railroad towns formed organizations to give financial assistance to the stricken family, for sympathy ran high for the missionary. Then another mission-ary told fundraisers they should take a look at an account in the Flagstaff bank. They found the "needy" missionary had more than forty thousand dollars in his personal account. This money was pure profit from farming with unpaid Indian labor. This situation so miffed the Tuba City Indian agent that he instituted proceedings to repossess the land that had been deeded—despite Navajos' objections at the time—to the missionary. Federal investigators looking into this case quietly examined others as well, and a month later two prominent missionaries disappeared from the reservation, leaving no forwarding addresses.

Early that fall Millie told me that the first of our children was on the way. Although I was greatly pleased, I was also concerned—we were more than a hundred miles from civilization. The risks of waiting too long or of being snowed in unexpectedly and unable to get her to a hospital worried me sick—especially as the months went by. The Tuba City government hospital wasn't even a good rest home for well people, and I didn't think the doctors there qualified even as third-class horse doctors. In fact, most of the local veterinarians were more skilled, even in obstetrical cases.

Only shortly before, one of the agency doctors had cut a baby piece by piece from an Indian mother who had already undergone hours of labor. Her screams aroused the villagers to murderous rage. The Indian agent who went to the hospital to try to reason with the doctor was told that it wasn't any of his business and that it had to be done. "Then at least give the poor woman an anesthetic!" begged the agent.

"Waste expensive drugs on a damned Indian squaw!" the doctor retorted. "I'll sure as hell not!" And he didn't. Tuba City people insisted that the brutal doctor should be taken out and hanged, but, instead, he was simply transferred to a midwestern Indian agency.

The first snow of the year fell late in 1925, and, before the ground was quite covered, I decided what to do. Taking no more chances by remaining longer at Shonto, we packed and went to where good doctors and hospitals were available. The first day of the following March our oldest daughter, Cecile Darlene, was born (thirteen years later she got a sister, Toni Dale).

Navajo Country

During the early 1900s the vastness of the western Navajo country, set with blue mountains, cut by canyons, and spaced with verdant valleys into which few roads entered, was still terra incognita to most Americans. The climate was notoriously forbidding. Great beds of sand dunes and masses of bare rock made it seem impenetrable. To the unknowing, it was the country of nowhere, inhabited by Indians existing in a savage state. Four hundred years ago, however, the Spaniards were already exploring the ruggedness of Navajo country. These intrepid adventurers, who came searching for gold, were followed by precursors of the fur trade—the beaver trappers, some of whom found their final resting places along the rims of canyons in Navajo country. But that was much later—the daring *conquistadores* were first.

A detachment of Coronado's men, led by Pedro de Tovar, explored Black Mountain eastward from the Hopi villages in 1540: they named the mountain Mesa de Vaca. At the same time, another small force under Garcia López de Cárdenas discovered the Grand Canyon. Captain Juan Melgosa, after whom the desert near Cameron is named, ventured across canyon country toward Navajo Mountain in search of gold. Another exploring band, from Antonio de Espejo's forces, went all the way to Navajo Mountain, which they called Sierra Panoche, in 1583. In a Colorado River canyon they found gold. A long time elapsed, however, before many other Spaniards came and carved their names, now illegible, on cliff walls in the area.

Awesome Navajo Canyon dwells in somber mystery. The break between White Horse Mesa and Red Mesa, on which Inscription House Trading Post stands, affords access across several small canyons to Kaibito. These canyons combine to form Navajo Canyon, which runs seventy-seven miles to the Colorado River. The Navajos call this formation "Where-the-canyon-runs-like-finger-into-the-hand." The Kaibito road crosses the fingerling canyons, and here on most maps is shown Navajo Creek, a spring-fed stream. Lake Powell, behind Glen Canyon dam, later filled a large portion of Navajo Canyon. Later explorers called it West Canyon: this identification for

A band of sheep climbing out a steep, rock wall rising from the floor of awesome Navajo Canyon.

the longest non-river canyon in all of Navajo country was to set it apart from those canyons coursing north (at right angles to Navajo Canyon) into the distant San Juan River. These northward canyons have their headings not far from Navajo Canyon, and, in one instance, the land bridging them is only spitting-distance wide.

From the wide floor of Navajo Canyon, Poverty Butte (the white man's Tower Butte) is outstanding on the southwestern skyline. It is one of the Navajos' three War Peaks. Here in the olden times of bow and arrow and lance warfare, Navajos defeated five times their number of Ute and Paiute Indians in a lengthy battle. No dead were buried or carried from the field. Blowing sand repeatedly covered and uncovered mouldering bones, and the process still goes on; the yellow sand is filled with flint arrow and spear points.

At the head of the main canyon, gaunt cliffs of salmon pink and vermilion and myriad side tributaries are filled with aboriginal ruins of ancient cliff dwellers. There was an inscription of some fifteen lines on a cliff shoulder in Navajo Canyon where Long House Canyon breaks into it. Long House Canyon, the longest of all the side canyons, enters Navajo Canyon just east of a twelve-foot-high pictograph of a potbellied man. The canyon was long used as a route to Kaibito Plateau, and, after World War II, I made a special trip to photograph this inscription for the scholars. But I had waited too long—the letters, never cut deep, were worn away.

In the first side canyon below this place grows native cotton of a type used centuries ago by inhabitants of nearby dwellings. The word "cotton" produces an image of cultivated plants as we know them. The wild variety, however, is a vine, dull green in color, with pods no larger than a man's thumb. But the fluffy white substance is real cotton. Going there with Hosteen Zon Kelli, I could find only a dozen plants. They clung to high-wall cracks and crevices beyond the reach of sheep and goats, which he said eat wild cotton because the vine tastes sweet.

Canegrass grows almost everywhere in Navajo Canyon. The sharp blades, which no animal will eat, are about sixteen inches long. As this grass matures in the fall, the dew on the blades dries in the warm morning sun, leaving a residue of grayish powder. This powder tastes sweet and was used by Indians as sugar long before the coming of the white man. Many old trappers and explorers in that country—Bill Williams, Ed Randolph, Buckskin Billy Ross, and Jim Black—assured me that they also used the sugary dust. A certain species of cactus (most likely *Opuntia* spp.) that grows in the area was eaten nearly to extinction by Navajos. Baked in stone ovens, it slowly roasted into a favored delicacy. Adding the pink berries of cliff-rose (*Cowania*) during the cooking process gave the preparation a sweet-tart taste. In later times only the Havasupai Indians made this delicious food, and Navajos went to them to trade for it.

Opposite Inscription House Trading Post is Red Valley. There is no other valley in the West more storied and holding more natural treasures. It has been inhabited by a succession of people since the dawn of Man: Indians lived in and around it more than twenty-five hundred years ago, and one Basket-Maker site dates from 600 B.C. People before these left no record that has yet been discovered, but the valley gives a feeling of history without beginning and a haunting sense of past glory. The original Richardson-made road, reaching deep into Navajo country and following the Ute War Trail, passed along the eastern sandhills, north twenty-odd miles, before pitching back inside Red Valley. About 1934 the Indian Service rerouted and built a new road, shortening it through the valley. On the west side, where the great stone walls of White Horse Mesa jut out from a corner between two deep and narrow canyons, stands Hole in the Rock Natural Bridge. Off the Kaibito road are several great natural wonders—among them are Square Butte and The Door of Red Sandstone. Farther along and off the road, but part of the mesa, are huge natural bridges of white Coconino sandstone.

In thirty-mile-long Red Valley there are several dug reservoirs and natural lakes. All are filled with water most of the year, and transient waterfowl pause to rest on them. In the old days they were often covered almost solid with ducks and geese, and a few minutes of sunup shooting would fill the larder for a week.

Red Mesa, which forms the other half of the northwest side of Red Valley, is gashed by several washes. Dished on top like a valley, it rises between side canyons and the main rim of Navajo Canyon. Off the Navajo Mountain road—at the upper end, on the rim of Gishey Canyon—lies the pit where a meteorite crashed within the memory of the local inhabitants. Somewhere around Red Mesa and Inscription House Trading Post is the legendary lost Hopi town of Kwashtima. According to Hopi mythology, this was the first pueblo established by them after their emergence from the bottom of the Grand Canyon into this world. From Kwashtima, clans spread to the east, north, and south, and this is the holy place they must return to after fulfilling their mission on earth. They have searched for it since long before the Navajos can remember. Aged Hopis appeared annually in this area, seeking the ruined town, although often claiming to be on other pursuits. Occasionally they even brought along some white man who, they hoped, might be lucky enough to find it.

Some centuries ago the east rim of Red Mesa, near Inscription House, caved in and left a few hundred thousand tons of clay and sand that completely hid an aboriginal ruin. When heavy rains washed tons of the cover from one corner, I asked Dr. Harold S. Colton, an archaeologist of southwestern cultures, to come out for a look. He dated potsherds as twelfth century, which is nowhere near old enough to be from Kwashtima.

I am certain that some generations ago Navajo Indians did know the location of Kwashtima. The town was noted for a prehistoric, highly polished, peculiar yellow (or golden), glazed pottery. Hopi potters have never been able fully to duplicate it. Specimens have been found in graves of the earliest Hopi pueblos; from then on, however, it completely disappeared from their craft.

East of the sandhills bordering Red Valley runs Cow Springs Canyon and Wash. Up this canyon from the springs, George McAdams set up a summer and fall trading camp in 1882; two years later two brothers, Benjamin and Bill Williams, ran the outpost for him. While stationed there, the brothers went to Navajo Mountain, Rainbow Bridge, and down into Navajo Canyon, looking for gold. The following year they accompanied their father, J. P. Williams, from the family trading post at Blue Canyon to Navajo Mountain, where they traded out of a tent. Navajos were induced to bring whatever might appear to be mineralized rock. The ore was tossed into a seamless bag; no identifying marks were attached. When one large chunk proved rich in gold, the Williamses hunted its source for the next several years, hiring Indians to help, but they never picked up another piece.

Before the stock reduction program of the 1930s to save eroded ranges, Red Valley served as horse roundup grounds for many years. Riders would drive bands into it from mesas, smaller valleys, and canyons where other riders held them in a common herd. Using a system of smoke signals by day and fires at night, the roundup crews slowly compressed the horses into the lower end of the valley. New colts were branded by owners, young horses and fillies removed for breaking. At times as many as eight thousand feral animals darkened the gramma-grass flats of Red Valley. In these wild bands, crossed and recrossed, appeared the last of the true palomino horses. Invariably, they foaled from line-back buckskins, which, in turn, were throwbacks to the broomy-tailed Spanish mustang.

Directly west of Poverty Butte, on a Colorado River canyon wall, is fastened a bronze plaque commemorating the 1776 crossing of the Spanish padres Silvestre de Escalante and Francisco Atanasio Domínguez. The ford is named Vado de los Padres (The Crossing of the Fathers). The plaque, however, is in the wrong place. Any local Navajo could have taken those who selected this site to the real one—Kaiparowits Plateau—where the early padres actually crossed the river en route to New Mexico from their wanderings in Utah. Probably accessibility had much to do with placing the memorial where it is. The crossing, in fact, took place at Ute Ford behind Navajo Mountain; a segment of the Ute War Trail, it is a difficult area to reach. Escalante and Domínguez must have come over this route, since it is the only ancient trail through the country around Navajo Mountain.

The historian who incorrectly located Escalante's river crossing also traced the Spanish party onto Kaibito Plateau, via Antelope Wash, far to the south, but he failed to produce evidence sending Escalante downriver and out eastward along the base of Echo Cliffs. Actually, the padres must have passed through Navajo Mountain country to Red Valley, and from there into the region of the present Tuba City. In his journal Escalante mentioned Indians, cornfields, watering places, and natural features of terrain, and he described specific sites that could have been nowhere else. Many theorists too often disregard the fact that Escalante used Ute and Paiute guides from each area that he explored; their ancient trails were the logical ones to follow.

The misnamed Vado de los Padres never even existed until Jacob Hamblin's men cut steps in the stone there in 1858–1859. The Mormons had tried crossings all along the Colorado River, from the junction of the San Juan to several hundred miles downstream, where Pearce's Ferry finally came into being below the Grand Canyon. And I have seen inscriptions that lead me to believe Escalante crossed at Ute Ford; one, no longer clearly decipherable, is in a Colorado River canyon high in Utah. If it does happen to be an Escalante date, then the padres probably came directly downstream to Ute Ford, rather than through the edge of what later became known as the Arizona Strip. A second canyon in the same area holds another Spanish inscription in which the date 1642 can be read easily; this offers additional proof that the Spaniards followed Indian trails which must have been ancient even at that time.

South of Navajo Mountain, emerging from hostile canyon country, Escalante's party passed into the northern tip of Red Valley. The hardy adventurers were out of food, but, fortunately, they found a few ears of corn in a harvested field only recently deserted by Havasupai Indians (who once lived in the Tuba City area). In a chronicle of this journey, Father Escalante is said to have blessed the region in thankfulness for such a provident circumstance. This cornfield, according to Navajo sagas, occupied floodlands between two washes passing Eagle Nest Rock. When this story is repeated in Navajo clan history, special mention is given to "Gray Robe" or "Long Gray Coat."

The legendary Gray Robe has, since Escalante's time, been a benefactor and a savior on desperate occasions. According to many stories I heard, in times of extreme distress, to lost children, and before impending danger or disaster, the form of Gray Robe appeared to aid the unfortunate. He is not described or referred to as a ghost or a spirit. There is no superstition connected with him. He is casually accepted as a mysterious being—neither Spanish, American, nor Indian—who appears and disappears on his errands of mercy. Navajos living in the region believe in him as faithfully as they do their own most revered holy one, *Yeibetchai* (Grandfather of the Gods).

My only near contact with Gray Robe occurred during the summer of 1940. Almost every evening, accompanied by two aged Navajos, I drove a pickup from the post at Redlake to Tonalea for the mail. On one return trip, around ten o'clock on a muggy, dark night, we were within the steep dugway approaching Eagle Nest Rock Wash, when both Navajos yelled, "Stop! There stands Gray Robe beside the road. There is danger!"

Off to the right, amid the sagebrush, I caught the mere impression of something filmy gray, but I didn't really see anything clearly, and to this day I have never been sure. When I cut the motor of the pickup, the roar of the wash, running bank-full, echoed clearly. It had not been raining in the valley. No clouds were in the sky, and the dugway over the wash had been dust dry when we crossed it less than an hour before. However, rain on distant mesas often sent down sudden flash floods, and the possibility always made the crossing somewhat dangerous. Several cars had been caught in it and had been washed downstream for a mile or more. Fortunately no fatalities had resulted, but the automobiles were always lost. A few yards more and we would have plunged into at least twenty feet of swift water; probably none of us would have survived.

Of course, my friends never doubted that Gray Robe had saved us. Navajo stories of him are legion, and the people believe them fully. Few in the vicinity haven't at some time or another encountered their singular benefactor. He is faceless—I could never obtain from anyone a description of his features. They simply could not recall ever seeing him except as a shadowy and indistinct form.

Latter-day dwellers in this storied valley were just as unusual as its ancient history and its natural wonders. Halfway down its length, for example, under the high walls of White Horse Mesa, lived John Boone. He had served as a cavalry scout, chasing Geronimo and his warriors, for which service he was entitled to a pension. Over seventy years old when I first met him, the wiry little man still had not applied for his pension, and when he did, considerable time passed before the government granted it. When Boone cashed the check for $1,894 at Redlake Trading Post, trader Johnny O'Farrell asked him how he wanted it. The old man replied, "Give me silver dollars!" Johnny started piling them in twenty-dollar rolls into a hat, but it wouldn't hold them, so the huge pile of cartwheels was stacked on the counter. From this, Boone bought his entire family silver jewelry, concho belts, and all the clothing they could possibly wear. The rest he took home and buried in a sand dune.

Boone in his old age could travel comfortably only in a car or wagon, and whenever I drove over to take him somewhere, he always made me delay long enough to eat mutton ribs baked in beds of hot coals. When I brought him back home it was the same—a meal of mutton ribs and coffee before he would permit me to leave. He lived to be a hundred.

One of my closest Navajo friends, Julius Sombrero, lived on Red Mesa at the edge of Red Valley. All of his many children, except one daughter and his eldest son, were well educated and held good jobs in Arizona and Utah. Julius, thirty years older than I, spoke no English at all. Sometimes I

Lambs in a brush corral.

asked him to help at the post. His mind on figures was absolutely incredible: he could add, subtract, and multiply faster in his head than I would do it on paper—or even with an adding machine. He could read scales, too, and I often sent him to the corral to buy lambs. Unable to write, he kept every single item filed in his head. Each lamb was weighed separately, and the weight multiplied by whatever we paid per pound. Whether fifteen or fifty head were bought, Julius gave the figures one by one while I made out the sales slips. He named the weight and the amount that each lamb came to, and the total sum for each bunch bought from individual sellers.

When we bought lambs we always knocked off six pounds for water. But not Julius—he subtracted fifteen. Navajo sheep had small stomachs and couldn't hold much water, so I suggested to him that we should give the Navajo sheepmen a better break. "My younger brother, you know that they stop by the water tank before they bring sheep to sell," he replied, "but perhaps you don't know that these people salt them overnight first."

Years ago Sagney Yazza, S. I.'s friend of a lifetime, lay on his death pallet at eighty-eight years of age. As was the old custom, he began giving away personal property to each of his heirs. One afternoon I took him some special food, and he asked me what I wanted. I stared at a cougar-skin quiver containing a medicine bow and arrow which he had always used in the *endah* rite (a nine-day religious ceremony). The three-hundred-year-old wood came from a bow that had been carried in war against the Spaniards in New Mexico. Being "dead" now, the bow was solely symbolic. "You wish that," he commented. "It is well." Three days later, when I opened the store at dawn, in walked his son-in-law with blackened face, carrying something wrapped in a robe. Wordless, he opened it on the counter, placed the quiver and bow there, and walked out. Sagney Yazza was dead, and I helped bury him that afternoon.

Inscription House

After a few seasons of handling dudes at Rainbow Lodge, S. I. couldn't stand their feisty ways any longer. Regardless of how much money they spent, it took the profits from the store to keep the packing outfit going. Being a topnotch trader, S. I. made money, but, wanting to engage exclusively in the Indian business, he began looking around for a likely place. In the stock-raising country around Red Mesa, he found well-traveled trails that crossed the canyon country to farmed valleys. Other trails led north toward Kayenta and eastward to the smoldering darkness of Black Mountain. The nearest trading posts—Kaibito, Shonto, Cow Springs, and Redlake—were far enough distant not to interfere with local trade. So, in 1926, S. I. decided to build a store on Red Mesa.

Camping out while he selected the site, he talked to leading Navajos in the area. One of them was Hosteen Navajo Mountain, who at census-taking time had selected the English name of Frank Richardson. He and his family had always journeyed the long distance to trade at Rainbow Lodge, so he greeted S. I.'s plan delightedly. A medicine man of important standing, he got other Navajos to express their approval.

Many of the Navajo Mountain Indians promptly followed S. I. to his new store to do their trading. The automobile road there made it easy for their wagons to haul supplies to distant hogans. The new trading post, called Inscription House, was named after the ancient Inscription House Ruins in the canyon, to which S. I. blasted a four-foot-wide trail down a stone wall.

The largest of the ruined cities on the Navajo Reservation is Inscription House in Neetsin Canyon. It is the only ancient city in the Southwest having T-shaped doorways. Dr. Byron Cummings, then with the University of Utah, excavated seventy-five rooms in 1909; at least thirty-five others had eroded away. The high village takes its name from a purported Spanish inscription. Archaeologists reported it as reading "S------ *Haperio Ano Dom* 1661." Unfortunately, the lettering could not be matched with any known Spanish explorer of any date. The inscription is long gone—it was never firmly cut into the thin mud plaster, anyway. Partly discernible when I first saw it in the 1920s, the letters spelled nothing like the above, but the date was definitely 1661. Western author Dane Coolidge carefully chalked and photographed it in 1925, but nothing more than "*An Dom* 1661" shows in his photograph.

In the early years at Inscription House Trading Post, we packed many archaeologists into the canyon. These parties were from nationally known eastern museums holding valid permits to excavate burial sites and cliff ruins. At least a hundred mule-loads of material came out of a small area around Neetsin: pottery; basketry; horn; turquoise and shell beads and bracelets; fabrics woven of human and dog hair, wild goat hair, and native cotton; wooden fetishes; carved stone objects; copper bells; yucca sandals; atlatls (throwing sticks) and stone hammers of several types. Indeed, on one occasion we brought out eight loads of stone hammers and hatchets from a single long shelf.

Prior to World War II, Inscription House Ruins were unprotected. Many times I rode a horse up the steep, slick, rock wall to the base of the bench on which the ruins stand. Navajo sheep, seeking shade provided by the great, overhanging, massive rim, destroyed most of the interior wattled walls. Too late, the Park Service installed a protective fence; yet the ruins had since 1909 been part of Navajo National Monument. Later, a water spring surfaced under a saddle into Jones Canyon, and its rapid wearing action soon cut a forty-foot-deep arroyo which blocked direct access to the ruins.

The inscriptions cut into cliff walls in this area by non-Indians before 1900—especially in the wide-mouthed cave—should have been preserved. Among the ones that I saw in 1928 were:

G. R. Choistlan   Oct. 24, 1888

W. Brookway   May 10, 1883

Ben & Bill   1884 (The two brothers were Benjamin and William F. Williams from Blue Canyon.)

W. C. Young   1882 (The initials might possibly be M. C.)

J. E. H.   March 1880

H. L. W.   Pole   1882 (H. L. W.'s identity is unknown, but "Pole" was Pole Hongrave, a well-known Hopi Indian from Moenkopi village, near Tuba City.)

W. Williams   1885 (This name, which occurred in three places, was no relation to Ben and Bill Williams or to their father, J. P. Williams. He might have been "Barney" Williams, an Indian trader.)

R   llred (The letters in between and the date had been rubbed out with sandstone.)

John Hadley   Nov. 17, 1885

C. M. Cade A.D.   18-- (The date is either 1869 or 1889, and it is more likely the earlier one, since C. M. Cade's name was carved in 1869 in the Rainbow Bridge vicinity.)

George Emmerson   1881

W. A. Ross   8/1879 (This man was "Buckskin" Billy Ross, who showed J. P. Williams the land where he claimed a homestead in Blue Canyon in 1882.)

Ed Randolph   1880 (When too feeble to prospect any longer, Ed Randolph homesteaded and lived in Doney Park, near Flagstaff.)

Jim Black   1881 (This was "A-One" Jim Black.)

Most of these names were also once cut on Rainbow Natural Bridge, and could be found in nearly every canyon of western Navajoland. Others at Inscription House ruins were indecipherable in 1928 when I copied the above, and at least three dozen more, which had been painted on cliff faces with wet charcoal, were disappearing.

When Millie and I arrived at Inscription House Trading Post in 1928, no improvements had been added to those my father had made two years before. A row of wooden buildings stood inside a fenced area facing the Redlake–Navajo Mountain Road. At the north end a huge, dirt-covered hogan served as a warehouse. Next to it stood the main building containing the store, an adjoining bedroom, and two more bedrooms behind the main section. Two wooden cabins followed to the south, and next to those were the cookhouse and dining room. Gasoline lanterns provided light, and rain, pouring off the metal roofs into cisterns, furnished domestic water. A small log barn and two pole corrals had been built a quarter of a mile away. Below them, S. I. had dammed a draw and dug out a reservoir for stock water. Across the road, on the east mesa edge, he had erected a long, flat, dirt-roofed, cedar-log garage for several cars.

Inscription House Trading Post was the largest, most ambitious post yet established on the western Navajo Reservation. Most places never consisted of more than a store, with attached living quarters and a water supply. But S. I.'s estimation of the business potential here soon proved

Gladwell "Toney" Richardson in front of Inscription House
Trading Post. Toney's father, S. I. Richardson, said that the stone
building, shown here soon after its completion in 1929, was built
by "me and seven other Indians."

warranted. Almost at once the store became too small, so in 1929 S. I.
"and seven other Indians" (as S. I. always said) built a new, sandstone
post in front of the old kitchen, facing the road. (The year after that, Frank
Banks [a young man employed by S. I.] added six more rooms. The telephone arrived in the mid-1930s, and my brother, Cecil, installed a light
plant during World War II. Stokes Carson, who bought the post from S. I.
in 1951, drilled a water well.)

Millie, baby Cecile, and I occupied a two-room cabin, and the cowboy
employees, Coil Davis and Henry Smith, had a room behind the store. S. I.
really needed help when we went there: three big truckloads of merchandise were required each week to handle his trade. There was no pause
between wool-, sheep-, and cattle-buying seasons, due to the different
climates in the high and low altitudes from which our customers came.
The store became so inadequate we had to close up to stock shelves on
rush-day afternoons and, frequently, at night. Our last customer seldom
departed before midnight.

The interior of the store at Inscription House Trading Post. Toney's brother, Cecil Richardson (with pipe), stands behind the counter; open door leads to the warehouse.

The Navajos who traded at S. I.'s store came from Navajo Mountain, Kayenta, Black Mountain, the Colorado River, Copper Mine, The Gap, Tuba City, and other places closer to Inscription House. "Close" meant not more than twenty to thirty miles away. Trading competition roiled keen, since all traders tried to keep Navajos in their districts from buying or selling elsewhere. When the Indians did, the trader lost charge and pawn accounts, and a lot of his profit. Although in those days people in this hard land didn't hope to make much money, every trader in this cut-throat business had his own schemes and methods for holding and pulling in more barter trade.

Old Luke Smith, then trading at Shonto for my uncle C. D., employed a tricky scheme, thereby laying himself wide open to retaliation: he sold three one-pound packages of Arbuckle Brothers' coffee for a dollar (the whole-sale price of that brand was then forty-eight cents per pound plus freight, and a one-pound package retailed in trading posts for sixty cents). Smith assumed a direct loss on the coffee because he claimed his deal brought in more customers, so the difference could be made up on other merchandise. His coffee business became absolutely ruinous to other traders, most of whom stayed in line on general prices for self-protection. The price cutter could always be handled, and we decided to take care of Smith.

Every few days we sent a different, trusted Navajo in a wagon with several blankets to Shonto with instructions to trade for coffee. He would tell Smith he was stocking up for winter when deep snow would prevent him from getting out to a post. Our stooges bought Smith's coffee by the hundred-pound case (in those days Indians usually did). Even after two months of this, Smith didn't tumble to what was going on, and we supplied our post customers with coffee that was far cheaper than what we usually paid for it wholesale.

One day C. D. came by—out of his way—en route to Shonto. After visiting a few minutes, he opened the warehouse door. Smith's cases of coffee were stacked from the floor to the ceiling along one wall. He didn't blame us at all, for he would have done the same thing to put an unruly competitor back in line, but he was mad. "When I checked Luke's wholesale bills and saw all those coffee orders," he said, "I knew he was supplying the rest of you traders for the winter. Well, you've bought your last coffee at my expense!" Going on to Shonto he laid down the law to Smith, who couldn't believe what he heard. He agreed to go back to the customary price and forget his expensive trade-getter, but a few weeks later, he again started selling coffee at three pounds for a dollar, so C. D. fired him.

Smith then went down on the Kayenta road, putting in a small stone trading post at the mouth of Cow Springs Canyon. When I saw him there, as he was building, he told me, "I am going to break C. D. Richardson for the ornery way he treated me!" His business methods and refusal to stay in line with other traders nearly bankrupted him at first. Finally, he settled down to behaving and made a good living at Cow Springs the rest of his life.

The heavy volume of business at Inscription House meant that we men were pretty well tied down at the post. Fortunately, the women had a little spare time for recreation, such as it was. Susie and Millie often hiked or rode horses to the mesa edge to view a wide panoramic beauty. They also traveled to the canyon country, where defiles offered spectacular views in fantastic color. Susie had one particular spot she claimed as her own: from near the head of a side canyon into Jones Canyon, against Senijeni Mesa, a giant, flat, natural bridge provided a wonder she always marveled at. On the mesa, when we kept cattle there, you could ride across the immense bridge without even realizing its existence: the flat top, several acres in size, made up part of the regular range.

Sometimes there were slack periods in late afternoon and the lengthy dusk, when we pitched horseshoes; then Susie sent to a mail order house for a croquet set. It was almost impossible to smooth out a level place to play on, so some of the wickets posed uphill hazards and handicaps.

On their trips Susie and Millie gathered different species of cacti—Susie had a great collection. In rock-lined beds she replanted about eight hundred cacti, trying to have no more than two alike. Once she found a variety that she could not identify in her colored picture books. The silvery spines of the plants were not sharp—they were more like cotton whiskers to the touch. I suspected from the first what they might be, and, sure enough, before many months passed they were identified as a species of peyote, *Lophophora lewinii*; Susie immediately burned them in the fireplace. Many wild tales have sprung up about peyote. It seems, however, to give the user a form of exhilaration and little else. In the 1920s peyote ceremonies of the incorporated Native American Church had not yet come west from Four Corners country; later, however, in a number of states, it was used in Indian religious ceremonies.

The district chief and medicine man in the area, Hosteen Navajo Mountain, had been a family friend since George McAdams's days. His two wives, many children, and in-laws were constant visitors at Inscription House. The wives were at the post one afternoon telling me the story of another Navajo, Hosteen Behegade, when the man himself entered. Trading a blanket to pay for a small bill of goods, he took out of pawn a string of glass beads worth, new, about fifty cents. They had been hocked for fifteen dollars, and before leaving he wanted to repawn them for half that. Since they were absolutely worthless, I declined, wondering why on earth a trader as smart as S. I. had ever taken them in the first place. The two Mrs. Navajo Mountains (whose English names were Mrs. Frank Richardson No. 1 and Mrs. Frank Richardson No. 2) continued telling me his history after he departed.

After the women had left, Behegade returned, having gone to the corral to see S. I. Silently he handed me the glass beads and a note in which I was told to accept them in pawn. Later S.I. explained that the deal with the beads allowed Behegade to keep his pride and his belief in himself as a trustworthy man. Navajo Mountain's wives had told me that Behegade was running from a *chindi* (evil spirit). The *chindi* wasn't exactly after *him*, but after a sixteen-year-old girl, the last surviving member of the Long Salt family. In some way she was Behegade's adopted niece. Her last relative had died when she was ten years old, and she had been given refuge among clan relatives by marriage.

The tragic circumstances had begun more than a hundred years before, when the Long Salts lived near Navajo Mountain: a blind medicine man held a small *b'jene* (a three-day healing ceremony) for a member of the family, and the pay arrangement for his services included five butchered sheep. However, a family smart-aleck killed five antelope, instead, and a few others thought making the switch was a good joke. Only one man in the family warned that they had better not do it—when the medicine man learned of the trick, he might put a *chindi* after them in revenge.

Nothing untoward occurred for some time. Then a member of the family took sick strangely and promptly passed away. In short order, so did other Long Salts. Obviously, a very powerful *chindi* was after them. A delegation visited the medicine man, asking that he remove the *chindi* before others died. As they feared, he knew of their duplicity. He told them he would have to think over what price to charge for calling off his evil one. They should return in ten days, and he would have the answer ready; but when the delegation went back to see him, the medicine man was dead. He had passed on without removing the *chindi*, and all Long Salts would now die, because no other medicine man knew which one he had put after them or how to remove it.

The years went by with Long Salts dying off faster than they reproduced until, by 1928, only the unfortunate young girl remained. Behegade sought frantically to save her. Loading his goods and family on a wagon, he would drive aimlessly, crossing his tracks several times to confuse the *chindi*. Then suddenly he would take off in an unexpected direction for a hogan, where he would stay. In two or three days he would repeat the process. Meanwhile he prayed and chanted every night, beseeching the gods to intercede for the girl.

His scheme appeared to be working until deep winter snows fell; then the *chindi* caught up with them and the girl died in the night. The rest of the family fled haphazardly through the snow to friends who took them in, and the girl's body remained in the hogan, wrapped in a robe. Behegade himself paused long enough to nail a few boards over the door to keep wild animals out, but now, after three years, the body still lay in the hogan.

A government employee, Carl Beck, was in the store one day and I told him about the girl. He asked if I knew for a fact that the body still remained unburied. "The dirt has washed off the logs and now you can look through the cracks and see her," I replied. Millie and I had ridden horses there occasionally and looked into the hogan. Now, taking white helpers, Carl dug a grave inside the hogan; with the burial of the girl's astonishingly well-mummified body, the last of the Long Salts was laid to rest.

Another prominent local Navajo, Hosteen Zon Kelli, we knew best as Old Man Jones. At eighteen, in 1864, he and his wife and baby had been taken as prisoners to Bosque Redondo by the Army. Fleeing from there, he came all the way west into Navajo Canyon to escape recapture. Often he talked to me about a party of Mormon colonists who had come down from Utah to where Inscription House Trading Post now stood. He said they had almost gained access into the big canyon. No one else knew of any evidence of such Mormon immigrants (who had appeared about 1874).

One day the old man agreed to show me proof, and we started out on horses. Not far from the post we found a short piece of what was once certainly a wagon road—now grown over with timber. On the rocks and in hand-dug trenches existed other evidence, and in a gash against the base of a hillside more unmistakable signs remained. The Mormons had made it that far with their wagons. Camping, they set about breaking out ledges of rock in order to descend into the canyon proper. While they did so, men of the party went down into the canyon, cutting logs to bridge an arroyo and to erect three small cabins. The apparent intention to make a permanent settlement in the tillable canyon at last alarmed the Navajos, and one night the Indians burned the bridge and the cabins. Then they hid in the rocks where the road had been almost cut through, and at daylight they opened fire on the camp. Unable to reach them or hold a parley, after nearly a week the Mormons reloaded their wagons and, driving their stock, pulled out for Tuba City.

Senijeni, who had herded sheep for me at Shonto, was Old Man Jones's eldest son—the baby prisoner at Bosque Redondo. A nearby mesa bore his name. It wasn't a true mesa—two canyons off Navajo curved only partway around it. The one entrance onto the high range—over slick rocks, twenty feet wide—could be closed easily by a brush fence. Cattle put in there could stray nowhere, and this saved herding expenses. During the cattle-buying season we rented this range from Senijeni, because animals coming from the canyons had never seen a wire fence and would have walked right through one.

The local Navajos were industrious and they were wealthy in sheep, cattle, and horses. Those who were poor had once been rich like the rest, but a *chindi* had been after them and they had spent everything on medicine men, trying to get rid of the devil. Our woodcutter, Hosteen Tsinclithly (Mr. Matches), once owned sixteen hundred sheep and five hundred cattle

Many of the people who lived in the area of Inscription House were industrious and had accumulated a great deal of wealth, which was evident in the good quality of their jewelry, blankets, and horses.

and horses. As a boy he had had a taboo fastened on him—never to leave off his penis wrapping, but soon after marrying, he had discarded it entirely. His children were either born dead or were mentally defective. A girl and two boys survived to grow up and marry, but they were half-wits. As soon as the cause, a *chindi,* became apparent, Hosteen Tsinclithly returned to his penis wrapping, and he hired medicine men to remove the evil with prayer. They were never able to do so, however, and he spent all his wealth futilely.

In November 1928 we bought and started trailing to market twelve hundred head of Indian cattle. The stockman stationed at Redlake, George Creswell, cut thirty head from the herd and put them in holding pens. He claimed that they had been illegally purchased because they were young heifers under seven years of age. The ranges were dangerously overstocked as usual, and Indian agents had asked traders to buy every four-footed animal possible to get them off the reservation, regardless of what the regulations said. The rules concerning cattle prohibited only the purchase of young cows—but that wasn't what happened to be wrong with the thirty Creswell cut out.

After I ramrodded the drive on to Flagstaff, we sold and shipped the cattle. Soon after I returned to Inscription House, the agent at Tuba City, C. L. Walker, arrived to spend the day. Before leaving he said, "By the way, I stalled Creswell from making an official charge over the young cows you bought illegally, because I had told you traders to get rid of all the Navajo stock possible. So send down and get them out of that holding pen. Of course, you'll have to pay the feed bill and herding expenses."

"Not me," S. I. replied. "Those cows were cut out illegally, and I am putting in a claim for them, attaching the Indian sellers' ownership affidavits as proof."

"Come now, I did say buy everything and all that, but Creswell refused to go along with it in the case of your heifers. But we're just going to forget it."

"I'm not," S. I. assured him. "I'm out the price of thirty head. Tell me something, how did Creswell ever get a job as stockman?"

"He grew up as a cowman and knows his business."

"Maybe you think so, but in my book he doesn't savvy a barren cow when he sees one." Walker considered this. If the thirty head were full grown, but barren cows, then the stockman's seizure had, indeed, been illegal. The next day he took two government veterinarians to Redlake; they looked only once at the barren cows before bursting into laughter. Agent Walker had the cows sent back to the trading post, where they would run with one of the herds until next trailing-out time. And Walker made Creswell pay all the expenses connected with their seizure and their return.

Christmas at Inscription House trading post was the most important family event. No matter where her three children might have wandered to, Susie always expected them to be present then. Our family members were closest and happiest at those Christmases of Mother's. They lasted one glorious, unforgettable decade, ending in 1938, when Susie left the trading post in its magnificent setting to live in Flagstaff. She had most of her children and grandchildren with her at Christmas time then, too, but the group lacked the interlocking spiritual interests we had had on the reservation. Out there, back of beyond, things were considerably different. In those days we possessed few worldly goods, especially during the depression years, but we all spent happy occasions enjoying to the utmost of what we did have.

When our special Christmases began, Cecile was two and a half years old and was the only grandchild in the family during the entire period that we gathered together on the reservation. Susie held rigidly to one rule—family exclusively. Christmas Eve became the one evening of the year when the store remained closed; only at this time could the entire family be together without interruption. Indeed, barring an accident, it would be the only occasion we could also enjoy dinner together each year.

For this fatted-calf feast Susie outdid herself in the culinary arts. She had long been famous in the Indian country for her meals—a fact mentioned in several published books. Travelers who knew, Indian Service and other government officials, Indian traders and their families, and Fred Harvey tour cars always made it a point to pause at Inscription House to eat. Often Susie produced meals at odd hours for anyone arriving hungry, and no one was ever charged. We who worked in the store ate in relays, for the post never closed until the last customer was gone—usually deep into the night. I cannot recall ever going to the table—if the roads were open—when at least two outsiders were not present—and often two or three Indians as well. Frequently, there would be a dozen or more there.

Like all old-time Indian traders, S. I. believed that flour, sugar, coffee, salt, canned tomatoes and peaches, sateen, velveteen, overalls, and a few pairs of work shoes adequately stocked a post. Anything else became unnecessary folderol. In the kitchen, however, Susie reigned supreme, and she had a hundred ways to get around staid basics for meals. She slipped her own special orders to truck drivers, who hauled the merchandise in. For Christmas dinner she needed many extra items, and she started accumulating them in late summer. Turkey, lettuce, celery, and other easily perishable foods arrived last, about a week before Christmas.

Her Christmas Day menu, besides the usual turkey and brown-sugar-baked ham, contained every other goody she could think of—so much that we spent the next ten days gorging. She produced some things that seemed impossible so far from civilization. For instance, whipped cream for pumpkin and mince pies she would contrive from condensed milk. Homemade ice cream she enriched with chopped cherries and peach or apple preserves in the days before we ever saw a tin of fruit cocktail on trading post shelves. Especially for Christmas, and occasionally during the year, she made a huge tamale; everything in it was found locally—the meat, tallow, Indian corn meal, dried red pepper, and shuck wrappings. Susie started her Christmas cooking three weeks before, with Millie helping. Fruitcakes of several kinds were cooked first and allowed to age. Chocolate, fudge, caramel, and other assorted candies were also made and boxed. Fruit, coconut, and pumpkin pies came next, with cream pies last. Usually a score or more were prepared. Nuts, having been purchased in bulk, were roasted and salted.

The Christmas meal always began the same ritualistic way: the family seated themselves quietly, Susie at one end of the long table, S. I. at the other. A minute of complete silence followed, and the saying of grace; then the turkey was served to S. I. and the baked ham to Susie. (Susie never ate turkey, or any chicken she had raised herself, and we never knew why.) After that we were on our own. An hour later we could leave the table, but food would not be removed—only used dishes and silverware. New places were set and more coffee made, so that during the balance of the day and night, anyone wanting a tidbit—if he could possibly swallow it—helped himself.

For the Christmas holiday, white employees would be gone outside to civilization, and Indian ones to their hogans. Christmas Day was given over to family and our Navajo neighbors. Presents were handed out to them that day, or whenever they appeared (sometimes deep snow delayed them).

Several days before Christmas Eve, Susie personally selected a piñon tree on the mesa, which we cut and set up in the long living room directly off the store. Only once did we bring in a fir tree from the San Francisco Peaks, and Susie didn't favor it at all; she preferred the branchy, perfumy piñon, with added purple sagebrush.

The tree was decorated with small bells, colored glass globes, strings of popcorn and red cranberries, strips of tinsel, and imitation icicles from a mail order house catalog. In the center of the ceiling hung a huge, red, paper bell of the accordion type, from which lines of varicolored decorations radiated to every corner and side wall of the big, white room. On a thick, cotton mantle—representing snow—directly beneath the tree were stacked presents in shiny, colored wrappings and ribbons. All wall space between pictures and rare blanket hangings contained hundreds of Christmas greeting cards from distant friends.

While the womenfolks busily engaged in this tree-trimming, the men paid a visit to the store office, where S. I. had a jug cached under stacked blankets. For this special occasion, we were permitted to nip a few without being fussed at for having whiskey at the post.

The evening began when the front store door was locked. The family ate in the dining room before a blazing log fire. Coleman gasoline lamps illuminated the scene, with a few candles flickering in the dim recesses of far corners. After dishes were washed and a few eggnogs passed (when we could persuade Susie to allow it), the family gathered around the festooned tree. Meanwhile, either my brother, Cecil, or my brother-in-law, Ed Ford (they alternated), slipped into S. I.'s bedroom at the east end of the lean-to porch to don a red Santa Claus suit used every year.

Cecile met her first Santa Claus on Chrismas of 1928. She was so excited she couldn't sit still. His entrance from the side door followed an established routine: he advanced slowly, talking in a disguised voice. "Well, little girl, have you been good this past year? Do you have a kiss for Santa Claus?" It required considerable urging the first year, but after that Cecile hastily bussed the jolly mask because in a few minutes, she knew, she would be transported into a dream-world of presents. Being the only grandchild at those Christmases, she queened it. Her loot filled the entire corner of the room, and it required days for her to get around to playing with all the toys.

S. I. possessed the Richardson trait of no sentimental nonsense worse than any of us. To him Christmas was just another day—and one that cost money while people engaged in damned foolishness. Susie purchased all the gifts delivered in their names, his position being that, "If I want to buy something for somebody, I'll do it right now, not wait for some special day to come along!" His attitude included even my mother; but at an early Inscription House Christmas, we partly broke him of the habit.

That year Susie wanted more than anything else an antique Navajo silver belt that he had up for sale. It was one of the early belts Navajo silversmiths made before learning to solder. The conchos had diamond-pointed holes through the centers by which they were fastened to belt leather on a thong over the metal strap. Mother worried constantly that S. I. would sell it to some rich tourist. That particular Christmas Eve various family members tried talking him into giving it to her. My sister, Irbymae, could usually wrap him around her finger, but not this time, so she appealed to me. "Everyone else has worked on him," she said. "Now you do it."

"He won't listen to me."

"You are the only one who can get him to!"

"Me, the family black sheep? I stand less chance than you!"

"Father has a lot of respect for you," she declared. "Sometimes I think he loves you more than any of us—you do it!"

I thought it over. If approached right, the Richardson protective armor could be pierced. Folding the belt, I boxed and wrapped it, then tied it with store string. Placing it before him on the counter, I said, "Hosteen, write on it, 'To Susie from Irb'," and I handed him a pencil.

He exclaimed, "Ee-god! I can get two hundred and fifty dollars for that belt any day!" Yet he wrote what I told him to, and the next year he bought Susie a present on his own. Thereafter he sometimes got gifts even for the others.

When the mail went out a week before Christmas, Susie sent almost a pickup-load of individual boxes packed with candy and fruitcake to Navajo children away at distant schools. She never forgot any of them; she often mailed them something on other special occasions, and always for graduation. On Christmas Day she gave food, clothing, and shoes to Indian children and a few adults who needed outfitting. She doled out common medicines all year long. While much of what she gave came from money she earned machine-sewing squaw dresses, some items were contributed by people living in distant states.

The donations had begun coming to her before she moved from Rainbow Lodge to Inscription House. The first three contributors were Mrs. Karl Krippendorf, whose husband manufactured shoes under that name; Miss Ruth Harter of Colorado Springs, who drove an ambulance in France during World War I; and Miss Jeanette Tandy, a tobacco plantation owner from Kentucky. Each had said to Susie, in almost identical words, "Instead of donating to missionaries, whom I have been considering, and who will do as they please with it, why can't I send my contribution to you? Then I will know needy Indians are receiving it."

To these gifts were added many others as the years passed, including two huge cartons of new shoes. Among these shoes were high-heeled, rhinestone-buckled, Paris models. Just imagine the gruesome performance of an Indian woman trying to negotiate rocks and sand dunes in them! But it was the spirit of helpfulness behind all the donations that counted, and Susie faithfully forwarded the Navajos' thanks to kind-hearted donors.

Every Christmas we gathered for the family reunion regardless of climatic risk. My brother, Cecil, and his wife, Alma, came over from Kaibito Trading Post, which he managed. My sister, Irbymae, and her husband, Ed Ford, drove out from Flagstaff, and later from Crown Point, New Mexico, where he served as an employee of the Bureau of Indian Affairs for fourteen years. Millie, Cecile, and I went there from Flagstaff when we were not living at a trading post. Often we had to fight a storm going in or get out quickly ahead of being snowed in. A couple of times we were all marooned there for four to six weeks, but for our second annual Christmas—1929—no snow lay on the ground at all. Susie, S. I., Millie, Cecile, and I remained at the post after the others had departed. Early in January, S. I. took Susie and Millie to Flagstaff (leaving Cecile with Cecil and Alma at Kaibito). Susie had to rush to Cleburne, Texas, to her aged mother's bedside, while Millie hastened to Modesto, California, due to her mother's serious illness.

The Richardson family and a Navajo neighbor outside Inscription House on Christmas Day, 1928. *From left:* Irbymae Richardson-Ford, S. I. Richardson, Edward S. Ford (behind S. I.), Alma Rodgers-Richardson, Susie Richardson, Cecil Richardson, a Navajo neighbor, Millie Green-Richardson, Gladwell "Toney" Richardson, and Cecile Richardson (age 2½).

They had hardly entrained before a heavy snowstorm struck the Indian country, blocking all roads and trails. Alone for the next three months, I saw no one but Indians and heard no English spoken. When Susie and Millie returned from their visits, they stayed in Flagstaff for some time. When, at last, the roads were opened as far as Kaibito, S. I. took them there. During their absence the temperature at Inscription House dropped far below zero, remaining there until spring thaw blew in. At night, extreme cold seeped in through the several doors and windows in the stone walls of the living quarters. Timbers in the roof popped and cracked all night long. The back-to-back fireplaces had to be kept blazing continuously. Luckily, they were huge, as Susie had wanted them, taking forty-inch logs of piñon wood—some logs were almost two feet thick. Much of the heat from the living room entered the store, where only one outside door and four windows broke the thick, mud-plastered walls. One stove, constantly stoked, prevented canned goods and soda pop on the shelves from freezing.

I left the building only to fetch water for the kitchen and to get a small quarter of beef—each time I brought in sufficient water and meat to last several days. Four to six feet of snow covered the ground behind the main building, so I shoveled a narrow path to the cistern and to a tree where the beef hung, but it immediately started filling again with windblown snow. This snow froze so hard that the next path had to be cut around it. It was impossible to knife-cut or saw the solidly frozen beef, so the quarters were laid on the kitchen floor and thick pieces chopped off with an ax. Meat placed in a pan at the side of the stove thawed out by mid-afternoon and could be cooked for supper.

Indians never showed up before noon, by which time I would have had my first of two daily meals. They traded desultorily and sat around warming, smoking, and talking as late as midnight; then they ran all the way home through deep snow in far-below-zero cold. They not only kept from freezing that way, but actually worked up a sweat. Horses were too weak to carry them, and horses that strayed on top of the mesa and were not quickly found either starved or froze to death.

Finally, incoming snow plows cleaned a large space before the trading post, into which S. I. drove Susie and my family. As soon as she entered the building, Mother hastened to the kitchen. She returned satisfied. "I knew you would keep a clean house," she said in a pleased tone. "But you should see it sometime when your father is alone!"

While I usually managed to keep living quarters clean, especially the kitchen, this time she had almost caught me napping. No cleaning had been done for several days, and chips and bark from fire logs, a little mud, and stains had disfigured all the floors. Also, a stack of dirty dishes and cooking utensils had filled the frozen-up sink. About three o'clock that afternoon an arriving Indian had announced, "I hear a truck coming along the road." That being an absolute impossibility due to snow depth, I went outside to listen. Wind brought the roar of powerful motors very clearly, but this was no truck; cats and snow plows were negotiating the steep incline of the mesa four miles to the south. That distance gave me sufficient time to chase all the Indians present into the living quarters with brooms, mops, and cleaning gear to give it the works. We finished probably fifteen minutes before the first of two snow-plowing rigs appeared through the timber.

The last Christmas we spent at Inscription House, in 1941, proved a hauntingly sad affair, at which ghosts of once supremely happy years intruded.

Susie and S. I. were then living in Flagstaff, and I was running the post for them. Cecile, then fifteen and ready to graduate from high school, came out for the holidays. Our second daughter, Toni, was two and a half years old, as Cecile had been for her first Christmas there. Millie, the girls, and I were alone.

The tree had been decorated as of yore, and presents from friends, members of absent families, and from each other were stacked beneath it. Millie spent two weeks preparing a bounteous feast, as Susie once had, but this time no Santa Claus appeared in all his glory. Other than the happiness of being together and enjoying good health, we had the most lonesomely sad Christmas we ever spent anywhere. The others were scattered too far. One of them, my sister-in-law, Alma Rogers Richardson, had passed on, but the unseen presence of them all seemed to be there. The memory of their excited, joyous laughter echoed out of the white walls of the living room, and their silent steps on the floor were a reminder of wonderful years beyond recall. Never again would they be there; yet something of them all had been left behind, hovering protectingly, even if sorrowfully. Nothing is more true than that you can never go back to what once was. This Christmas heralded the end, an irrevocably closed chapter in the lives of us all.

On Christmas Eve it started snowing and turned very cold. After New Year's Day the road to Tonalea remained partly blocked, and only the big truck could get through. Frank Hill, the range rider stationed below the mesa, had returned early from visiting his family in New Mexico, and he drove the truck to take Cecile to Tonalea, where S. I. picked her up for her return to school. She was to stay in Flagstaff that year with our dear friend, Ethel Wallace, and her family. Despite their loving care, Cecile would spend a miserable nine months—it was the only time in her teen years she had been away from both of us. As for that, we missed our big girl as much as she did us.

Another storm hit, and in the dampness and cold, disease fell upon the Indians. Deaths were many, especially among small children not in school, where medical attention was available. The country was closed tight, once more an isolated, lonely world of glistening white under a bright sun. Millie, at thirty-eight years of age, got the measles again from Indians who came to the post, and she suffered after-effects of swollen glands on her neck. Somehow we made it through to spring, when warmer weather and vanishing ice and snow returned good health and peace to the far country. One day early that summer we departed (I was to run Kaibito Trading Post for my Uncle Hubert), never to return again as resident traders at Inscription House.

Kaibito

In 1929 my brother, Cecil, was trading for our uncle Hubert Richardson at Kaibito. Previously he had run Leupp Trading Post (where he and Alma Rogers were married), and when Hubert had sold Leupp to Stanton K. Borum, he had sent Cecil to Kaibito. That spring Cecil wanted to take his wife on a vacation in California, so he propositioned S. I. to have me hold down the other trading post. S. I. decided he could spare me, so Millie, Cecile, and I drove there, twenty-eight miles from Inscription House to Tonalea and twenty-five more around White Horse Mesa to Kaibito. The plateaus, mesas, and canyons stretching from Kaibito to the Colorado River (where Page and Glen Canyon Dam are today) were all good trapping country. Coyote, lynx cat, and fox thrived thick as fleas, and parties of trappers were there all winter. Cecil said that two of them were liable to show up to sell their furs, as he had promised to buy them, and the approaching spring meant the end of trap lines.

Another of my uncles, C. D. Richardson, had built Kaibito Trading Post in rich sheep country, in a canyon against White Horse Mesa in 1914. He had held ownership, hiring various managers, until selling to Ed Morris in 1921. Although Morris had had backing from Louis Ilfield in Albuquerque, after two years he had sold to my uncle Hubert. A small, stone house for use by missionaries had been built on a rise behind the post under the mesa rim. Before our arrival, a missionary who had recently returned from the Orient camped there with a bedroll brought from China. With the bedroll, he introduced the large, vicious Chinese bedbug.* These insects invaded the post and multiplied like crazy. Their bite was extremely dangerous to babies and small children. On hearing about the flying insects, Millie grew very scared, and for the next several weeks she practically sat up day and night guarding Cecile. We did not see any of them, but they were around.

---

*From the cursory description given by Richardson, a Northern Arizona University biologist, Glenn Anderson, believes the insect thought to be a Chinese bedbug was in reality a *triatoma*, popularly called a kissing bug, which is known to fly as well as to inflict a stinging bite.

The old post interested me because of the historical surroundings and tragic events connected with it. Near here in 1916 the Navajo outlaw Taddytin had been killed. Walter Runke, Indian agent at Tuba City, had sent three white policemen after him for a score of crimes. Ashley Wilson, the chief of police, headed a posse composed of himself, Ed Nash, and David Robinson. They found Taddytin in a hogan which he refused to leave. The officers argued with him through the doorway, which was covered by a saddle blanket, and Taddytin threatened to shoot the first one trying to enter. No nervier man ever lived than Wilson, who quickly grew tired of bickering. He said he was going in, and, throwing the blanket aside, he leaped into the hogan. The Navajo pointed a .30-.30 Winchester carbine at him, but Wilson knocked him down before he could fire. Taddytin hurled his body beyond reach, leaping up to snap the hammer of the carbine at Wilson, who then shot him dead.

A furious outcry was raised that Taddytin had been murdered on orders of the Indian agent. Runke, a school superintendent and Indian agent for more than twenty years, was removed from office five years later and tried in federal court for giving orders to bring him in. Instead of backing up their agent, the Indian Bureau actually prosecuted him. The trial went on for two years before a jury found him not guilty. Immediately after the shooting Indians were in an uproar around Kaibito, so my uncle C. D. went there to stay with his resident manager in case of worse trouble. None appeared in the offing until one night Ashley Wilson showed up, riding across the country on police business.

Wilson stopped at Kaibito and ate supper with the family. Near the end of the meal C. D. said, "Of course, you realize the Navajos already know you're here. You should either fort up or slip out on your way quickly. They will kill you when they can come in force." Before Wilson could reply, loud knocking sounded on the trading post door. C. D. and Wilson went into the store, carrying a dim oil lamp. C. D. proposed talking to the Indians outside, but Wilson vetoed this move at once, since it sounded like a considerable bunch out there.

"Just let them in when I tell you," he instructed. He assumed a position against the wall between the high, right counter and the barred door. "Now, let's see what they look like."

C. D. unfastened the door, opening it wide. He had returned to the end counter before the block of dark night beyond was broken. A Navajo stepped in slowly, followed by others, until fifteen of the band were inside. They never looked to either side, yet were well aware that Wilson stood there, partly crouched, his right hand resting above a holstered gun for a quick draw. They proceeded to the far counter, on which reposed a free tobacco box. Silently each one took his time rolling and lighting a cigarette. Leaning idly against counters, they spoke to C. D. and his manager, who remained nervously near a double-barreled shotgun under the counter top. Half an hour elapsed before they made a move. Then, the leader asked for a sack of smoking tobacco, paid for it, and walked unconcernedly from the post, again being very, very careful not to notice Wilson. The rest soon followed, and the band rode off into the dark night. Nothing whatever happened because Wilson had faced them down. A few weeks later the federal government charged Wilson with the murder of Taddytin. Three months later a judge released him from the Prescott jail, although trial was still pending. When the U.S. entered World War I, Wilson went into the Army and was killed in action in France in 1918.

The third day we were at Kaibito, a rainstorm came up and lightning killed three ewes in the flock belonging to Fat Goat, one of the Kaibito headmen. The old man took sacred pollen and a basket and made medicine around the bunched band to ward off further danger from the sky. Afterward he had to remain in his hogan for four days, in accordance with Navajo custom. After the storm Crooked Finger, another headman in this area, asked me to go with him to investigate tracks near the burial place of a former district chief. Fat Goat told us only a demented person would prowl the vicinity of a grave, where all Navajos were afraid to go. We drove several miles into Standing Rock country. The huge masses of stone, some as large as buildings, contained expanses of bare yellow sand between them. Crooked Finger directed me to one of the rocks, where we parked the car. Slipping to the base, he paused at a scrawny cedar tree, where the grave was located. Rain had wiped the sand clean in the immediate area of the grave, but he found mysterious tracks directly opposite where we stood. He would go no closer, but I could safely do so, despite evil spirits, because I was a white man.

Old burial sites in Navajoland are dangerous places to be fooling around. Those of an important district chief, such as this one, contained valuable silver ornaments. Jewelry buried with the remains here was probably worth between five and six thousand dollars, which accounted for Crooked Finger's wanting the site investigated. The man buried there thirty years before had been known as Spanish Horse. Probably a dozen head of horses had been killed around his grave. Whitened bones were scattered over two or three acres, from one domed stone to another. A few cooking utensils had also been "killed" for the dead man to take along.* Near a tree two saddles had been chopped useless; rotting leather was still clinging to parts of them. In the lowest cedar-tree fork reposed an undamaged Winchester rifle, merely rusted by the elements. No identifying mound marked the actual gravesite. Under smoothed sand, it might have been right near the tree or anywhere from ten to twenty feet off.

So far as I could determine, nothing had disturbed Spanish Horse's final resting place. Certainly there was no fresh sign on the rain-cleaned sand. Passing a near rock, I investigated the space beyond it, where the tracks Crooked Finger had seen came into being. He had followed no sign in, and backtracking him, I discovered none either.

Going south around more obstructions, I entered a wide space between two other rocks affording a direct view of the grave. Right under my feet in one narrow opening appeared fresh moccasin tracks. They went on for ten feet; the sand there revealed that an intruder had spent at least fifteen minutes reconnoitering. On turning right to leave, he had circled halfway over the opening before taking off running. His feet punched deep marks that were easily followed to where a horse had been tied to another cedar tree half a mile away. Against the cedar bark, clinging hair revealed the horse to be chestnut brown with a black mane. Tracks showed the left rear shoe to be loose and badly worn. The right forefoot had been recently shod and the other two were medium worn. Measuring with a stick, I cut notches to show the size of each shoe.

I gave Crooked Finger the stick and described all evidence carefully. On the return trip he asked to be let off at his hogan, not making a single comment on what I had told him. As I drove off, he began yelling for his sons; they would, I knew, grab someone quickly—and they did. That night they came to the post with half a dozen other Indians. And they brought Gisheybeta, a third Kaibito headman. All were in a happy mood and teasing the old man, for it turned out that he had been the one there. A kinsman of the late Spanish Horse, he had secretly watched the grave. He was leery of the Paiute Indians who often rode across the country from Boschini on the San Juan River to another village at Willow Springs down on U.S. Highway 89. The Paiutes were known as grave robbers among the Navajos, but it is doubtful that any of them ever knew where Spanish Horse slept.

---

*"Killing" meant damaging (either through knocking a hole or badly denting) a utensil so as to render it useless.

Cecil's two Mormon trappers came in, ready to leave the country. They brought two mule-loads of furs, which were graded and priced. After paying their supply bill, and having been given all money at hand at the post, they still had two hundred and fifty dollars due. For this I wrote them my personal check—later I would be reimbursed by the post. Eighteen months later the check showed up at my Flagstaff bank. The trappers had taken it home to Utah, where it had passed through many hands in a dozen small towns as a medium of exchange; it contained so many endorsements that a piece of paper had been pasted on to hold them. Among the furs these trappers had sold were a dozen beautiful cross fox. Three were not the usual gray, but a very rare red. Cecil sent them to Denver to be tanned, and we had them made into neck pieces for his wife and Millie and Susie.

Another trapper, Red Eldridge, spent three days at Kaibito before heading south. He could talk about one subject only—gold. He had located a mesa top south of the Verde River where gold nuggets dropped from the roots of pulled bunch-grass. He did not explain why he had failed to make a hay-crop then and there, so, naturally, I considered him another windy hopeful who dreamed of sudden riches. He did say the mesa would be his next stop and that he intended to sack up enough gold to engage in business for himself—which is exactly what he did do. You can't always tell about the blowhard type.

As a group, the main Kaibito families were the wealthiest Indians I ever traded with. They kept their money in the post safe. When it had been spent, they went on the books for credit amounting to one to three thousand dollars each until next wool-shearing or lamb- or cattle-selling season. Family units would load their wagons with coffee, tomatoes, and canned fruit by the case. Sateen for skirts and velveteen and silk plush for shirts were bought by the bolt. Shoes and Levi's pants went by the dozen, and flour was bought twenty-five sacks at a time. While sometimes buying bacon and salt pork, they never bought eggs—they claimed that people who ate the chicken's little ones would have twice too many children. These rich Navajos, first to own automobiles in the western Navajo country, paid no attention to time. They were liable to appear any time between sundown and sunrise. When I protested they should arrive at least by midnight to trade, they replied smugly, "Your fathers (meaning my uncles) will be unhappy if you do not let us trade now!"

The Indians liked to tell me about the joke they pulled on my uncles Hubert and C. D. the first time they appeared together at Kaibito, many years before. While both spoke the Navajo language fluently, apparently they were years learning the meaning of one particular word. At the post they asked the Indians all day long where they were from. Every one of them answered, *"Nizady"* (meaning a long distance off, far from here). One night at supper Hubert broke from a spell of deep concentration to say to C. D., "You know, Claude, you made a mistake building your store here. You should move it over to Nizady, where all these Indians live!"

Kaibito once came near losing all Navajo trade when C. D.'s brother-in-law, Tom Turpin, who was running the post for him, passed on suddenly of influenza in 1919. Knowing that if Navajos learned someone had died in the building they would never enter it again, his wife locked up tight. She refused to open for customers until she managed to get word out to Tuba City by a rider. C. D. hurried there, taking his friend Joe Lee and Tom's younger brother, Tobe Turpin, with him. That night they concealed the body in a touring car and departed at three o'clock in the morning. The Indians were told that Turpin had moved elsewhere. To this day, when it no longer matters, they still do not know he died in the post living quarters.

One afternoon in the store a woman whispered to me, "See the brother and sister looking at silver jewelry in the glass case? The brother is both a man and a woman." The pair at the far end of the store were much alike, slender of build, and favoring each other as to features. In their late forties, they lived together in a remote area. It did seem to me that the man's shirt bulged with breasts behind blue percale fabric, and I recalled having heard it said that a hermaphrodite lived somewhere in the Kaibito country.

A little later the pair came over to me. The sister placed a very fine blanket on the counter top. When I bought it, they traded out the money. The brother then sacked their purchases and left. I asked the sister confidentially, "Is it true about your brother?"

"It is," she replied casually, unconcerned. "I do not weave. He made this fine blanket. Surely you have heard that *nahtgla* (hermaphrodites) are the best makers of blankets among The People?" (Indeed, legends claimed that these people were expert artisans who originated all arts and crafts among the Navajo.) While I admitted to such knowledge, the brother re-entered the store.

She said to him, "He doesn't believe what you are." Instead of being embarrassed, he was tolerantly amused.

"There are many *Denah* (Navajo people) who do not believe I am the fortunate one, either."

"Show him," the sister added.

To my astonishment he proved not a pseudo-hermaphrodite, as I suspected, but the real thing. With his very expert weaving drawing top prices, and the income from her sheep, they were quite wealthy. When I stayed three nights at their hogan in 1940, while taking the district census, they showed me a secret cave in Echo Cliffs. The walls were covered with ten-foot-high colored paintings of Navajo *yei* (gods). When or by whom they were put there no one knows. Navajos living in the area have no story to account for the paintings, which are not mentioned during the annual telling of clan history. The brother and sister claimed I was the only white man ever to enter the cave, and they could not recall any Navajos who had seen the paintings in recent times.

The Kaibito Indians frequently tried to get me to ride to the base of White Horse Mesa with them, to look at several natural bridges. They described them as being larger than huge Hole-in-the-Wall Arch off the Tonalea-Inscription House road on the east side. Perhaps, they speculated, they were larger than famous Rainbow Natural Bridge. A few years later I did visit several smaller ones, but not those they had described. After World War I, Senator Barry Goldwater and his son, jeep-exploring fingerling

The blouses and skirts of Navajo girls were made of velveteen, sateen, and silk plush—materials which were bought by the bolt by wealthy Kaibito-area families.

canyons that form Navajo Canyon, discovered a huge white arch which they photographed; Goldwater called it "Margaret Bridge," for his wife.

Missionary Butler, who headquartered at Tuba City, had an oblong, red sandstone building down the canyon from Kaibito Trading Post, where once or twice a year he preached to Navajos through an interpreter. To acquire even a small crowd, he would throw a big feed and gave away presents each night. While we were at Kaibito, he came and stayed a week, and not one Indian attended his meetings. One day, near sundown, he showed up at the post in a real dither. "I have just learned why no Indians come to hear about God and the Bible," he informed me. "They are over there every night at Bert Tso's house, gambling—men and women both—so many that they can't all get inside!" That night after supper I drove over to Bert Tso's rock house, a couple of miles out on the plateau. The son of rich, old Gisheybeta, Bert had recently gone to Flagstaff, where he had bought a battery radio. Butler was right about one thing—people sitting on the ground near fires filled all the space before the house. But he was wrong about the reason they were there. An oil lamp burned inside and Bert's radio, turned as high as it would go, had been placed in an open window so that people inside and out could hear it. They had gathered in droves to listen, even if the programs were all in English.

Ever alert against Cecile's being bitten by a Chinese bedbug, Millie was very happy when Cecil and Alma came home from California. Before returning to Inscription House, all the clothing we had taken to Kaibito was boiled, just in case one pesky insect might have hidden in a pocket or seam.

The Big Snow

The winter of 1931–1932 produced the most disastrous freeze-up old traders claimed they could remember. The first deep snow fell about the middle of October, and it still lay on the ground when another piled down on top of it. Trails and roads had been broken, but now snowfall continued intermittently into December and January. The heavy pack crystallized, roads drifted and froze solid, and all western Navajo Reservation routes became impassable. Much the same conditions existed down around Flagstaff, a hundred and seventy miles from Inscription House. With early winter, coyotes began running in packs, which was most unusual for them. Wildlife as well as domestic livestock starved to death.

The heavy snow and the below-zero temperatures which occurred in the canyon country of southern Utah forced wolves southward through defiles into the tribesmen's range. Gaunt with hunger, they spread over the slightly warmer valleys in packs, hunting anything to eat. Big stock, like cattle and horses, weak from hunger and unable to fight or flee in the deep snow, were easily pulled down. When wolves got into a sheep corral, they killed thirty-five or forty head before they could be driven off. Navajos built huge fires and sat up all night on guard with rifles. Still, the starving, voracious wolves made deep inroads.

Range feed was impossible to get to under the deep snow. Indians dug trails through the snow—as deep as their heads—to water and into stands of timber, where limbs were chopped off so that their sheep could eat twigs and bark. Those that died were covered by succeeding snows, and coyotes, wolves, and flocks of crows dug down to the frozen carcasses. The huge, black birds appeared in masses, quarreling and fighting for anything they could get at. Navajos reported that the crows would even fly in among their sheep to pick the eyes out of the living.

Stockman George Creswell arrived at Inscription House on a horse, after riding the high, windblown ridges. He had orders to try to break the road through to Navajo Mountain, where conditions were even worse (if that was possible). The Tuba City agency hoped to truck stock-feed through before the Indians lost everything they owned. Creswell, who had no equipment

whatever, planned to construct huge "Vs" of logs to be pulled by ponies to clear the road. Unfortunately, no one had taken into consideration the weakness of all the Navajo stock. None was strong enough
to do much more than stand up, so the plan fell through before it was even
initiated.

Starvation, disease, and death rode the land. Traders' supplies neared
the exhaustion point, since no trucks could get through with merchandise.
Not many Navajos could reach the nearest stores, anyway. At the height
of the emergency, Indian agent C. L. Walker wangled food and procured
Army bombers from March Field, California, to drop supplies. His unofficial
action—"Operation Bread"—covered remote areas of western Navajo country. It was the first air drop therein; others were to be made in later years
under conditions of far less disaster. The big planes circled hogans and trading posts, bomb bays open. Seamless bags contained flour, dried fruit and
beans, coffee, sugar, sow belly, salt, and some canned goods. When these
bags hit the frozen tops of snowdrifts, the heavy cloth split, scattering contents for a considerable distance. Many sacks of flour and dried beans spread
all over the landscape and were unrecoverable.

It was impossible to send word around of the drop, so the Indians didn't
quite know what to do about this packaged food from the sky. Were they
supposed to use it? Could it be poisoned? Some concluded that it must be
a special Christmas gift from Washington. They were unhappy, however,
about the items, wanting to know, "Where is the candy? Did they forget
it?" Sometimes the Indians threw away the beans in the few containers
that didn't break, much preferring to eat the lean, stringy meat of their
frozen sheep.

A sudden break came in the violent weather, and the sunshine lasted
seven days. Two tractors and a road blade got through to Inscription House,
making a one-way passage through packed snow. Six miles above the post,
where canyon country began, tractors were forced to turn back. Snow filled
all the deep places completely, and the machines couldn't possibly bore
through snow and ice twice their own height. S. I. left by pickup over the
one-way trace south to see about getting merchandise trucked in before the
roads closed again.

Two days later Mother asked me to get the mail at Redlake—we hadn't
received any since before Christmas. My brother-in-law, Ed Ford, and I
started out in a big Chrysler sedan. We should have realized that if the
roads were open, S. I. would have returned at once. Five miles into Red
Valley the heavy sedan bogged in ice and snow, ripping the rear end out.
We had to walk back and the car remained stuck until spring thaw. Food

supplies at the post were dangerously low, however, so I decided to walk out to see what could be done. Hiking proved easy as far as the broken-down sedan, but from there on windblown drifts filled one-way cuts. At the lower end of the valley, snow had melted off in patches on the sides of sand hills that faced the sun. As I walked along, sleeping robe slung over a shoulder, what I assumed were coyotes on hillsides paused while digging out prairie dogs to watch me. In other places crows were busy tearing at the snow crust, trying to get at carcasses of dead animals buried below.

I made it to Redlake, where trader Johnny O'Farrell reported that the highway was only now barely open to Flagstaff. Catching a ride, I arrived at Cameron, fifty-four miles from Flagstaff, to find S. I. waiting there with a truckload of supplies. He had tried unsuccessfully to get through for several days. The next morning we started at daylight and made good time to Redlake. But at Eagle Nest Rock a new storm had filled the wash and road cuts solid. We turned back to Tuba City, where we were informed by the agent that roads would be opened immediately with new equipment that was being sent in. We went forth every day for a week, but no road was broken, and another storm was approaching.

My brother-in-law, Ed, was at the isolated post with Millie, Cecile, Susie, and my sister. Since they were surely in worse than desperate straits by this time, I determined to hike in. S. I. let me off at Eagle Nest Rock. I didn't figure that walking twenty-eight miles to Inscription House would be much of a chore; in fact, I should reach there along about three o'clock in the afternoon. Only to please S. I. did I agree to take a couple of oranges. We separated and I started walking over frozen crusts. Eleven miles into Red Valley, I slipped and fell over a sharp, pointed ridge of ice, injuring my right side. Half a mile farther the frozen crust began to break through under my two-hundred-pound weight, and, every fourth or fifth step, down I plunged into dry, loose snow.

I was too far from Redlake to go back, but I reasoned that before long I would surely see smoke from a Navajo hogan, where I would seek refuge with friends. Sand hills visible off the road were covered with what I still assumed to be coyotes. Before much more time passed, I would discover my sad mistake of not identifying the beasts correctly.

About an hour before sundown, the clear ring of an ax echoed across the valley. Unfortunately, it wasn't possible to separate the true sound from the echoes reverberating in every direction. Pausing, hoping to spot smoke, I ate one of my oranges, throwing the peel away. Deciding that some wood-chopper must be half a mile ahead to the right, in a stand of junipers, I set forth. My right leg was now dragging, lamed by the earlier injury. Arriving even with the timber, half a mile to the east, echoes sounded from every compass point, as before. Frozen ground creates echoes and re-echoes in fantastic array. Despite the yellow ball of the sun, still slightly above the horizon, I realized that the temperature was well below zero and that I was in real danger.

Knowing it was physically impossible to proceed much farther, I decided against the risk of moving away from the road into deeper snow. While moving on, I ate the last orange, but this time I stuck the peelings into my pocket. It seemed that I was getting closer to the ax-chopping sounds, but the sun was touching the horizon and soon disapppeared. A grimly cold, bluish white world surrounded me. Then the wood-chopper quit. The sound of his ax, indicating that a least one human being was near, had been comforting in my distress. Now, with it gone, extreme sadness struck. I cannot recall another moment in my life when abrupt cessation of a sound plummeted me into such depths of hopelessness.

Struggling on, knowing my strength was waning fast and that I must soon halt, I hobbled around a low hill west of the road. Near its base the oval dome of an abandoned hogan stuck up higher than the snow. Turning toward it, I fell, crawled, and hobbled a couple of hundred yards to the nearly buried, beehive-shaped structure. I had to claw and kick out ice to get down to the east entrance, which proved to be covered by a door made of Arbuckle-Brothers-Coffee-box boards. I tore off enough boards to crawl through. Snow lay piled in the center of the hogan under the overhead smokehole; otherwise, the floor was dry sand and red clay.

The structure proved to be a travelers' hogan, of the kind that occupied a trail junction and was used by people passing through the country. According to custom, a baking-powder tin, containing coffee and a small amount of salt, should be buried to the right of the door. This was for emergency use—afterward to be replaced for the next hungry person. A boiling can for the coffee stood against the log wall over the cache. Being half frozen, I couldn't dig the rations out yet. It required most of my strength just to strike some matches to fire a small pile of bark and wood chips against the base log on the north side of the hogan. That done, I collapsed in the sleeping blanket.

The fire caught, and presently cloying warmth drugged me to sleep. I awoke with hands and feet stinging from thawing out. For a moment the hogan interior seemed too hot—the log wall had caught fire! But it was so far below zero, so inhumanly cold, that the hard logs burned very slowly. The prospect of coffee became irresistible, and with renewed strength I dug where the rations should be. Bringing out a large can, I yanked the lid off, only to find it completely empty. In despair, I melted some snow to get water and ate pieces of orange peel.

A glance outside revealed a cloudless sky bright with stars; bluish white, like diamonds, they matched the frozen world hemming me in. Rolling into a blanket before the burning wall, I lay down to sleep. But I slept only for brief periods—while freezing on one side, I burned on the other. From one doze I awakened suddenly when a heavy object fell inside the hogan through the smoke-hole. Staring me in the face loomed a big grayish-colored wolf. It wheeled sideways and out through the door opening when I jumped up, yelling. Ringing the smoke-hole overhead appeared several furry heads, with eyes that gleamed in the leaping firelight—not coyotes, but wolves like the one I had just chased out. These were the animals I had seen on the sand hills.

Wall ice had loosened up near the fire, and I managed to pry out a short length of pole that had been used as chinking between crooked logs. With it I drove the wolves from the smoke-hole, but they were soon back. While they were gone I replaced the boards of the broken door, pulling big chunks of ice in the passage up against them. The fourth time I beat the wolves away from the smoke-hole rim, a paw hanging over got smashed. The damage drew blood, and, when the beast fled, the night was suddenly rent with howls and a great noise of fierce fighting. The starved pack may have attacked the bleeding wolf; in any case the scrambling mass spilled off the north side of the hogan, creating an awesome racket for quite some time.

Soon glowing eyes ringed the smoke-hole again. My only weapon, if it could be called such, was a small pocketknife. If they came down to attack, I wouldn't last long. Then I remembered that wolves were supposedly afraid of fire. Now able to extract bark chinking and smaller wall-logs, I kindled a blaze on the ice surface directly under the overhead opening. Although it never flamed high, it did seem to hold them at bay. But I certainly must remain awake; walking around to do so—often slapping my face—I managed to keep at least partly alert.

Then the situation developed into a numbing nightmare. Snarling wolves fell into the deep hole I had dug up to the door. A long nose broke through between boards, but I immediately slammed a log against it, and a dog-like howl was raised as it scrambled backward. Then the hole behind the door became a fighting pocket of maddened beasts. The space couldn't contain them, and their pressing weight broke out the boards altogether. They spewed inside, all snapping teeth into one other. The scene was unimaginable: an injured wolf going down bleeding was seized by half a dozen maddened jaws all at once. They piled on each other to get at the fresh meat.

The smoke-hole was my only route to escape. Three times I leaped, with hands reaching for the log rim, before I managed a hold. Desperately pulling myself upward slowly, I knew if I fell now I would never make it again. Coming over the edge, I lay looking down, watching the fighting wolves that filled the hogan interior. Taking a heavier club from the smoke-hole rim, I settled down to wait. The crunching of teeth on bone went on for what seemed hours in my distraught condition. Likely no more than one hour had passed when a wolf came out of the hogan and loped away across frozen snow. A second followed, and more and more appeared in a dark line, making off under the bright whiteness of a rising moon. Checking the hogan, and finding it empty, I dropped back into it. Bones and pieces of furry hide lay around where three of the pack had been eaten. One other wolf had been consumed in the hole before the east door. Even the terribleness of what had happened, however, could no longer keep me awake.

I fell asleep, completely dead to the world, and awoke to find bright sunlight shining through the smoke-hole. Only flickering flames licked at the logs. After extinguishing the fire, somehow I struggled back out to the buried road in glaring brilliance. What had happened in the hogan seemed momentarily to be a dream, yet the bones and fur were clear evidence that a life and death battle had occurred.

Perhaps I had gained a mile in three hours, when again, the sound of a wood-chopper's ax rang out. This time I could see someone on the other side of a timbered hill half a mile to the west. As I started struggling toward him, the Indian spotted me. He yelled at another, and they both came running. The ax wielder was Jack Gambol, a Navajo practitioner of witchcraft (a few years later, he landed in a federal penitentiary, where he hanged himself in his cell). The two Indians carried and dragged me into timber cover, where a small fire blazed. They had hot coffee and flat bread, which had never tasted so good. Gambol's friend carried a note to Ed Ford at Inscription House to send me a horse, which Ed very nearly didn't do, because Indians had been making up excuses of dire emergencies trying to borrow the one horse that we kept up and grain-fed all winter. But the Navajos did bring the saddled horse, and at sundown, I fell out of the saddle in front of the trading-post door. The next day tractors opened the road and truckloads of supplies followed them in. The big freeze had ended, and melting snow and ice began to flood the country. Wolves withdrew to the north toward their usual habitat and were not seen in this area again for another ten years.*

I talked to Luke Smith, the trader at Cow Springs Trading Post—about twelve air miles from where I had had such a harrowing experience with wolves. He told me that on that night his weather thermometer had registered minus thirty-one degrees and that it had varied from minus twenty-five to minus thirty-four during the past three weeks (Luke always kept a weather log wherever he operated a post). When the skulls of the wolves eaten in the hogan were later examined, we thought they must have been a coyote-wolf cross because the heads seemed shorter than those of wolves as we knew them. But when a story I wrote about that terrible night appeared in a national magazine, letters from cowmen across the southern Utah line claimed it wasn't true. They said the brutes were plain wolves—the same ones that gave them trouble every bad winter. I must add that the coyotes around Navajo Mountain and Inscription House were as large as the biggest of wolves, which might account for my not immediately seeing that they were, in fact, wolves.

The family still had a little food left at the trading post, but they had run out of wood. Fires had been built only to cook and keep canned goods from freezing in the store. Each day, shortly after noon, they had had to go to bed to keep warm: only enough green wood could be cut and packed through deep snow to keep the post from freezing up. Fortunately, with my return, the bad storms ended, and with roads open we soon had plenty of wood and supplies.

---

*Some scholars have questioned whether wolves ever inhabited the Navajo Reservation, but David E. Brown, big-game supervisor with the Arizona Game and Fish Department and foremost authority on wolves in the Southwest, observes: "Wolves were present on the Navajo Reservation—at least up to around 1920. As in northern New Mexico and Arizona, however, they were largely—if not entirely—eliminated by 1930. The wolf was also extirpated by this time in southern Utah, so accounts of wolves after 1930 should be viewed with great skepticism." David E. Brown to Editor, October 2, 1984.

Sunrise

In the spring of 1932, after the big snow melted off western Navajo country, my uncle C. D. needed a trader at his Sunrise Trading Post. C. D. used to travel all over the West, wholesaling Navajo rugs and silver jewelry, while Aunt Trula ran her own curio store in Winslow. The man they employed at Sunrise and his family were swiping everything but the walls and roof. Because the post was in precarious financial condition, Millie and I agreed to go there temporarily.

We went to Winslow one afternoon, staying overnight with C. D. and Trula, and going on the next morning with them to the post. The man working there had not been informed of his impending release, but, when paid an extra month's salary, he and his family rushed their packing to leave. As soon as they finished, C. D. shook down their baggage and bundles. From their belongings he recovered twenty-eight hundred dollars worth of silver and turquoise jewelry pawned by Navajo owners; the post would have had to make this loss good to the Indians. In addition, they had taken better than two thousand dollars in jewelry from the store stock (much of this must have been stashed away before our arrival). Also, the employee's wife had gathered all the newest linen at the post and packed it.

Sunrise Trading Post, standing two and a half miles down the Little Colorado River from Leupp Navajo Agency, occupied high ground between two bridges. The first spanned Canyon Diablo (hardly more than a good-sized wash at this point, before emptying into the river); the other extended over the Little Colorado on the old Oraibi road.

Somewhere around 1905, Babbitt Brothers Trading Company had built a store across the flat from Tolchecko Mission, against some low bare hills. When the mission burned down on Christmas Eve of 1918, the small trading post practically went out of business for lack of customers. While they still operated it—mostly for wandering Indians—their trader, Nebby Smith, proceeded secretly to construct the large, stone building that became Sunrise Trading Post. Closer to Leupp than the old store, and situated at the junction of two main roads, it held promise of being a good spot.

One day C. J. Babbitt came along in his car and discovered workmen putting finishing touches on the roof of the new building. Having his driver stop, he strolled over, asking whose trading post it would be. "Babbitt's," came the answer from the workmen, who didn't know him. This was news to him. No authorization had been given to build another store near Leupp. For one of the few times in his life, he got mad. "You men quit working right now and board up the front door!"

Going down the river to his store, he nailed Nebby Smith, who confessed everything. In the end Smith talked Babbitt out of dispensing with the project, and some months later, Sunrise store was finished and stocked with goods for both Indian and white trade. C. D. acquired it in 1928 through a deal with Babbitt Brothers trading company for his stores at Tuba City and Shonto.

The new building was not the first post at this spot; across the road from its northeast end, sections of the stone foundation of a former one still remained in place. It had done business from about 1904 (when Wolf Post, farther downriver, had closed) until 1911. Leupp was also nearby. The first river crossing near the old building had become a cable ferry during high water, and at the crossing, under a cottonwood tree, Indian Bureau Commissioner Francis E. Leupp had camped in 1908, en route to the Hopi snake dance; on his return trip he inspected the vicinity and ordered construction—a bit upstream—of an agency and boarding school which were named for him.

Sunrise Trading Post, located on high ground between the two bridges
that spanned Canyon Diablo and the Little Colorado River,
in the early 1930s.

Sunrise has always stood solitary and alone, blasted by harsh winds. Domestic water was a problem—it had to be hauled in. While Millie and I were there, C. D. hired a well digger to put down a hole on the near side of Canyon Diablo below the bridge. The water table lay only thirty feet below the surface, and the digger got down to twenty feet easily. Then, one morning on his way to work, he heard a peculiar noise. Taking a look into the uncovered well, he came away fast and quit on the spot. The previous night sidewinder rattlesnakes prowling for water had fallen into the hole; the bottom held a large mass of them, and they were buzzing like mad. I covered it with heavy timbers to keep animals and people out of danger, but snakes continued to get in there somehow until, when we left there, the well held a stinking mass nearly to the top.

Once or twice a year, when rain came to Sunrise, it fell in torrents, but it very seldom snowed there. Winter and summer devil winds (miniature cyclones) tore across the countryside, ripping grass and weeds out of the ground, whirling them with sand a few hundred feet skyward. Occasionally a dozen at once could be observed moving across the higher plateau.

Sunrise enjoyed an excellent Navajo and Hopi Indian business. We bought an average of ten rugs each day, and, when boarding school ended in 1932, and parents came for their children on the day set, more than four hundred passed across the counter. The trade was all barter, but that spring wool purchases were half trade and half cash when customers wanted it. The highest price per pound went to Indians taking all merchandise and paying their bills; the sellers taking half cash and half merchandise got the lowest. Now and then we encountered a smart Indian scheming around this deal for all cash at the higher price. One such man, educated and from another district, brought a truckload of wool to Sunrise. After dickering for some time, he asked for the half-and-half deal, so we weighed his sacks. The total came to twelve hundred dollars, of which he received six hundred in currency. Saying he would trade that afternoon, the Navajo departed. Thirty minutes later, he brought Indian Agent Jack Balmer from Leupp to the post. Balmer strode around the large bull pen, furiously puffing smoke from a fat cigar stuck in his mouth. "You owe this Indian six hundred dollars?" he demanded.

When I explained the deal to him—which he apparently already knew, as all traders were doing the same—he listened impatiently. I knew his angle here, because he and the Leupp trader together had worked many scurvy money-making schemes. He wanted to get Sunrise in a jam so as to stop our heavy competition against his buddy. When I finished, he wheeled on me anew. "You owe this Indian six hundred dollars. You claim the deal one way, he says another. All right, you admit you owe him the six hundred, so pay him and pay him right now!"

"I'm coming from behind this counter," I told him, "and directly when I get into the bull pen, you'll be picking pieces of that cigar out of your insides!" When I started for the closed gate leading into the customer space, Balmer beat me out the front door. Jumping into an agency sedan, he roared back to his office, and I never heard any more about the matter. He is the only Indian agent I ever had any trouble with.

A little later the Little Colorado River came up in a sudden flood, threatening to wash out the great clay dikes protecting the Leupp agency and school on low land. Balmer came to Sunrise on this occasion, asking if he could bring the boarding-school children there before the dirt embankments broke. They could be camped on high ground around the store building. I told him to come ahead with his truckloads of kids, and we would take care of them. Agency employees sandbagged the dikes day and night, and fortunately they held. Eventually, to protect the Leupp agency, the Indian Service had to cut the river from its main channel and send it down Canyon Diablo and back into an old river course.

A few weeks after the flood, I saved Balmer his job. An inspector from the Bureau in Washington and his wife, who wrote poetry, stayed with us at Sunrise; we had known them for several years. Every morning the inspector went to the Leupp agency, returning after sundown very close mouthed. The next weekend he told me, "I have uncovered sixteen gross violations of regulations involving several people. All are government employees except the Indian trader over there. If I recommend prosecution, it will cause terrible confusion and probably end with penitentiary sentences for several. My concern is only what is best for the Indian Service—it's a tough decision to make." After he explained the cases in detail, I shook my head. "Give the agent a break if you can. I happen to know some of his assistants have done crooked things behind his back."

Leupp-area Navajos soon learned I was the elder son of S. I. Richardson, and the old people who had known my father at Wolf Post began coming in to talk. One thing the venerable hosteens liked to do was to spin yarns for endless hours. They gave their versions of the Elliot Canyon gun battle and how S. I. had played a part in the aftermath (see chapter on "A Dynasty of Traders"). One of my visitors was B'ugo Ettin Begay, who had been a leader in that fight. Another, Red Woman's Son, was a half brother of Hosteen Navajo Mountain at Inscription House Trading Post.

Jim Silversmith, speaking a scant dozen English words, made silver and turquoise jewelry for me. He created fine pieces the old-fashioned way, using a goatskin bellows and cannel coal (a fine-textured and volatile bituminous variety), although he did employ machine-made stamps which I got for him. As was customary with silversmiths everywhere, two-ounce silver slugs and polished turquoise stones were counted out to him and entered in the account book, and the finished article was weighed back on delivery. This method prevented silversmiths from cumshawing a little silver. I don't think, however, that Jim ever held out a single stone or a drop of silver on me. Thoroughly honest, he remained my friend until his death.

The missionaries at Leupp—associates of F. G. Mitchell, headquartered at Indian Wells—were a particularly mean bunch. They kept all the district trading posts closed on Sunday. In this case it worked no hardship, and traders were glad to get one day off each week for recreation. However, the missionaries also took it upon themselves to snoop, seeking violations of trading regulations to report. Missionary Mitchell employed what he imagined to be a sly trick to catch traders. Taking two "Christianized" Navajos, he would enter a store and engage himself away from them. Pretending not to be with him, the two would then, in Navajo, state that they wanted to buy imitation turquoise stones because they were cheap. At that time sale of these stones had been banned in order to maintain high standards for Navajo handmade jewelry. No honest trader stocked spurious stones, anyway.

Mitchell pulled this stunt on me at Sunrise. His Navajos kept wheedling and insisting that I must have imitation turquoise hidden somewhere. Finally they became convinced otherwise. Realizing they would make no buy, Mitchell started out, disclosing they were actually with him by ordering them in Navajo to come along. Both Indians began cursing him feelingly and at length, using white man's oaths. I started laughing, finding it very amusing to hear middle-aged Navajos swearing in English. Later, one of these men said to me, "I believed that man did good work for our people, so I felt very proud to help him. And I worked for him three years before discovering even white men hate him!"

Blanket weavers living near Sunrise were some of the best on the entire reservation. They were especially noted for storm-pattern blankets and were also the first to put red on them. For thirty years Babbitt Brothers Trading Company at Flagstaff used a colored reproduction of one of these blankets

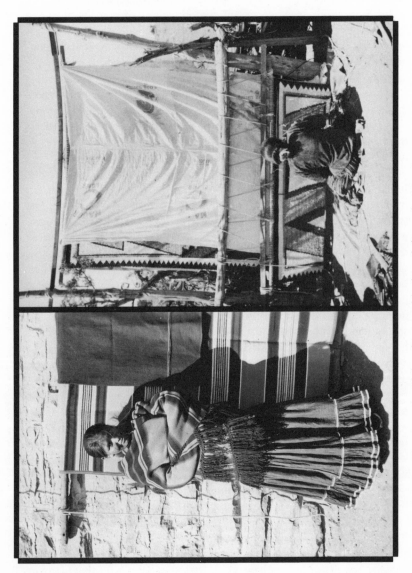

A young Navajo girl with hand-woven blankets (left), and a Navajo woman weaving a large rug on an outdoor loom.

on its stationery. The blanket design from which the printing plates were copied had been fabricated especially for C. J. Babbitt. Briefly, the story told by the storm patterns, when the symbols are used in a sacred sand painting, is of the emergence of the original Navajo tribal clans into this world. According to legend, they came up through a hollow reed onto an island in a lake near Four Corners (where Utah, Colorado, Arizona, and New Mexico join). The center of the design represents this hole and the island. Four lines to cardinal points represent where that number of thrown stones landed to drain off the water so Navajos could walk ashore. A slightly different version holds that the badger dug four holes, after trenching to cardinal points, through which roiling water disappeared (this is why the badger has black marks on his feet today—stains made by bottom mud).

The storm-pattern blankets began to appear in the Sunrise area as early as 1890, copied from natural-colored ones of white, gray, and black, woven at famous Two Gray Hills. While not responsible for them, C. J. Babbitt did popularize them through his firm's extensive mail-order business. When he received an order for a dozen five-by-six-foot blankets having a red background and a sacred figure in the center, he consulted my father and my great-uncle George McAdams at Wolf Post in 1900, and they agreed to have them made on special order. However, Navajo weavers were deathly afraid of putting a holy figure in a blanket. But a Hopi kachina proved entirely different, and represented no source of possible danger to them. Thus, the first Navajo blankets woven with human figures had kachinas, not *yei* (Navajo gods) on them. Of course, as S. I. declared in later years, "Who would know the difference except an expert on Navajo mythology?"

Weavers were still turning out the same type of blanket when I traded at Sunrise in the early 1930s, but they were slowly beginning to use the *yei* to displace the kachinas. We paid weavers fifty dollars for this type, whereas a blanket of the same size in a contemporary design brought only eighteen to twenty-five dollars, depending on weft and craftsmanship. The two patterns enjoyed a ready sale, as did the large (nine by ten feet) blankets that we bought at Sunrise; Mrs. Adaki Yazzie, for example, turned out an excellent large rug in natural colors, for which we paid her four hundred dollars.

When passing to Winslow from his Oraibi store, Lorenzo Hubbell, Jr., always stopped to see if I had any large rugs on hand. He bought them for a special eastern customer who wanted the largest ones he could get, and Lorenzo often declared, "A good Navajo blanket is better than having money in the bank."

In a picket-post warehouse at his Oraibi store, Lorenzo never had less than seventy-five thousand dollars worth of blankets on hand. He also stocked a like amount in the basement of his Winslow place, which he had bought from Hubert in 1928. Several years before his death, he had a special blanket made which was exhibited all over the U.S. Valued at twenty thousand dollars, it was twenty-six by thirty-six feet in size, and for some years it held the record as the largest ever fabricated in Navajo country.

Lorenzo was a man who, when he liked anyone, could never do enough for that person. Often, when I visited Oraibi, it was a full day before I could get away. It took a meal and at least five or six hours just to tell him hello and good-bye. On quite a few occasions I sat in his office while he carried on conversations in four languages—Navajo, Hopi, Spanish, and English. He could shift from one to another flawlessly and, most astonishingly, never lose track of what he was saying.

Annually, from his Oraibi store, more Hopi pottery, baskets, and wooden dolls were shipped to market than from all other reservation posts combined. The very best Indian craft items—most of them priceless antiques—were displayed in the living quarters built behind his store. This special collection contained highly prized silver concho belts made during the period when Navajo artisans shifted from ironsmithing to silversmithing.

Although a little heavier, Lorenzo resembled his father, "Don" Lorenzo, in general build, and his manner of conducting business and his personal association with people was much like the old *don's*. Lorenzo, Jr., was married late in life to a woman with a nine-year-old daughter from a previous marriage. The breakup of this union, after slightly less than a year, drove him to the depths of nervous despair and brought on an illness that eventually killed him. Toward the end, the man who had never criticized or had an unkind word for anyone grew very bitter. I last saw him in the early 1940s sitting in a wheelchair, watching post trade and shaking hands silently with old Navajo men and women he had known since his boyhood. When I prepared to leave, he said flatly, "The medico tells me it won't be long now. I hear you're going away to war—I won't be here when you return. Good-bye, my friend." Lorenzo died in April 1942.

Chee Dodge, grand old man and the last universally recognized tribal chief, served a long time as chairman of the Navajo council. He and Lorenzo had been close friends, and Chee, who was many years older than Lorenzo, took his passing in deep sorrow. He told me in Gallup, where I talked to him last, "The time is not now long for any of us. The years have passed swiftly. For the few remaining to me, I will miss him every day."

Cameron

In the early 1930s Millie and I decided to devote all our time to producing western stories, which were then selling well, and we stayed at home in Flagstaff to do it. This decision held only a short time. About once a week someone came around offering a deal to manage some trading post. The owners knew that during one period of nine months at Inscription House I had made the store a profit of nine thousand dollars. They could see only that thousand-dollar-a-month net; what they weren't considering was the favorable position of the post and that, in fact, Susie had run the store while I bought stock.

Late one night my cousin Jack Richardson rushed in bearing an urgent message from my uncle Hubert. He wanted me to run Cameron Trading Post on the Little Colorado River for a while; it was an emergency, since he needed to take Aunt Mabel to a California doctor, so I went. Millie remained in town with Cecile. Perhaps she still retained some faint dislike of Cameron from the first time we had stopped there together in 1925. Just married, we were en route to Navajo Mountain. Cameron then consisted of a drafty, wooden store building and four small, one-room-shack cabins overlooking the bare river canyon. Not only did the cool weather turn colder, but the Navajos' fourteen different kinds of wind blew downriver all night long. Especially did Talking Wind shake the flimsy cabin walls while conversing with himself around sharp corners. I was used to all this— neither bone-chilling cold sweeping through the thin wooden walls nor howling wind bothered me in any way. Coming from a very mild California climate, Millie never slept a wink. In addition, what we considered good roads in Indian country had already filled her with dire apprehension of worse yet ahead. In those days travel by car from Flagstaff to Navajo Mountain consumed two days. You remained one night either at Cameron or at Tuba City; otherwise, you had a choice between sleeping on sand or in the car.

Stanton Borum and his wife Idamae had managed the Little Colorado River post for Uncle Hubert that year. Hubert and Aunt Mabel were visiting from Winslow, where they resided in order to send their three children to school. Millie made an immediate hit with my relatives and the Borums, but she abhorred Cameron for some years afterward. The most barren and desolate place on the river, it hardly compared with today's million-dollar village of hotel, restaurant, motel, service station, post office, electric power, and apartments. At the time of Millie's visit, there existed no running water, electricity, or indoor restroom. In fact, Cameron wasn't any different from any one of a hundred trading posts in outback Indian country. It became her introduction to unusual living conditions in the land she would know intimately for forty years.

The only employee at Cameron in those old days was a Tennessee Negro cook known as "Happy." He produced fine meals, always going around singing. Susie had first hired him through a Phoenix agency to cook at Rainbow Lodge, where Happy became friends with everyone, went on horseback rides, and generally made himself useful. The tourist guides there considered him tops, swearing they would make a dude hand out of him. Near the end of his first month, however, much to everyone's astonishment, he said to S. I., "Mr. Richardson, I ain't staying no longer. This is the scariest place I ever been, 'scusin' the Ku Kluxers. Even the rocks here is wild!" Unable to prevail on him to remain, S. I. sent Happy out on a freight truck to Cameron, where Stanton Borum hired him.

Built in 1916 by Hubert Richardson, Cameron wasn't as old as most other trading posts, and it was the second store on the site. The first was just a tin shack put up during construction of the bridge over the Little Colorado River in 1910–1911. S. S. Preston, then trading at Tuba City, had obtained a very remunerative contract hauling bridging iron and cable from the railhead at Greenlaw siding near Flagstaff to the construction site. He got another man to run his Tuba City post, as Mrs. Preston did not want to stay there alone. This man soon burned out the Tuba City post (robbery was suspected as the motive). The Prestons had erected a corrugated tin shack south of the river, above the bridge construction, and stocked it with merchandise. Mrs. Preston ran the small trading post, where workers' checks were also cashed, while her husband freighted. As soon as the bridge was completed, in about a year, Preston tore down the tin shack, and they returned to Tuba City, where he rebuilt the burned-out post.

After my uncles Hubert and C. D. Richardson opened their Blue Canyon Trading Post in 1913, both began looking around for places to put in individual stores. In 1914 Hubert surveyed possibilities at Cameron. The site did not appear to be good, but the following year cattle buyers purchased more than three thousand head from Indians living there; Gray

Stanton and Idamae Borum managed the Cameron Trading Post
for Hubert Richardson in 1925.

Mountain Navajos might not be numerous, but they were wealthy cattlemen. Changing his mind, Hubert put in a wooden store building at Cameron in July 1916. Carpenter Thomas F. Long of Flagstaff built it, taking
his son, Thomas V., along to help. Hubert squatted on seventy-nine acres
of bare rock masses and began trading. While living in Winslow, operating his wholesale house, and after moving to Cameron, he employed resident managers. Several men who became famous Indian traders learned
the business at his Little Colorado River trading post.

Cameron does enjoy a little history. Captain Juan Melgosa in 1540 was the first European to explore the region. Early beaver trappers and prospectors used this gateway passage west and north, and several U.S. Army expeditions went through long before Arizona was declared a territory. History does not reveal how early the first Americans were on the scene, trapping or prospecting near Cameron. Some speculation exists that it might have been before Jedidiah S. Smith entered Arizona in 1826. This probability is based on the discovery in 1940 of a musket-rifle from the time of the American Revolution in a cave near Tappan Spring. Not rusted and in astonishingly well preserved condition, it bears the Tower of London stamp.

Among several aging Navajo leaders in the Cameron area, who for a brief time insisted on calling me "Beni Doclissey Begay" (Hubert's son), were hosteens Huskon and Sagney. These old men were born on hulking Gray Mountain, where they raised large families and spent their lives. In them reposed a wealth of local history. When we could spare the time to listen, their trading-post visits grew lengthy. Huskon and Sagney were boys in their teens when the first pack-train trader entered that part of Navajoland (from their recollections, it would seem he appeared there in 1850 or 1851). They remembered him well because he gave them their first drinks of whiskey.

Called "Billakona Sani" (Old Anglo), he arrived with several camp tenders. One of them was an aged Mexican driving a two-wheeled wooden cart. Most traders of those olden days sold what they called whiskey. They packed grain alcohol, or "Taos Lightning," undiluted, in small wooden kegs, then mixed one gallon with three parts of water to make four for selling or trading. Chewing tobacco added color, and a generous application of cayenne pepper gave bite. These were the ingredients of the first Indian whiskey on the Arizona frontier.

Huskon and Sagney watched Billakona Sani mix his concoction. Like their elders, they considered it sheer magic. The white man took plain ditch water, did some hocus-pocus and, presto, the exhilarating strong drink came into being. Years passed before they knew whiskey traders actually diluted firewater to increase the volume. Tobacco and pepper disguised the fact that it was less than fifty percent alcohol. Both now chuckled over their teenage ignorance, while relating how Billakona Sani fooled them.

While I was at Cameron, Dr. Barnum Brown, a curator of fossil reptiles of the American Museum of Natural History, brought out a collecting party from New York. Goldtooth Semolley, an old Navajo who lived near Cameron, had told Hubert about a large number of three-toed tracks in the sandstone of a canyon fifteen miles east of the post. After investigating, Hubert informed Dr. Brown, and his expedition uncovered three hundred tracks in what was named Dinosaur Canyon. Later Hubert found larger dinosaur-track impressions in light-colored strata on top of a seven-hundred-foot cliff overlooking the find below, which, as far as I know, has never been scientifically investigated. While working the area, Dr. Brown recovered, among other skeletal remains, those of a labyrinthodont, an alligator, and a crocodile ancestor. His most important discovery was the remains of a small Jurassic-period reptile not previously known to paleontologists. These finds brought optimistic predictions that this section of the Melgosa Desert would become a fossil-hunter's paradise. Except for one other small expedition, however, the area received little attention.

Whenever he could, Barnum Brown dragged me away from whatever I was doing to play bridge, which he enjoyed more than any other entertainment. Every night he tried to get me into the lobby of the small hotel at the post to be his partner. His friend Gilbert Gable and whoever was around were our opponents until Hubert eventually returned from California to play against us. A shrewd and skilled player, Brown proved hard to beat, and enjoyed cutthroat games for weeks until suddenly a moving picture company arrived at the post.

The company was there to shoot a picture between the river and Tuba City. From director to business manager to lackeys, this Hollywood crew was a hairy bunch. Most were drunk all the time. Even their technicians stayed looped on some of Flagstaff's finest bootleg, doped with cinnamon bark instead of cayenne pepper.

One day an explosives expert mined a cliff in the Melgosa Desert for a special scene. Unfortunately, he did not take into consideration the conglomerate composition of a high wall, which consisted of little more than loose, water-worn stones and blue clay. Digging tunnel-like holes, he packed in an enormous amount of dynamite, and then let the whole works go. Cars parked a mile away were damaged by falling stones, and at least twenty-five people were seriously injured—one of them, Marion Wallace of Flagstaff, fatally.

The movie director turned into a determinedly individualistic extrovert. Still feeling his firewater at four o'clock one morning, he rushed outside with trusty six-guns to shoot off every recently built cabin stovepipe on the post. Such shennanigans, however, hardly interrupted our bridge game; the incident that *did* occurred one night between midnight and 1:00 A.M. Dr. Brown always sat with his back to the ornamental fireplace. This position afforded a direct view of the cougar-skin-decorated stairway to

Loading a wagon with furs and sacks of wool in front of the warehouse and cabins at Cameron Trading Post in 1925.

the second floor, where high-salaried moving picture stars were quartered. When Brown's turn as dummy came, he laid down his hand. Then he glanced upward, blinked his eyes, and took a fast double gander. Surprised, the rest of us turned our heads toward the stairway. Descending toward us hip-swiveled a female star of the picture, stark naked. (She was a former high-priced New York artist's model.) Advancing slowly, she husked out, "Any of you gents got a match?"

Someone handed her a light to fire the cigarette dangling between red lips. That done, she ambled unhurriedly up the stairway and from view. The next day Dr. Brown announced, "I've had it!" and went back to New York.

While Hubert remained in California with Aunt Mabel, a lot of money flowed over the counters—yet much of it disappeared by closing time. While counting up each night, I could recall big deals for more money than remained in certain cash registers. The situation aggravated me and I wished Hubert would return to resume the responsibility of bossing his outfit. Everyone thought that "Dad" Welch (retired from the Indian service and a real loafer at the post) slept away the afternoons, lolling in a big chair, but I had a different idea. When I told him there must be several sticky-fingered people working at Cameron, his face actually showed considerable relief. "I've been wondering when you'd get wise to them," he replied. "They're dipping in with both hands!"

After Welch told me how he had watched certain ones pull their thefts, we laid plans to catch them red-handed. Contriving to leave just one clerk, always one of the prime suspects, alone in the store, I would go away. Returning unexpectedly, I would glance at Dad Welch. If the clerk had taken something during my absence, he would give me a high sign. The plan worked, and five thieves were canned in short order—one of them an Indian. The rest must have gotten scared, for they either stopped stealing or quit their jobs. At any rate, no more money strayed by mistake into clerks' pockets. When Hubert returned to find once-familiar faces missing, he inquired what had happened. When told, he insisted on hiring the Indian clerk back. "Most employees will take something, including money," he observed, "but an Indian will steal much less than a white man!"

Educated Navajo Maxwell Yazzie worked at Cameron about fifteen years. He believed strongly in education for Indians, while disagreeing, in some anger, with methods used to get children into schools. Maxwell cited his own personal case as an example of how officials had handled it in former days, when they had rounded up students just like going after stray animals. He got caught when he was eight years old. The Indian agent sent riders over the countryside to swoop down suddenly on hogans. Grabbing all children who were obviously of school age, they herded them, bawling and squalling, to the nearest sandy road. Presently a wagon with a trailer came along, and children were loaded in like canned sardines. The wagon continued until not one more child could be crammed in, then proceeded to the Tuba City boarding school. Maxwell said that the "whipper" (disciplinarian) took away all his clothing, shaved his head slick, and stuck him in a tub of blistering hot water. Thus deloused, he received school clothing to wear, and wasn't allowed to go home on visits because he would get body lice again.

After several years at the Tuba City school, he and fifty others were loaded into wagons for the trip to Flagstaff to board a train for Sherman Institute at Riverside, California. En route the wagons arrived at Tanner Crossing on the Little Colorado River, six miles upstream from the present bridge. Students were made to get out and walk over because of steep dugway inclines. Maxwell fooled around on a gravel bar, getting his feet wet. Discovering a small, bright, golden pebble, he picked it up. At the Indian school, a science teacher tested the pretty rock and declared it pure gold. Sometime later, when needing money, Maxwell sold it to a Riverside jeweler for five dollars; soon afterward, he learned that the big nugget was worth at least a hundred dollars. On returning to the reservation, he tried to find the gravel bar to get more, but it had been washed downstream a long time since. For years, and occasionally while working at Cameron, he hunted futilely for more river nuggets.

Tourists off the highway were over-filled with curiosity in those days, just as they are now—especially about Indians and anyone working stock. At Cameron the sheep corral stood in plain sight of the post (later it was moved farther away), and every time herders brought sheep in or took them out, tourists gathered with cameras to snap away. At the end of sheep-buying season, I stood at the corral gate counting the flock out for trailing to Flagstaff shipping pens. By the time the job was finished and the herders had left with the woolies, probably twenty or more tourists had collected to watch. When I announced the number of sheep we had passed—2,836—a big wise guy refused to believe it. "Those animals came out in a steady stream, some running," he observed sourly. "How can you possibly be certain of the exact number?"

"Oh, that's easy," I assured him unsmilingly. "You count all the legs as they rush through and then divide by four. Simple."

"Yeah? How is it possible to remember what the hundreds total?"

"Did you see black sheep coming through the gate?"

"Why, I believe so," he said.

"Black sheep are known as counters. For every one going past, you automatically count one hundred. Catch?"

"Ha, tricks in all trades!" he exclaimed, as if understanding everything by that explanation. He had not observed that I dropped one small pebble into my right side coat pocket for every hundred counted. Two days later six pebbles could have been thrown away: the Cameron flock lost exactly six hundred ewes and lambs that ate thick-leafed milkweed just beyond a canyon ten miles south. It is deadly poison to sheep, and the herders should have known better than to pass close to such dark green patches. Sheep raised locally will not eat the weed, but those from afar, not acquainted with it, will unfortunately take a few nibbles.

One day Jack Fuss, a Flagstaff friend, came by to visit briefly. Going to a sack of wool lying at the base of the warehouse wall, he lifted one end. When it raised upward without bending, he turned to me grinning. "Years ago I went to work here for Hubert's trader. He gave me two five-gallon cans, sending me to a sandbar near the river. I filled them and dumped sand in a pile inside the warehouse. By the time it grew into a sizable heap, I wondered what the trader planned on building.

"Then you know what? He told me to tromp down one layer of wool in a racket sack, shovel in one layer of sand, and pack in more wool. I did so for about an hour, getting madder all the time. Talk about a crook— that trader was the world's cheapest! That night I told him where he could put all that sand and went back to Flagstaff. The stunt cured me of ever wanting to be an Indian trader!"

Fuss knew that a sack of sanded wool will bend in the middle. But that trader wasn't as crooked-smart as he had believed. Sand has to be wet to be kept in a sack of wool. The bag must be hauled to the railroad and weighed before drying out—almost an impossibility if it has to be trucked any distance. Often enough, rough roads would shake all the dry sand out into the truck bed.

The trader Fuss worked for was probably one of the world's chintziest, though. His sly tricks nearly got him killed several times. Not long after Fuss's experience, several Navajos, selling piñons one night, bested him in the deal. Sore about it, he decided to keep the seamless sacks in which the piñons had been brought. He had sold them to the Navajos at one dollar each.

After trading out what their piñons brought, the Indians asked for their sacks. They had not even been emptied. Informed by the trader that he had bought them with the nuts, the group went very quiet. They asked once more, in a gentle way, for their sacks, and, when they were refused, the entire bunch ganged him. Backing him into a corner against the wall, they hit him with everything they could get their hands on, intending to beat him to death.

Luckily S. I. happened along and, hearing the commotion, went to the trader's aid. Never raising his voice, S. I. got them to desist. On learning the Indians' story, he turned on the trader, who didn't deny anything. Later on, when at Navajo Mountain, this same trader was shot at several times, and had to leave one night in fear for his life. Almost all traders were wonderful men, but there were a few like this one. In every case they came to grief; some were even killed.

Retaliation was often swift when a Navajo was wronged. Such cases might involve mere pennies, as in the following instance. Fortunately, no one got killed in the incident, which happened at Round Rock Trading Post, owned by Oscar Marty, on Lukachukai Wash. One day a Navajo brought in a small rug, which he proceeded to barter for supplies. When his dealings were completed, he thought ten cents remained unspent. Marty told him no, that he had nothing left. When the Navajo kept insisting, Marty remained bullheaded. The Indian said that he wanted these last pennies in peanuts for his children at home. In those days parched peanuts came by the barrel and were dirt cheap. Marty could easily have done what most traders would have—given him the ten cents worth of peanuts for "friendship." Instead he ran him out.

That night after sundown, the family and a clerk, a man named Almond, sat eating supper by lamplight. The Navajo slipped back, firing a .30-.30 rifle through the window at the back of Marty's head. The bullet missed, plowing through Almond's shoulder. Leaving his body, the bullet grazed the head of Marty's young son, but not fatally. The second bullet, slamming through the broken-out window, missed completely. By then everybody was down on the floor with the lights out. Marty hid out, sold his post to J. H. McAdams, and left the Navajo country. It was all he could do. Although the clerk recovered, his left arm remained partly paralyzed.

Hikers occasionally showed up at Cameron. They were real hikers, actually wanting to walk instead of riding whenever they could. A clean-cut, well-educated, and friendly eastern youth entered the store toward sundown one evening. After buying a few items of food, he stowed them in a pack and strapped it on. Then he picked up a coil of hair rope that I had not seen and looped it over his left shoulder. The hair rope, he informed me seriously, was his protection against rattlesnakes. At night, sleeping on the ground, he circled it around him. No snake would cross it; therefore he would be safe from being bitten.

He departed north on Highway 89, which at that time was a dirt road that swung east, away from the river bridge, far over into a long valley. Near Seven Mile Wash, after dark, the youthful hiker called it a day. Looping the hair rope around a spot, he stepped inside the circle and lay down in the middle of a narrow road cut by wheels between hummocks of bunch grass. He must have been sleeping soundly at midnight when Hopi trucker Walter Lewis approached. Lewis, barreling it for home at Moenkopi, saw the recumbent form far too late. By the time he could bring the truck to a halt, the hiker lay broken and dead, and inside the hair rope were two fatally injured horned rattlesnakes.

When he heard about it in the store, cowman Rimmy Jim Giddings, from Poverty Tanks, stomped around in his boots muttering, "S'too bad. S'too bad."

"Who would have thought even a dude didn't know enough not to sleep on a traveled road?" I commented about the sad case.

"Never mind him," the cowman retorted, shaking his head. "Dudes are a dime a dozen. It's them little rattlers—if they'd been let live, someday they mighta bit a sheepherder, don'tcha know?"

Gold and Dudes

On each occasion that one of us helped bury an Indian, Susie asked about the ceremony. She had long wanted to take part in one, but no convenient opportunity came until a morning when Harry Grisham's wife asked for a white-woman's lipstick. Susie asked her the reason. On being informed that Dick Tate's daughter had died less than an hour before, Susie found a lipstick and went back with the woman to the mesa death hogan, about two miles away from Inscription House. On her return, several hours later, she said to me, "Well, it was interesting, but I wouldn't want to attend another." She then described the proceedings in this instance.

The girl had died in a summer brush hogan from some undiagnosed illness. The women stripped and washed the body carefully. They put on the best clothing of the deceased, re-did her hair, and powdered and painted her face to make it lifelike. Personal jewelry went on the body, after which they wrapped it in a new Pendleton shawl. The men present were the girl's father, her oldest brother, Harry Grisham, and one other relative. A hundred feet from the hogan they started digging a grave, while the women prepared the body for burial. Susie went out to watch and even took part in shoveling out red clay.

At a depth of five feet, a six-inch-wide shoulder was left on each side of the grave, which went down another eighteen inches. Opening the west end of the brush hogan, they carried the body through in traditional custom and lowered it into the ground. Cedar wood, cut to fit the grave exactly, was placed crosswise on the hardpan shoulders above the body, followed by bark and grass that covered the rough wood to prevent sand and clay from falling through. While filling the grave, the men tamped the dirt hard so that, when it was level with the surface, no sink-in would follow after the grass and sage were replaced over the site. Removing residue, they scattered it widely, well away from the grave.

From the beginning of preparing the body until departure, no one spoke a single word. Signs were made directing the certain necessary things being performed. The shovel used to dig the grave, all cooking utensils, and everything else in the brush hogan at the time of death were "killed." This meant breaking shovel and ax handles, punching holes in all metal utensils, and tearing up fabrics to render them useless.

The men and women removed their shirts and jackets, took down their long hair, and let it hang loosely behind their shoulders; removed moccasins were interchanged and replaced backwards. This way the dead spirit, which hovers reluctantly around for four days, could not ascertain the exact direction in which the family departed and would, thus, be unable to follow. After the four days elapsed, the spirit of the departed would join the Sky People. When everything required had been accomplished, Tate gestured to Susie that they were leaving. In her case, being *billakona* (Anglo), she had no worries concerning the *chindi* (spirit). The Navajos, however, took off running through the purple sagebrush, zigzagging in many directions, until they were out of sight. In the early 1900s most Navajos preferred interring their dead this way. Only a few put them in wooden boxes. Babies were not buried at all, but wrapped in a robe and left in some distant cliff cave. In later times almost all dead were buried in coffins.

A few days after the funeral, Susie and I were alone at Inscription House when Hosteen Behegade rode in to report two tourists broken down in Red Valley just beyond the Kaibito fork. Driving there, I found them in a heavily loaded pickup. The truck carried two large, extra gas tanks and was equipped with special, over-load springs. From the way they sagged, obviously something very heavy lay under the strapped-down tarpaulin. One of the men was Amos Byers—a gray-headed old man in his seventies, who had been to Shonto in 1925. His companion—a big, dark-complexioned man, who was introduced as "Al"—was his sister's son Albert. They were having ignition trouble and the pickup motor had overheated. After cooling the motor and working on the wiring a while, we got the engine started. Other repairs were necessary, so they decided to proceed to Inscription House instead of going out by Kaibito as originally planned.

The spry, little Byers and I followed the pickup in my car. Nursing it along, Al managed to reach the post, where he drove inside the fenced compound. He went to work on the motor, but sundown had come before he had it running smoothly. Following a lengthy consultation with Al in whispers, Byers asked Susie if they could remain overnight. They planned an early start in the morning to traverse the canyon country in daylight. It developed now that they had entered the Navajo country off U.S. 89 at The Gap via Kaibito; this fact seemed very suspicious, for most travelers would have come over Route 160, turning north near Shonto.

Susie extended our hospitality by telling them they could sleep in a two-room cabin behind the post. Al drove the pickup to it, stopping in a position almost blocking the entrance. At the supper table that night, he purposely took a chair from which he could watch their pickup through a dining-room window. This seemed even more strange, and by now I suspected that the men were pottery hunters without permits: maybe, having cleaned out graves or a cliff ruin, they were hauling away whatever they had found. However, this didn't really seem reasonable—the pickup carried too much weight to be loaded with just aboriginal artifacts.

After supper Al immediately left. Byers remained in the gasoline-lighted living room, glancing through week-old newspapers. When a customer pounded on the store door, I left Byers there alone. After trading with the Indian, I returned to the living room, where Susie sat in a leather easy-chair doing needlework. Byers slouched on a long couch, talking about his early days in Arizona and New Mexico. The old man seemed to be in a very loquacious, reminiscent mood that night. He claimed ownership of a mine on Black Mountain that he called Copper Bell because he had found such an aboriginal article in an ancient pueblo close by. He mentioned the year 1882, so I asked him if he had been hunting the lost Merrick-Mitchell Mine. Chuckling, he shook his head. "No, I have the real article; rather, I once did. We found a mine on Black Mountain and worked it."

Byers went on from there with his story. He and another young fellow named Earnest Bladen, tiring of prospecting on Cripple Creek in Colorado, had gone to Santa Fe for the winter of 1881. There they fell in with Henry Jinon and Zeke Johnson. Jinon, an easterner loaded with money, spent most of his time trying to drink himself into oblivion. The four were constant companions in the cantinas and occupied an adobe house together. Almost every day they were pestered by a drink moocher, an aged Mexican wino named Emmanuel Gallegos. In his cups, Gallegos assured them in flowery language that he possessed the secret of untold wealth. Claiming his age as nearly a hundred, he swore that in his youth he had gone with a prospecting party three hundred miles due west and that they had found gold nuggets in the sand of a clear, running stream. They had brought back several buckskin sacks filled with these nuggets. Of course, the adventurous young men assumed Gallegos was telling lies purely for their entertainment while cadging more drinks.

One day, while Jinon and Bladen drank with him, old Gallegos began talking earnestly. "Señores, I am not long to live. For a gift of a hundred pesos, I will present you with a map to the world's most gold, lying in a canyon in far Navajo country. Fifty pesos for the padre to bury me, and fifty that I may indulge myself in forgetfulness before passing on."

Jinon, who considered the aged man harmlessly senile, promptly and solemnly accepted his offer. He left fifty dollars with the cantina owner, some sort of distant relative who assured him Gallegos had been "loco" all his life. Jinon then took Gallegos to an old mission, where he deposited fifty dollars with a priest to complete the deal. A few days later, Gallegos contacted Jinon and Byers; handing over a flat package wrapped in a filthy cloth, he departed. Tossing the package into a cowhide trunk, Jinon remarked, "We'll keep it as a souvenir, just to please the old man."

The four friends came home one night, bringing another man, named Ed Olden, with them. While sitting around drinking, Jinon got out the package; under the cloth several pieces of paper were fastened about a sheet of parchment. The black ink on it had run badly and the alleged treasure map was very greasy and dirty. Removing smudges carefully, they found landmarks and other natural features identified by Spanish names. As more details of the map appeared, Olden grew excited. "I've been in them parts," he declared. "This Mesa de Vaca—Americans call it Black Mountain. This here canyon through it is Blue Canyon. Damned if I don't think there's something to that old Mexican's yarn!"

Spreading the parchment on a table, Jinon, an expert penman, began redrawing the map on a large piece of heavy paper, producing a readable facsimile. The cleaner lines convinced Olden even more than before. He suggested that they cautiously have the Spanish translated item by item, not all at one time or by the same person. This they did, and Jinon inscribed the English names on the map. Olden and Byers were anxious to hunt for the place. Jinon declared if all went along, he would finance the expedition.

Stock and supplies were procured, and the following March—1882— the five men entered Black Mountain off a San Juan River route, ascending near Lolomi Point. Easily picking up an old trail marked on the map, they soon located guiding features—a square stone watch tower; canyon ruins of aborigines; some old graves; and a defile called Bluebird Canyon. The sandy floor of the canyon was supposed to contain nuggets waiting to be picked up, according to Gallegos, but they found only a little flour-gold. While exploring the immediate area, Jinon carefully marked the map with the diggings of other prospectors and the trails and tributaries of Blue Canyon. About ready to leave, they camped one night under a plateau rim near some ruins, where Byers found the small bell of native copper. Strolling around, pecking at outcroppings with a pick, Olden came onto a vein of quartz and summoned the others. Several pieces they broke out were laced with gold.

Much excited, they tunneled along the vein, back under a solid stone wall. The vein increased in size, and chunks of gold, falling out of rotten quartz, were collected in hide sacks. Convinced they would soon be rich men, they prepared a permanent camp by erecting a small, one-room log cabin. They labored every hour possible, burying the gold in the dirt floor of the cabin. At times they had to quit digging in order to cut mine timbers to shore the tunnel.

On their last excursion, Navajo Indians, whom they knew to be prowling about, fell on the intruders in the cedar forest. That April day in 1882 Bladen, Olden, and Jinon were killed in the surprise attack; Byers and Johnson escaped. Byers found Jinon's horse with the saddlebags containing the map, and he started north. Johnson soon joined him in the getaway, riding another horse that the Indians had failed to gather in before opening fire. Hardly pausing until they crossed the San Juan River, the two survivors proceeded into Colorado, where they separated.

Four years later, when they met by accident in Farmington, New Mexico, Johnson said that several white families had located not too far from their gold mine and that the country was generally being settled. They agreed to return for the gold, and, taking two pack horses along, they rode straight west past the Hopi villages into the fastnesses of Black Mountain. The cabin still stood, and there they dug up the sacks of gold. Johnson, somewhat apprehensive, refused to remain a minute longer than necessary. The two men started north, intending to go out through southern Utah, the shortest route. Near Lolomi Point, while coming off the mountain escarpment, a long distance shot from a hidden sniper knocked Johnson dead out of the saddle. Byers halted, only to discover Indians charging through the timber toward him. Keeping the pack horses running, he finally reached the river and Utah safely.

The old man did not state definitely what amount of gold he had brought out. From what he did reveal, it must have been worth about a hundred thousand dollars. Selling it, he went to Los Angeles, where his sister lived. He then invested in a mercantile business and did well until 1910, when he went bankrupt. That didn't worry him too much, because of the secret gold mine. Entraining for Flagstaff, he proceeded to Tuba City, where he purchased a saddle horse and two pack mules. Telling people he had come to the high, dry country to arrest a case of tuberculosis, he wandered around aimlessly for a while. On the day he considered his presence was no longer arousing curious interest, he hastened to the Copper Bell Mine. Taking out what could be carried on the mules, he returned to Flagstaff and went home by train. In 1919 he had come back for more gold, and again in 1925—this time by pickup truck. In 1925 he had brought Al along to help, and, just as on this trip, they had stayed at Inscription House.

Byers named places and men he had either stayed with or met on his several expeditions. This part of his story rang true; the men he mentioned were known to me. In addition, the section of Black Mountain that he described was very familiar. Indeed, S. I. and I had been there the preceding summer, inspecting a location where the Tuba City Indian agent wanted us to put a trading post. We had gone there in a small car; by using sheep trails and shoveling a little sand and filling ditches, even a passenger car could be driven within half a mile of what Byers called Bluebird Canyon. Byers then produced the map from a coat pocket. Because it showed names for natural features of the locality no longer in common use, or even known, I requested permission to make a copy. At first he said I could have the map; then he decided Al might want it as a souvenir; so I copied it.

Susie asked why Byers had never filed legal claim to his mine, and he replied that it didn't matter now, pointing out that it had been secure all these many years anyway. Besides, he believed the vein was petered out, and on this trip he and Al had blasted the entrance to close the tunnel forever.

Even though Susie had listened courteously, her skepticism of Byers's story finally showed through. We had heard dozens of lost-mine tales pertaining to western Navajoland. Furthermore, illegal artifact-hunters always gave some seemingly legitimate reason to account for their presence. Finally, she suggested in a roundabout way that he might have a pickup-load of pottery, metates, stone hammers, or perhaps mummies. Indeed, not long before, a party had emerged from the Navajo Mountain country with two station-wagon loads of mummies and pottery. They were sneaking out of the country, hoping government officials would not check on them. Through a California museum, they had obtained a federal permit, but they had none for Arizona—necessary at that time. Their important discovery of several mummies had been prematurely reported in the press, whereupon Arizona's governor had ordered them arrested. To evade state officers waiting at the reservation border, they had hurriedly departed by back roads, just as Byers and his nephew were doing now.

When the old man realized Susie's disbelief about his gold mine, he stared at her, saying testily, "Madam, I am not telling jokes. Have you ever seen sacks filled with pure gold?"

"Not recently," she replied cautiously.

Turning toward me as he got to his feet, Byers requested, "Bring the gasoline lantern along. Let's show your mother some real gold!" Susie followed us while I carried a light. Al sat in the cab of the truck with a .30-.30 Winchester rifle across his knees. Neither man apparently realized that standing armed guard would prove to every Navajo around that they had something valuable. Even so, not an Indian would have bothered them.

Unfastening one corner of the buckled-down tarpaulin, Byers threw it wide to reveal that the pickup bed was loaded with heavy cotton sacks in rows. Filled only to about a third of their length, they were fastened close above the contents with twisted baling wire. Byers opened one sack with a pair of pliers, rolling the top down to expose pieces of glistening metal mixed with gray quartz. "Now, Madam," he said respectfully yet triumphantly, "help yourself to a handful!"

Susie picked up half a dozen pieces, examining them interestedly in the lantern light. A minute later she dropped them back. "Real pretty," she commented.

"Madam, that is a fortune!" he burst out, somewhat miffed when she failed to be properly impressed. Around two o'clock in the morning, the roar of the pickup motor awakened me as the two men departed surreptitiously. For days afterward, Susie pondered about whether or not what we had seen was really gold and about how much truth there was to the old man's lengthy story.

Personally, I never doubted Byers's statement. What he had said about the country, trading posts, and people, I knew to be so. Later, those people he said he had contacted on his widely separated visits to Copper Bell Mine confirmed his statements; a few even described his personal appearance in a particular year. S. I. never doubted Byers's story, either. He knew of two mining claims on Black Mountain proven before the Navajo Reservation extended that far west; when John Collier was Indian Commissioner with the Roosevelt administration, he tried to seize these mines or have the private deeds to them revoked.

In the summer of 1940 three men, purportedly seeking the legendary Navajo "Cave of the Gods," hired Ramon Hubbell to guide them onto Black Mountain. At that time Ramon, one of the sons of old "Don" Lorenzo, operated guided tours for dudes from Gallup. Probably this supposed Cave of the Gods was the one that Navajos had shown me on the Kaibito Plateau. Quite a lot of publicity appeared in the press about the search for this cave, but the three men were really hunting "lost" gold mines. Hubbell took them into the least-known, northeast corner of the fabled mountain stronghold.

Three weeks later the expedition reappeared in New Mexico. They reported finding a number of canyon ruins never seen before by white men and claimed discovery of several Spanish inscriptions. Carefully, they refrained from mentioning either the Cave of the Gods or gold mines.

Ramon's personal characteristics were vastly different from those of his brother, Lorenzo, Jr.; he always seemed just a little bit lost. After the Black Mountain trip, he started driving across the reservation from Gallup. This time he was guiding a well-known woman dude rancher from northern New Mexico and her guest, a very rich, old woman. It must have been quite a tour even before they arrived at Inscription House Trading Post one night after sundown: the women were muddy and wet from their feet to the top of their heads and so angry they could hardly talk. The guest, a slender old woman, was almost completely deaf, as was Ramon, with whom she scrapped constantly. With Millie's help, the dude rancher got the old lady bathed and into fresh clothing so she could rest. The dude rancher then began the same kind of cantankerous, petty bickering, while Millie tried to get her straightened out from dampness and red mud. Since all this consumed time, their supper came late—they were already waiting and fussing about their meal by the time that overworked Millie managed to get it cooked. Ramon appeared in the dining room, whereupon the old woman took after him in renewed vigor. Ramon took himself away as soon as possible.

They continued to whine and to berate Millie until I very nearly ordered them to pack and leave. They raged about no inside bathrooms, no heating (and it was summertime!), no maid to wait on them, no electric lights—everything. They said they were being forced to attend to their own wants, but that did not prevent them from treating Millie like a personal servant to be rudely ordered around. Finally, unable to stand their treatment any longer, I sent Millie to bed and turned out the gasoline lights. That forced the women to their rooms, where they had to use kerosene lamps.

In the morning the same old arguments were renewed. At the breakfast table they argued with Ramon again about whether to proceed to Rainbow Lodge on Navajo Mountain or not. In the end, he fled the table with his breakfast only half consumed. Obviously something serious had happened to set this group at swords' points with each other and the world in general. In the store Ramon, mad as he was, began telling me what had happened.

Down the road, at the edge of Red Valley, he had found a sandy wash running with flood water. Mistakenly assuming it flowed over a rocky bottom, he had gunned his motor and landed stuck solid. Unable to move the car, he had waded out, pausing to tell his passengers that he would walk to Inscription House for help. Perhaps he might meet a truck on the way that could pull his heavy car out. Very promptly they had informed him they would not remain alone at the car. Ramon replied that they could hike with him if they wished. The dude rancher opened the car door, looked at the swirling muddy water, and said they would get their clothing wet. What were they going to do about that? Ramon, somewhat miffed, answered that if they didn't want to get their clothing wet and muddy, they should strip. He started walking on, then turned around to glance back at the wash. The women had removed their clothing down to their underwear and had started wading. The old one then slipped and fell, immersed immediately in two feet of muddy water. The dude rancher made a grab for her and fell down, too. By the time Ramon had extracted the raging women, a truck came along to pull his car out. Ramon, reflecting on his half-naked charges, said, "That was the first time in all the years I have been hauling dudes that one of them ever did what I told them to!"

Now, when he offered to pay for their lodging, I said that we did not run a hotel, and that we had accepted his party as guests because of the Hubbell family status as Indian traders and because his brother was a good friend of mine. Ten minutes later I came very near to changing my mind about being generous. Ramon faced a group of Navajos in the bull pen, speaking Navajo so fast he didn't believe anybody except a Navajo could understand him. His father had possessed the same trait—a belief that no one spoke or understood Navajo as perfectly as the Hubbells did. Ramon gave my customers his old man's same harangue: that they were the first traders in the country (which wasn't true), that they were the Navajos' only real friends, and that the Indians should always go to a Hubbell store to trade. Of Mexican descent, he declared that *billakona* (Anglo) traders were thieves interested only in robbing the Indians to get rich. (Be it said for Lorenzo, Jr., that I never heard him pull a similar stunt. But I had never liked old man Hubbell too well after he pulled a coin-tossing stunt on me when I was trading at Houck. Arriving there in a topless Ford, he had stood on the rear seat, throwing silver coins from a sack into a fast-gathering crowd of Indians, in order to lure them to trade at his place.)

When Ramon paused for breath, I called loudly in Navajo, so that his hearing aid would be sure to pick it up, "The *nocki* (Mexicans) are all thieves who took Navajo slaves in the old days, and are trying to treat you now as they did before Washington kicked the bear's brothers out!" That "bear's brothers" represented the highest of Navajo insults, since the bear is associated with evil, and my fiery statement shut Ramon up cold.

While the women's bags were being loaded into the car, the three of them started bickering once more about whether to go on to Navajo Mountain or not. Ramon ended the discussion by saying positively they were driving directly to Gallup and nowhere else. The very next day we had to take in six men in two cars, because they, too, had had car trouble. Immensely wealthy men, they were Hollywood big shots and corporation heads from California. In contrast to Ramon's cantankerous bunch, however, not only did they help get their own meals, but washed dishes afterward and had a good time doing it. Complaining about nothing, not even the atrocious roads, they expressed sincere gratitude for a place to sleep and eat out of the mud and rain. After their return home, although it was hardly necessary, several of them kept the trading post supplied with magazines until we left Inscription House. Especially appreciative was a moving-picture director, William (Bill) Shirreffs, who continued to correspond with us for several years. My whole family agreed that, of all the gold-seekers and dudes that had passed through our lives, these men were among the few gentlemen we had encountered.

The Witchcrafters

While I was trading at Inscription House in the late 1930s, a Navajo named Bisheyi, living near Shonto Trading Post, found four strands of human hair tied in four knots hanging on his hogan door-post. To superstitious Indians, this was the worst possible sign and was clinching evidence that a witchcrafter was after that person. Bisheyi immediately consulted Harry Rorick, the trader at Shonto, who scoffed at the man's expressed fear for the safety of his family. Had he been an experienced trader, Rorick would have known better than to ridicule an Indian's beliefs. Beside himself with fear, Bisheyi came to me at Inscription House. Certainly I didn't laugh at him, being far from amused. From long experience I knew incredible things could sometimes happen. "Let's go see a friend," I told him.

I took him a few miles away to a woman who was really death on practitioners of witchcraft because she was a hermaphrodite. She was known only as "Loolo," but I think S. I. gave her that name; before that she was called "Nahtgla" (dual-sexed). There is a singular story behind this woman and her work. It is almost unbelievable except to those who lived among the Navajo and know something of their history and religion.

Hermaphrodites, like the second-born of twins and multi-mammae, were customarily disposed of at birth. Somehow Loolo escaped detection until she was five or six years old. Killing a little girl that age would certainly bring prosecution in the white-man's court; had she been killed at birth, tribal laws and ancient customs would have protected the family. No Navajo would even have reported the case or given evidence.

Loolo had been born on Kaibito Plateau. I suspect she came from the same family as the male weaver I knew there, but Loolo herself couldn't remember enough to confirm that. When she was discovered to be a hermaphrodite, the family was stunned. Navajos believed that, while hermaphrodites originated all the arts, they also invented the degrading sexual sins of mankind. While her family stewed in a quandary, a medicine man named Jack Gambol (called One-Eyed Singer in Navajo) heard of her and offered to take the little girl off their hands.

From the moment the family disposed of the child, no one ever mentioned her again; nor did they care what happened to her, even whether she was murdered. One might like to think that perhaps the mother shed a few tears, but this is doubtful. Callous and brutal as this seems, we must remember several things. That she was *nahtgla* was a tragic disgrace to the family—something not only to be abhorred, but feared. Her presence meant that all relatives, friends, and every Navajo who knew about it would avoid them as they would a *chindi* (evil spirit). Her coming to them proved that a *chindi* had been inflicted on the family. One or more powerful *yei* (gods) were punishing them for some real or fancied offense of ironbound, ancient, religious customs. Years later, the family undoubtedly knew her real identity after she turned against witchcrafters, but they would suffer even death before admitting to such knowledge or ever accepting her again.

Loolo never speculated on who her family might be or tried to find out. Understanding the situation thoroughly, she accepted it uncomplainingly and held no resentment against those who had done her such wrong. No act of hers would ever harm those who under normal circumstances would have kept and loved her. It would have been physically possible for Loolo to have children and raise a family, but she could never marry, or even adopt an orphan. No man would touch her, and all people left her strictly alone. She was the loneliest person I ever knew. When no other Indians were around, Loolo would talk to me at great length. Often she invited me to her hogan, and I usually stopped by. Her native intelligence and superior knowledge of many things—even concerning world affairs—was absolutely amazing. Since she could not read and knew no English whatever, how and where she learned so much on thousands of subjects far beyond her limited life was a mystery.

One day Loolo told me her story. Gambol, the man who had "adopted" her, dabbled in witchcraft and occasionally practiced it (he is the same man who pulled me out of the snow—see Chapter 12). Using the girl, he conceived a colossal idea. A hermaphrodite witch would be the most powerful of them all—one who couldn't possibly be overcome. Some day he could become the richest man in Navajo country by training Loolo in witchcraft. So Loolo never went to school a day in her life—Gambol hid her, while instructing her in all he knew of witchcraft. He did a perfect job—among other things, he taught her the Blessingway Chant backwards and the use of dangerous herbs, poisonous medicines, and prayers. For some reason, perhaps because he feared her power himself, he hesitated to put her to work when she had absorbed all his knowledge. He then went into partnership in this sorry business with another witchcrafter, Gani Choi of Black Mountain.

This same Gani Choi had tried to cast a spell on no less a person than the administrator of Navajo services at Window Rock, E. R. Fryer. Brought before Fryer on charges of practicing witchcraft, Gani Choi flew into a rage, threatening to send demons of his cult after the white man. As a warning, he attempted a spell by using cigarette ashes in a tray on Fryer's desk. It didn't take very well with Fryer: he advanced from the administrator's job to Japanese relocation officer during World War II, then to a position in Bolivia, and later, still very healthy, he became a big-shot government official in Washington, D.C.

At seventeen, Loolo told me, she had learned everything Gambol and Gani Choi could teach her. Intellectually brilliant, she learned easily and showed promise of attaining everything the crafty Gambol desired. To finally finish off her training, they brought in a Hopi witchcrafter who taught her even more. The two partners were all set to go in 1935, and they tried their first deal against Old Man Peaches, who lived on Black Mountain. But the rich Navajo turned out to be a tough customer. He didn't bend to their will until one of his children died and another became seriously ill. From then on, they were able to bleed him of every dime he could get and take all his sheep and cattle.

The two witchcrafters moved from victim to victim, living lavishly and becoming such frightening ogres that Indians grew afraid even to whisper their names. Those refusing to believe in their power soon came upon sickness and death. Loolo never saw a single one of the poor victims: the medicine men would furnish her with a prized possession of their intended prey or something the person had worn, while all the time she remained secured in a secret medicine hogan. She didn't know, and couldn't know because of her training, that she actually practiced witchcraft. Her teachers had brainwashed her thoroughly to believe that her medicine-making was done to help people. Loolo suspected nothing untoward whatever.

The situation grew worse— the medicine men were flagrantly blackmailing all wealthy fami-

Special cigarettes placed in a sacred basket played a part in some witchcraft ceremonies.

lies. Western Navajoland suffered spasms of witchcraft fear. Finally one wise old woman, L'chee b'Assan, solved the problem. One day she walked into the hidden medicine hogan and found Loolo alone, which she was most of the time. L'chee had entered with a sharp butcher-knife in hand, informing Loolo that she had come to cut her throat. This was the penalty meted out to witches since the tribe's return to the Colorado Plateau area in 1868, when almost one medicine man out of every ten had turned to practicing witchcraft. Manuelito, Delgadito, and other noted Navajo leaders banded together to wipe them out by slitting throats all over Navajoland. Loolo, of course, knew nothing of this. When L'chee made her accusation, Loolo protested that she did no one any harm. She saved people!

"Did you save Hosteen Dugi'chon?" L'chee demanded.

"Yes, some time ago I made medicine for him."

"Dugi'chon went into the ground four days after you made *chindi* medicine for him!"

When Loolo declared sincerely that it couldn't possibly be, L'chee mentioned other horrible cases, and she became nearly as astounded as Loolo as their conversation developed. Out of it came the discovery that the girl actually did not know the truth and knew nothing whatever of the intricacies of Navajo religion. Instead of carrying out her intentions, L'chee dared defy all traditions and took Loolo to her hogan. Over a period of time Loolo came to understand how she had been tricked all her life. The facts appalled her, and she hardly knew what to do. Hiding from the medicine men, who sought her frantically, she finally reached a decision and proposed it to L'chee.

With the help of L'chee and a group of trusted friends, Loolo moved into the forest near Inscription House and formed what is best described as an anti-witchcraft cult. Its sole business was to eradicate the human monsters who disguised themselves in coyote-skin capes to commit dastardly deeds. Case after case concluded successfully in her hands, and soon no witchcrafters existed in western Navajo country. Shortly after the beginning of her change-over, the Hopi witchcrafter who had taught Loolo died under circumstances that were never explained. Next, Gani Choi, trying to witch a flock of sheep from an owner, fell out of his saddle while descending a Black Mountain trail toward Kayenta. He was dead from a .22 bullet. A small boy in the brush admitted shooting him because "a *chindi* suddenly commanded me to." Nothing whatever was done to the boy, of course. Jack Gambol, discovering that evil spirits were after him, fled to the safety of a Colorado River canyon for two years.

Loolo's advice to Bisheyi, when I brought him to her for help, was the same as to all: declaring no such beings as witches existed, she said they were pretenders. No man could will another to suffering or death. Fear came from lack of knowledge. She tried to talk common sense into Bisheyi, and her discourse sounded akin to the words of the sandreader. Bisheyi, although somewhat calmed by her words, kept shaking his head stubbornly. He or some member of his family would surely die in four days; this was the warning in the knots of human hair. No demand had been made on him for tribute, so the enemy must have hired a witch to remove him or a loved one from this world. He kept pleading for help and finally Loolo agreed.

As I left, she asked me to return that night—her ceremony never began before high moonrise. About fifty men and women were present when I arrived again at her hogan. They chanted steadily to thumping drums while two men constructed a dirt altar in a crescent shape. They covered it with a thin layer of ashes, under her direction, and painted on it in colored sand the two-foot figure of a man. At midnight Loolo halted the chanters and drummers. Standing in the flickering firelight before the altar in ceremonial attire—nothing but a G-string, with her body painted half white and half blue—she gave a lengthy talk. It could even be called preaching. Recapitulating the history of supposed witches, she gave an account of how sin came into this world, and warned of evil men who did wrong.

When she ended, she lifted her right hand briefly, and the chanters began prayers in series of four, accompanied by the drummers. The closely packed crowd swayed in rhythm to the chant—which somehow seemed designed to put you to sleep or in a trance. During the praying, Loolo placed a miniature, strung bow between the feet of the carefully drawn man-figure. On the buckskin string of the bow she dropped a tiny white bead. The chanting and drumming grew into a mighty crescendo, then ended abruptly. Had I not been close and gazing directly down at the bead, I would never have believed what followed. The instant that the sound stopped, the tiny white bead jumped from the bowstring and landed on the neck of the man-figure in the sand painting. Should I live to be a thousand years old, I shall never forget it. That was the end. Maybe it was trickery, maybe not.

Bisheyi didn't know the identity of the man who was after him, or he would have shot him dead on sight. He couldn't have given Loolo his name—but somehow she knew. She informed the assembled people, "The evil one who is trying to do this thing is Denetso Begay. Very soon, I do not know when, he will recede from this world by falling on his neck." It seemed to me that she looked extremely sad before turning to enter the medicine hogan.

The next week came news that a truck on a road near Comb Ridge, south of the San Juan River, had run off into a shallow ditch. The driver had easily pulled the undamaged truck back on the road, but not before the man riding in the truck-bed had been thrown out. The man, Denetso Begay, died from a broken neck.

Since nothing had happened to him, Jack Gambol now showed up into the Kaibito country, bold as brass; but Loolo had not forgotten him. Several old charges of witchcraft remained against him, but officers, including F.B.I. investigators, could not pin convicting evidence on him because too many lips were sealed tight. Many complaints about him, however, continued going to Tuba City and Window Rock, the Navajo tribal capital. Finally, in sheer desperation, lawmen did something about his misdeeds—they got him on an old polygamy law that was rarely enforced. Polygamy was common in western Navajoland in those days, and longhairs having several wives were considered as doing no more than what was customary. The educated ones with two or more wives might be warned to be careful, and were sometimes jailed briefly. But when Gambol took a second wife, a fifteen-year-old girl—apparently by threat—lawmen swooped in and arrested him.

Tried in federal court at Prescott and convicted, Gambol received a stiff sentence in McNeil Island Penitentiary. Raging at Navajo witnesses while being led away, handcuffed, he declared that all who swore against him would soon die—no matter where white men incarcerated him, his power would reach across great distances in vengeance. Supposedly that ended witchcrafter Gambol, and Navajoland breathed heavy sighs of relief. But it didn't turn out that way. Within a few weeks, members of families who had been involved in the trial began coming down with strange illnesses. One died, then another, and frightened Navajos rushed to Loolo.

After holding a ceremony, Loolo told them, "You are cleansed of all sickness. Fear no more. It will take a little time, but soon this evil one shall be beyond all things." Never once did she say anyone would be killed. They were just "going away." I asked why Gambol's retribution should take longer than in other instances.

She replied, "Because he knows almost as much as I do about these things. With such knowledge, he can guard against danger—except for one, which has not occurred to him. Only through his mind can he be touched." Loolo reached him across space, all right. Call it mystery or magic or mere coincidence, but Gambol was suddenly determined to be insane in the penitentiary. Transferred to a hospital for mental defectives in Springfield, Missouri, he hanged himself in his cell with a belt.

Gambol's hold on his enemies, however, proved so great that they refused to believe him dead even when the official reports arrived. Dozens went to Tuba City to see the paper, and still wouldn't accept it. For a year or two, many expected him to return to the reservation. A Navajo who thought the medicine man's ghost might appear to plague them asked me in all seriousness what he should do if he saw it approaching his hogan. "Shoot him and run!" I replied. "It won't be a ghost!"

Educated Paul Begay, who for years served as a tribal councilman, left a letter with me at the store. "Mail it as soon as possible," he urged me earnestly. "I've got to have a reply quickly!" When the mail was ready to go out to Tonalea, I found that the letter, addressed to Gambol in the Missouri government hospital, was unsealed and unstamped. Unable to resist, I read Paul's short letter:

We hear that you are dead. As soon as you get
this letter, write me right away and tell me
whether it's true or not you are dead.

Paul Begay is a common name, like Bill Smith or Tom Jones, but this one happened to be an unusual character and smarter than his neighbors—sometimes. Occasionally, however, he would let his imagination run away with him. For example, we used to sell Goetz beer (no alcohol content whatever) in cans; Indians drank it like soda pop. One day Paul slurped down three cans of near beer in a hurry—showing off to bystanders. Then he proceeded to act, or really believed himself, drunk. Becoming a nuisance in the bull pen, he turned on me when I told him to leave. The argument didn't get far before I went over the counter after him with an ax handle. Paul made it out the front door, sending a friend a week later to ask if I was still mad at him. When I re-entered the store after chasing him, I thought S. I. would be very put out over the incident, but he merely said to two other clerks, "When that boy gets mad, he gets mad, don't he?"

Paul was the second and last Indian I was ever angry at during all the years I spent on the reservation. The first case had occurred at Sunrise in 1932. When a Navajo started an argument over some inconsequential matter, I threw him out of the store. Being a friend, brother, or father to Navajos, the trader was never supposed to get mad at one—at least not openly. To do so would lower the Navajo's personal respect. The trader would then become one to avoid like the plague, for he was surely crazy. So, the next morning, when the man came back at sunup as the first customer of the day, asking to be allowed to trade there again, I complied, and that was the end of the incident.

In only one instance can I recall that S. I. ever became really angry at a Navajo, and he handled the matter in a strange way. Speaking gently, he handed the obstreperous Indian two silver dollars. "Here," he said. "I am paying you to stay away from this store—don't come back."

The very next day the Navajo returned nonchalantly to the post. "I thought I paid you yesterday to stay away from here!" S. I. said to him.

The Navajo laughed. "If I stay away," he said, "how am I going to spend the two dollars you gave me?" Unable to argue with such logic, S. I. let him trade them out.

Mysterious People, Mysterious Land

Over the years, a number of people in Navajo country simply vanished. One such mysterious case is that of a young man named Everett Ruess, who came to northern Arizona from Los Angeles in the early 1930s. An artist and poet, Ruess disappeared in 1934.* After his arrival on the reservation, he wandered alone over much of the Navajo country. Traveling with horses or burros, he went to the Hopi Snake Dance, Mesa Verde, Chinlee, Kayenta, Lukachukai and Navajo Mountain, Tuba City, and Monument Valley. His camps were lonely spots on the desert or in deep canyons. He had a passion for solitude and for expressing his emotions in poetry or art, which he sold to traders. Also a prolific letter writer, he penned accurate descriptions of scenery around him and wrote about his feelings under starry skies in the hinterland.

Crossing the Colorado River at Marble Canyon with two burros, Ruess wandered north, reaching Escalante, Utah, on November 12, 1934. From there he sent his final letter home; returning down the Escalante River toward the Colorado, he disappeared. His family grew worried, and search parties entered barren lands and hidden canyons seeking him. In March 1935 a volunteer posse found his two burros and last campsite in Davis Canyon, a tributary of the Escalante. All of southern Utah got into the act, and Ruess became such a celebrity that in August the *Salt Lake Tribune* dispatched a special expedition. But, like all those previously conducted, it came up with nothing.

Many theories, largely wild, were concocted to explain Ruess's mysterious vanishing. Some held that Indians killed him or that he fell to his death from some cliff ruin—he had possessed a mania for exploring them. Other suppositions were that he had been adopted into some Indian family (a total impossibility) or that he had married into a Navajo family and chose to lose his identity as a white man.

After a number of months, the Ruess case fell by the wayside until 1941,

---

*The disappearance of Everett Ruess was still unsolved in the mid-1980s. The following pages give Toney Richardson's explanation of the case after a four-year investigation.

when two Indians confessed to a murder on Oljeto Creek. Not one, but two bodies of prospectors, slain in 1930, were recovered. At this point a California journalist named Randall Henderson made a special trip to Inscription House to discuss the case with me. He thought that through my friendship with so many Indians we might learn something of the truth. No trader in western Navajoland believed that it would be possible for Ruess to take up with an Indian family for any reason, without letting anyone know. Sooner or later news of even the most minor incidents in the vast Navajo domain reached traders. And only the importance of the matter determined whether or not a trader ever revealed it.

My quiet detective work on Ruess bore no fruit until one night, seventy-four-year-old Wo'chan came in to trade a blanket, baskets, and willow water jars. Wo'chan was a Paiute woman who, as a teenaged girl, had saved the life of trader Joe Lee near Boschini in 1896. For all the years after the thrilling incident, she called herself his wife. Almost casually, she informed me that a white man had been buried many years ago on a sandbar in the San Juan River canyon. She had not been there herself, but other Paiutes had told her of seeing bleached bones and rotted clothing where wind blew the sand covering away. She named a Paiute who seemed to know most about the grave, a son of old tribal chief Nasja. When this information was reported to Randall Henderson, the journalist urged that everything possible be done to ascertain the facts. If it was Ruess, there should be some of his

Wo'chan, an old Paiute woman, who revealed that a body was buried on a sandbar in the San Juan River canyon.

manuscripts, paintings, and art materials with the remains. If they had been thrown away, they surely would have come to light long ago.

I knew most of the Paiutes from the north, and many of them were renegades and outlaws. If the San Juan River body was that of Ruess, it would be very possible that they had killed him. Paiute renegades came often to Inscription House Trading Post in the middle of the night. They moved fast if they had the least suspicion that federal or state officers were hunting them. All were wanted, and lawmen were constantly in pursuit. Leaving Utah camps, the Paiutes rode through uninhabited country, two hundred miles south, across western Navajoland to Willow Springs on Highway 89. There they remained with relatives or friends until officers came around making inquiries, whereupon they streaked back for Utah until the heat died. Their only stop was for a few provisions at Inscription House.

These men were wanted on charges ranging from robbery to murder. S. I. often warned me against opening the store for them after dark. But hungry men needed grub, and I knew them all as friends. Not one ever had offered offense or acted in any suspicious way toward me. Only one of them knew a little English, but all could speak the Navajo language, in which we communicated. Late one night, as they ate crackers and a can of tomatoes on the store counter, I maneuvered conversation around to the river grave. They knew only what they had heard from others, but they said that Nasja's son, Toby Owl ("nasja" means "owl" in Navajo), knew all about the dead man's grave.

I offered to pay a reward for any personal effects brought to me, and the Paiutes agreed to pass the word on. Months went by before Toby finally came in and agreed to bring me whatever he could find (in contrast to Navajos, Paiutes had no fear about digging up the dead). Nothing developed until 1942, just before I left for World War II, when Toby brought in several metal buttons, a rusted belt buckle, and a long-barreled rusted Colt .44. After examining the buttons, I commented, "This man has been dead at least fifty years."

Toby nodded his head. "Somebody killed him the year after those in Monument Valley were slain." He meant Robert Merrick and Herndon Mitchell in 1881. As for this ancient San Juan killing, some of his ancestors had been involved—which accounted for the details being so well known to him.

Some years later, Randall Henderson, always a desert wanderer, made an extensive tour of southern Utah in the region where Ruess had disappeared. Mormon cattlemen there gave him their version of what had happened, which appears in Henderson's book, *On Desert Trails,* first published in 1950. According to these stockmen, at the time Ruess vanished cattle thieves were especially busy along their side of the Colorado River. They were too crafty to be caught, so the stockmen devised a trick to scare them out. They "leaked" word that F.B.I. agents were entering the area in disguise to hunt them down. Of course, this couldn't possibly have been true—the thefts were not a federal case. However, according to cattlemen, the rustlers believed it, and when Ruess, a stranger, wandered into their midst, they killed him, buried him secretly, and fled elsewhere.

About seven years after Everett Ruess disappeared, his family—especially his father, who had been making quite an angry to-do over the affair—clammed up tighter than a bank on Sunday. At this time there was a theory that someone had found out Ruess was, in fact, alive. Supposedly he had checked into a St. Petersburg, Flordia, work camp for transients in May 1935 as Everett Runyan. While the stranger registered, a little white dog he had with him barked, attracting the attention of an elderly man named Burton Bowen, who then approached to get acquainted with "Runyan." Bowen worked with the man for several weeks on country roads, cleaning lawns and doing farm labor. During this period Ruess supposedly told Bowen his life story, readily confessing his identity, as he did to a number of newly made friends in Florida.

For some unexplained reason all transients in the work camp were then to be fingerprinted. This frightened Ruess, according to Bowen, who revealed his new friend's confidences only when questioned by investigators and officials of an insurance company. A few days later, the young man informed Bowen of his impending departure, which had been quickly arranged. Without a word to camp officials, he simply walked out to the road, where a minister picked him up in a car. Bowen believed that Ruess went back to Arizona—he had declared many times his intentions of doing so. After World War II, Bowen made many attempts to locate Ruess, but he failed, and the mystery was never solved.

In 1940 I took the U.S. census in the Kaibito and Copper Mine District, the largest in all Navajo country. The area stretched along both sides of Highway 89 from The Gap to old Lee's Ferry, along the Colorado River north to junction with Navajo Creek and east up the canyon to and including White Horse Mesa. I drove the few roads and some sheep trails by car; trailless areas had to be entered by horseback. The latter areas included several mesas almost as extensive as White Horse, remote canyons where few or no white men had ever been—L'chee Rock, Land of Standing Rocks, The Marching Giants, Sand Dunes, and Where the Trees Died of Fear. Navajo hogans were found in many hidden nooks and holes. Families living there seldom went to a trading post more than once a year. Many of these mysterious families actually hid out from other people—even their own tribesmen. The few necessities of life that these "wild ones" could not produce were sent for through an occasional passing relative.

After spending two days riding around searching for one particular family, that of Old Man Iron, I persuaded Paul Begay, who knew the area well, to help. He dubiously agreed, and by diligent searching and careful observance of ground signs, we finally pinned the "wild man" to one small area. We had to leave our horses a mile after we started. Passing down a deep wash with banks higher than our heads, we turned a bend to meet the "wild man" face to face. He wore only a pair of ragged Levi's, and his lice-infested, short hair stood out stiff in every direction. The sight of us seemed to turn his face instantly white, and his eyes glared in terrible fear. In an instant, before we could speak to him, he twisted on bare feet and took off running. Paul yelled for him to stop, but it didn't slow him down. We gave chase, gaining a few yards, when he suddenly leaped for the exposed roots of a tree hanging over the bank in order to escape. The one he seized broke and he fell down on his back among water-worn pebbles. As we came up, piteous moaning escaped his lips, and he panted in fear like an exhausted dog.

Sitting down on either side of him, Paul and I began smoking, while talking to him in a soothing manner. In about half an hour he was calm enough to sit up. Although he accepted a cigarette, he still refused to utter a word. Finally, we told him the nature of my business at his hogan. In response to my request, Old Man Iron rose and moved ahead, up and out of the wash, to the rudest kind of shelter. In and around it were two women and seven children, who were almost as scared as the old man himself. Some of the youngest children never did come out from behind bushes. The interview with this group took considerable time—at the rate of about one word a minute. Eventually I managed to guess the approximate ages of the children from their size and the knowledge that a Navajo mother suckles an infant two years, during which time she usually does not become pregnant. None of the wild man's family, however, possessed either a name or a tribal census number.

Continuing my census work, in a small, remote canyon I ran across Cara Nutgloa who was supposed to have been dead for the past twelve years.

Behind that lies a strange story: Cara had come to Inscription House accompanied by her husband (she was one of his four wives) in 1928. From glandular tuberculosis, her throat had puffed out to nearly the width of her head. When the doctor from Tuba City finally showed up, he announced, "Her throat must be lanced; otherwise, in a few days the swelling will cut off her breathing entirely."

Naturally, I supposed he would take Cara to the hospital. Instead, he asked me to interpret while he operated immediately. We took Cara to an iron bedstead under a piñon tree behind the trading post. Covering the springs with a tarpaulin, we placed her on it, stripped to the waist. Without giving her any anesthesia, the doctor reached in with a curved knife and slashed one side of her throat. Then it became obvious why he had partly undressed her. Blood and corruption spewed from the wound. He lanced the other side of her throat in the same quick motion. Cara did not utter the least sound of pain, but the slashes must have hurt. The rough job the doctor performed angered me. She certainly experienced considerable pain, too, when he cleaned the wounds. Soaking a roll of gauze in iodine, he probed deeply into each wound, leaving the packing inside.

Medicating two more rolls, he wrapped them in waxed paper. Handing them to her husband, he said to me, "Tell him to pull out the packing two days from now. Put these in the way he saw me do it."

When informed, her husband asked, "Two days after that what do I use to treat her, when these are gone?"

That having also occurred to me, I asked the doctor. He glared at me with, "Hell, two days from now he won't even need what I gave him. She will be dead. Tell him so!"

Her husband asked me twice what the doctor had said before I formed an evasive answer: "The doctor says she will be all right then and won't need any more." Neither Cara nor her husband questioned my statement. Despite the doctor's grim prognosis, Cara lived to age seventy-five.

I did the census job by special request because I knew the country thoroughly. In previous decades families therein had been only partly enumerated. I received extra pay and horse hire for this work, yet I lost money; expenses were unusually heavy and the lack of roads ruined a new car. More than four months were required because the jumbled terrain was so difficult to negotiate. Also, delays occurred on all hogan visits, except with the hidden families who wanted no one around longer than necessary. Most family groups, however, insisted I remain to eat and to stay the night. I spent hours listening to accounts of their everyday affairs, reminiscences, and legendary narratives. Not that these stopovers were not pleasant; they

were. But it slowed my work while S. I. waited impatiently for me to return
to Inscription House as resident manager. On these trips I carried a small
camera. I took a large number of pictures of unusual natural features and
people. Later these were used to illustrate articles in *Desert Magazine* and
other magazines of national circulation.

In the early 1940s Randall Henderson, the journalist who had investigated
the Ruess case, visited us every few months at Inscription House. We
made several horseback trips into Navajo Canyon and to Inscription Rock,
five miles away in a corner of Red Valley. Henderson loved this far country and its people, and he had a reporter-writer's inevitable inquisitiveness. Hearing us mention Inscription Rock, he could not rest until he had
explored it for himself. This flat-topped, round mass of stone lifts sheer
skyward three hundred feet. The names of a few white men were cut on
eroded walls. However, the rock's name derived from the many petroglyphs
made in the twelfth and thirteenth centuries by aborigines inhabiting a
pueblo on top. Under the stark rim of the east side was a series of small
caves, used for many years by Navajos as a repository for dead infants. While
the graves were usually protected by mounded stones, vultures and rodents
got to the small bodies anyway, scattering bones over the edge to sand
dunes below.

Henderson and I used to climb to the top without using ropes; here he
made innumerable photographs. We did not manage to get down into the
caves, and were unable to figure out how the Navajos did it. Footholds
once used by them had probably sheared off. Local Indians said that no
bodies had been placed in these caves during the past twenty years. Indians
were, however, still disposing of infants by ancient customs. In other cliff
caves, I found many such small bundles. Like the Indians, I always made
hasty retreat from such sacred places.

Henderson wanted to see an old trapper's stone cabin in Jones Canyon,
a tributary of Navajo Canyon. We rode a long time, but I was unable to
find it. For the next couple of hours he must have entertained grave doubts
of my being the knowledgeable expert on Navajo country he had long
assumed me to be. Using the Mitchell-Siewert inscription for a starting point,
we retraced our way several times into Jones Canyon. Always we were right
back where the cabin should be—except that it wasn't. It had once stood on
a prominent knoll among several cottonwood trees below the saddle into
Jones Canyon from Neetsin Canyon. Behind the cabin, at the base of the
eighteen-hundred-foot wall, had once been a bubbling spring, which occasionally sprayed high into the air, the water running toward a canyon-floor

creek. Many times, while exploring the canyons, Millie and I had watered our horses and eaten lunch there.

The mystery of the vanished spring, trees, and cabin puzzled me, but Henderson's knowledge of geysers saved the day. Carefully examining the scene, he pointed to layers of a black substance on the sandstone cliff wall. "Your spring was once right under here," he declared. "The black comes from water bubbling that high." It turned out that three years before, while damming the canyon stream, workmen had torn the cabin down for the wall stones. The cottonwoods had also been cut and the stumps burned. A sudden flood had then completely obliterated the old trapper's cabin site. Rushing waters had deepened the arroyo, lowering the water table at least thirty feet and destroying the bubbling spring. No one ever knew who had built the cabin; it had just always been there until now.

The dropped water table also affected the Turquoise Shrine. This huge mass of solid rock stood barren and craggy in the center of the main part of Jones Canyon. At least five hundred feet high, it could be scaled, with ropes, to a dish-shaped depression on top. In the center was a hole, twelve feet in diameter, passing straight down into nowhere. The Turquoise Shrine had nothing whatever to do with Navajo tribal clan history, nor did it come into being during their antiquity. The shrine stood there when the first Navajos arrived. In some way it was connected with the bubbling spring, for water sometimes roared up the hole to froth around the dish-sloped rims. With the water came pieces of unpolished and some crudely polished turquoise. Not infrequently small stone carvings were also lifted to the top. High winds often blew these objects off the rock mass to the sand below, and for many years we bought turquoise and some grayish stone fetishes from Navajos who had picked them up there.

Indians had been trying to get down into the shrine since long before the first white man appeared in the country. At certain seasons of the year, rushing water came no higher than a table-like rock about two hundred feet below. Those who lay watching the surging water for days and weeks might have been able to predict when to go. None, however, had ever managed to reach the table rock and get out alive; several had disappeared while trying. In my time, they made a windlass and tied lariat ropes together to make several attempts. Todachene Nez had spent years trying to figure out a means of recovering turquoise from the shrine. He and his friends believed tons of it lay below. Surely former inhabitants of the ruined cliff towns had been sacrificing it there for centuries.

After reading my story about the shrine in *Desert Magazine* a friend in Flagstaff came up with a plan. City Water Superintendent Hayes Weidner drew up specifications for a bail that automatically opened and closed. The operational principle lay in hoops and bars in the mouth of a fine, wire-mesh bag. The bail opened when lowered to drag the bottom and closed when raised, no matter what the force of water below. In due course we constructed this bail and went to the shrine to give it a try. Todachene Nez and his friends were most anxious to recover the treasure while the water remained low. After much difficulty we reached the top of the shrine and lowered the bail from a windlass on a rope. One man held a powerful flashlight with the beam pointed on the table rock, which glistened slick in the light.

The first haul brought up, among many pieces of gravel, twenty-some broken chunks of low-grade turquoise. This proved the bail worked. Elated, the Navajos proceeded industriously, and a second haul produced drilled turquoise (certainly from a string of beads) and two bear-like carvings. "Zuni!" Todachene Nez exclaimed. "Only they should be red instead of white." When the lime deposit was knocked off, the objects, carved from pipestone, were, indeed, red in color.

The bail could not be used in crevices or cracks, and it was only partly successful in the black openings of subterranean passages showing below the slick rock. It also hung up occasionally and was hard to work free. Subsequent hauls after the first few produced nothing except gravel. As the day waned, we hooked onto an unknown object below the flat rock. It took half an hour to loosen it, and a gush of air roared skyward as the bail came free. Following almost instantly, water boiled clear to the top of the hole, and we had to rush from the rim to escape. "The Water Monster is angry!" Todachene Nez cried, aghast. "Let us leave at once!" We left and did not try bailing again. Later, when the water had receeded, perhaps it would have been possible to lower a man safely into the hole, but I doubt that any Navajo would have volunteered for the project. Returning to our daily routines, we left the secrets of the Turquoise Shrine still locked in its depths.

Changing Times

Probably no one escaped draft registration after 1941 when the Selective Service Act was passed by Congress. We registered all Indians at Inscription House, even those who spoke no English. On request of the Navajo Service, following the bombing of Pearl Harbor, we organized Navajos into watcher brigades for the possibility of enemy planes crossing inland from the coast. Of course, that never occurred, but it so happened that Inscription House stood below a regular airline path of transcontinental travel. From then on, the Indians suspected every plane heard in the air.

By then rationing had gone into effect, and sugar coupons were handled as regular business. Too, the European war had already reached us in the persons of Jean and Elizabeth Weber-Marshal, a couple who had escaped from German-occupied France. On the afternoon of their arrival, I had been out behind the post shooting coyotes—the varmints were somehow managing to get through a wire-mesh fence and were rapidly killing all the laying hens. The Weber-Marshals entered the store from their loaded station wagon parked in front. Elizabeth asked where they could camp on the mesa. Feeling out of sorts and that the question was superfluous, I gave her a short answer: "Lady, there's a few million acres out there," I told her. "Pick your camping site anywhere you feel like!"

Only later did we learn that they had recently escaped from the Nazis. Elizabeth, daughter of an old New York family, had spent the previous fifteen years in France. Her husband, Jean, and his brother owned a wholesale electrical equipment business in Paris and Casablanca, Morocco. When German armies invaded and the nation surrendered, Elizabeth, on her American passport, entered Spain. Jean's brother was taken, along with the business. Jean managed to hide out, eventually making his way to the Mediterranean coast. Stowing away for Casablanca, he fell into the hands of German sympathizers. Escaping them, too, he reached friendly officials who secreted him until Elizabeth could arrange his entrance into the United States via Spain.

Seeing store lights burning late that night, the couple came back to the post for water and a few supplies. Millie, waiting for me to finish trading with a customer and close up, fell into conversation with the Weber-Marshals. Most of that week they called at the post and took several meals with us. They became good friends whom we later visited in New York. Elizabeth never failed to remind me goodnaturedly of my first short answer.

At about this time, in 1941, Navajo rug sales once more crashed to the very bottom. The single and double fuzzy saddle blankets, originated at Inscription House, could hardly be given away. This thick blanket, woven of hairy wool, brought the trader even less money than the wool alone would have if sold in the fleece. S. I.'s previous trader had been paying a dollar or a dollar and a quarter for singles. The post was lucky to sell them for a dollar and a quarter, if and when a buyer could be found.

Trading-post profit depended on what its Indian customers had to spend. In those years their economy was based more than sixty percent on weaving. What the trader sold their blankets for governed what he could pay for them. Most traders I knew scrounged around everywhere, seeking better markets for Navajo blankets. We did it all the time, even advertising in magazines and newspapers. When blankets failed to move and hit rock bottom prices, weavers' families were often hungry and traders could go flat broke. The Navajos' welfare and the trading business depended on a nearly stable blanket market. I decided to try something to improve the intolerable, practically nonexistent, fuzzy-blanket trade, and S. I. gave me the go-ahead.

Young Dr. Solon T. Kimball, anthropologist for the Navajo Service, had visited us frequently from Window Rock. On his first trip, Millie prepared Navajo fried bread with chili. Made of chopped beef or mutton with all the necessary ingredients added, it is a far cry from that found in restaurants. The fried bread, really a thick tortilla cooked in a dutch oven or cast-iron pan, was made from Indian cornmeal. We used this meal-flour, which produced a bluish-tinged tortilla. Dr. Kimball liked the chili and the tortillas so much that, if he was ever anywhere in the area, he came by for another meal. To help him in his work, I kept a detailed account of the economic condition of several selected average families. He had a few surveys going in every land-management district. About the time I began trying to change the fuzzy-blanket situation, he happened along.

Knowing the hardships of a bare-living income for Navajo families, he became most enthusiastic over my plans. We sat up until nearly daylight going into the entire problem and theorizing the solutions. The center body of the fuzzies was woven in a single, dull color, and the end was decorated by plain stripes. What would happen if simple designs were placed in the corners and, on some blankets, a center one was added? The blanket could become a dual-purpose item: it would continue to be a saddle blanket and also be attractive enough to use as a floor piece. To obtain satisfactory color combinations, the wool would have to be scoured better than usual before carding and spinning. The next day we finished planning the project by creating assorted designs in different colors with crayons. The weavers could now be called in to talk it over.

The proposition was discussed with half a dozen local weavers. They were eager to give the idea a trial. We set a date and dispatched word all over the country. Inscription House would buy blankets from as far as a hundred and fifty miles away. Not only did these six weavers produce samples of what we had in mind, but they set up their looms under shading cedars near the post to demonstrate the new method. Help from Window Rock—Navajos who were experts on washing, dyeing, and spinning native wool—had arrived the night before.

Indians were hired to prepare a big noon feast of mutton, bread, coffee, and whatever else they could fix from canned goods. The session began at eight A.M. and paused only for an hour at noon so that the families attending it could eat. Altogether, we fed about five hundred Indians. Not only my weavers, but tribal employees from Window Rock, gave instructions and lectured on what we planned. The meeting proved a great success. Weavers learned how to prepare and dye their wool far better than in the past. Once they grasped ideas of what design or pattern to use, they were eager to get to work. As encouragement, I offered two dollars for corner-designed fuzzies and two and a half dollars for the same with an additional center pattern.

The singles were approximately thirty-one by thirty-one inches, as before. Within the week we began buying five to ten a day at double the former price. As stacks of them built toward the ceiling, I started worrying over the selling end. Unable to get away from the store on a promotional trip as I had planned, I sent several special samples to a wholesale firm in Gallup. Handling charges and freight raised the cost even more; merely hopeful, I quoted prices at three and three and a half dollars. If they were willing even to negotiate, then perhaps we could make a deal for at least a quarter or so above our cost.

To my surprise, by return mail the company sent a check for the samples at my stated price and asked that two thousand fuzzies be sent to them as soon as possible. Now I must obtain the required number. The weavers wanted to work at these higher prices, and soon Inscription House had a stupendous rug business. Other types of blankets began to come from the

177

Nellie Sombrero carding wool.

same families. Quite often a truckload of Indians arrived bringing different fabrications from their looms.

After several weeks a letter came from the company, wanting to know when they might expect delivery. That same afternoon they telephoned, urging us to send whatever was on hand (we had nineteen hundred). A truck came in at sundown with merchandise, and we were unloading it into the warehouse when S. I. arrived from town. After taking a look into the rug room, he came tearing across the store to the warehouse. "What did you pay for all them fuzzies?" he demanded. "And what are you going to do with them?"

When told, he gasped in horror. "Ee-god, boy! You've busted this trading post!"

Of course, he already knew something of what had gone on, because traders encountering him in town had been quick to report that Inscription House had gone crazy buying fuzzy blankets. Taking him to the office, I produced all the correspondence. He read the letters several times, continuing to shake his head and refusing to be convinced. "They won't take them," he said. "I know that outfit."

After supper everybody went to work bundling blankets. We did not merely tie a hide rope around them and toss them into a truck. They were first wrapped in heavy paper to protect them from soiling, and burlap was sewn around an entire bale of fifty. Five of us had them ready to go by midnight. The next morning S. I., still insisting the deal was impossible, decided to truck the load to Gallup instead of shipping by rail. "Better give me that letter," he said. "It's some kind of contract, but I'll probably have to hire a Philadelphia lawyer to collect!" Five days later the truck returned from Gallup with a big load of piece goods, shoes, robes, and shawls. S. I. followed it, smirking broadly.

Our competitors knew what we paid for fuzzies: Indians had told them from the beginning. What they didn't know was where we sold them and for how much. Of course, they didn't rest until they found out. What S. I. knew was certain to follow, did. Other traders raised the weavers' pay above ours; to gain back this loss, they hiked prices of their merchandise—which we did not do. The biggest trading-post item was flour. Mormon flour millers in Utah delivered twenty to thirty tons at a time to Inscription House. Any loss of even a few cents soon mounted up with this commodity alone. My competitors paid the weavers four dollars for single and eight dollars for double fuzzies. At the same time, they jumped flour to two dollars for a twenty-five-pound sack—no baking powder included. Their price-raising didn't worry me at all. One thing was sure, I never sold the Navajos short on their trading ability. They could, and did, readily see that a four-dollar blanket bought two sacks of flour without baking powder, which was an additional fifty cents. At Inscription House, where we included baking powder with our $1.25 sack of flour, a $3.50 blanket paid for two sacks of flour, and fifty cents remained for something else.

We kept buying more and more fuzzies. The whole country seemed to rain them on us, a thousand to fifteen hundred a month. Inscription House alone could have flooded the market and thereby slumped prices. This was what I feared would soon happen, and I believe it would have if World War II had not come along. When I left Inscription House for that fracas in the South Pacific, weavers were receiving four and a half dollars and nine dollars for fuzzies.

By the mid-1940s, sadly, the real fuzzy blanket was no more. None were woven after 1946, for the reason that no hairy wool was available. "Improved" breeds of sheep replaced the old native types that stayed fat on hardly more than rocks, sand, and dry woody browse. The saddle blanket called a fuzzy after 1946 was entirely different from the old one. But the same designs were employed in its fabrication, and that was actually what sold them from the beginning. The phoney fuzzy retailed at such standardized prices as seven and a half dollars for singles and fifteen dollars for doubles in the Southwest. Elsewhere the same blanket was priced for anything dealers could get—often two or more times those figures.

Early Sunday morning on December 7, 1941, S. I. drove in at Inscription House to stay a couple of days during our absence. Millie, Toni, and I were going to Flagstaff to visit Cecile in school and to attend to personal business. Noon approached, and a few minutes prior to our departure Susie telephoned from town, sounding very excited. "Haven't you had your radio on this morning?" We seldom had time to turn the battery radio on except late at night, and, when I replied in the negative, she gave me the astounding news: "The Japanese have bombed Pearl Harbor!"

En route to Flagstaff we stopped at Gray Mountain. In Earl Reed's trading post I sat with a bottle of beer while listening to details of the infamous attack from an excited newscaster. Incredible that war had come, but nevertheless a fact. For some weeks after Pearl Harbor, it did not appear the war would reach into our lives. Then I went on active duty with the Naval Reserve. When we started packing to leave for our Flagstaff home, a solemn delegation of old friends, led by Julius Sombrero, came to the store. "We want you to come with us," they said.

Their seriousness halted any questions on my part. Obviously they were greatly concerned over something, so I went with them to Julius's hogan two miles away on the mesa rim, against the canyon country. In the medicine hogan he handed me a G-string and a pair of silver-button-decorated moccasins. "Put them on," he said. "We are going to hold the going-to-war ceremony for you. This is so that you will return safely, my brother." Who can say that their prayers didn't work? About all I got in the South Pacific was a mild case of malaria and heat rash.

The old trading days I had known so well actually ended during World War II, a fact that hit me when I returned to Inscription House in 1946. No more did I see thin, dusky, half-starved faces. The Navajos' economic standard had improved astonishingly. Six thousand young men returning from the armed forces had much to do with this new, upward mobility. Their attitudes were changed by knowledge of other people, of far lands. Now, for the first time, The People were not forced to live in a circumscribed world peculiarly their own. Wide awake, they were ambitious and going places, acutely cognizant of changing times.

Revitalized and enthused by the generation that fought the war, even the longhairs demanded employment. No longer were they forced to sit around their hogans hoping that a little wool woven into a blanket would buy enough coffee and flour to sustain them. Now they not only wanted jobs, but insisted on them as their right. The Navajos had never been lazy, and, when obtaining jobs on or off the reservation, they stuck to them faithfully. All these changes in the Navajos' outlook ended the old form of trading, which had outlived the years when tribesmen existed on blankets, poor sheep, and hairy wool. Blanket weaving became scarce, as the native craftsmen in all lines were turning to other pursuits for a livelihood.

The Navajos were now "living like a white man," with radios, washing machines, and passenger cars and trucks. They demanded more than the barest commodities once available in trading posts, so a new, better, more expensive line of drygoods was brought in, along with a wider variety of canned foods. Along some of the paved roads, over former sheep trails, trading posts had become community markets, even selling fresh milk and vegetables.

The first day I walked into Inscription House Trading Post after the war, the change had moved far toward what it was to become. One thing proving it most was the absence of a particular item on the shelves. Vacuum-packed coffee in all sizes of containers and assorted brands occupied space once filled with ground and whole-bean Arbuckle Brothers Ariosa coffee. The absence of the Navajo's long favorite *Hosteen Cohay* (Arbuckle Coffee) seemed to signal the end of the glamorous, even romantic period of adventurous barter-trading. This coffee had played an important role in the daily lives of trader and Navajo alike. We could, and did, make a satisfying meal on nothing more than the strong brew and a chunk of fried bread. Even the boards from coffee packing-cases were used for every purpose imaginable. They went into trading-post walls and into construction of outhouses or sheds. Everything connected with the coffee was valuable, including the paper in the packages. This paper contained a black-printed signature for which the Indians received one cent or a stick of candy. The trader then shipped these coupons to Arbuckle Brothers premium department for merchandise, which furnished the post's living quarters with many niceties the family could not have enjoyed otherwise. Traders of the old days lived just about as close to the bare subsistence level as their customers.

The trading post itself had changed, also, during the war. During my absence my brother, Cecil, who ran Inscription House, had put in an electric power plant. Now the post had good lights everywhere, a decided improvement over keeping sand cleaned out of the bowls and generators of gasoline lights so that they would work at least part of the time. With the juice wired into every building at the post came household appliances for better living: washing machines, refrigerators, deep-freeze boxes, soft-drink-bottle coolers, and meat saws.

Cecil returned to Flagstaff in the mid 1940s, and S. I. then hired a succession of traders—at least, men who made a weak stab at it, as he said. Now, in the twilight of a long and eventful life, he wanted to relax in town with Susie. After the war, I had decided to stay exclusively with the writing that made my family a living, but very soon most of it would be done at Inscription House. S. I. telephoned, "Don't you want to write up here awhile, where people can't bother you? You can help me out at the same time." So back to the post I went.

For some months Navajos came to renew friendships and reminisce about old times and the escapades of our youth. I had encountered many of their sons in the Marianas and on Okinawa during the war. Among them were Bahe Ketchum, Billy Goodman, Edgar Cling, John Luther, Bill Redshirt, and George Littlesalt, all of whom I had known as small boys. They had written home about seeing me and, on their return, had given larger accounts, until their families were convinced we had won the war together. When these boys came around periodically, we fought it all over again.

When Hosteen White Horse, now very feeble, held a nine-day *yeibetchai* (healing ceremony) just off the mesa, Millie and the girls came out to stay awhile. They went to the afternoon sandpaintings and spent the final night of public performances in the cold, enduring the smoky fires surrounding the dance corral in a mass of four to five thousand Indians attending from distant localities. The family insisted on seeing the *yeibetchai* all over again, although they had seen dozens of previous ones, right to the concluding Bluebird Song as the sun rose over the eastern horizon. The ancient healing ceremonies were changing, as were the land and its people: now they served largely for spiritual salvation. The Navajos accepted fully the white man's medicine and hospitals. Their sons and daughters had moved into the profession of medicine. The sandpaintings were somewhat different than in former years—no longer were they created with fanatical devotion to religious symbolism. Chants were not the same or as lengthy. The costumed clan dancers who made mistakes escaped without reprimand.

The vastness of western Navajoland changed rapidly with new and better roads, community centers, chapter houses, and local day schools. The young people returning from the war found living standards far above those they had left. These Navajo youths had made good soldiers and had served honorably. Yet the old desert warriors, the battle-scarred ones (perhaps from envy), were not convinced on this point. "These boys had no real war training," Hosteen Redshirt assured me confidently. "They were not taught how to track and how to hide from enemies as we did. Washington should have sent us older men who know all those things. Look, I will show you how we did it!"

Walking a hundred yards to a two-foot-tall sagebrush, he dissolved his body behind it. I moved toward the brush; no part of him was visible until, at about eight feet, I saw the muzzle of a six-gun pointed directly at me. "See?" the old man chuckled, leaping to moccasined feet. "Had you been an enemy, you would have died by my bullet, without ever knowing I hid there!" The grandsons of these old warriors had endured the cruelty of Bataan and fought from Guadalcanal to Okinawa; many had won medals for valor.

A few things in western Navajoland had not changed. A deputy U.S. Marshal and an F.B.I. man arrived one afternoon. They were loaded down with six-guns, rifles, and a Thompson submachine gun. S. I. considered their armament in astonishment, remembering the days of yore when law-men, in their ignorance, deliberately invited a shooting scrape. They wanted to hire horses to enter Navajo Canyon in armed force, searching for a bad Navajo. S. I. shook his head sadly. "If you ride down there with all them shooting irons, you'll never see the Indian. He'll shoot you from his hiding place in the rocks."

The officers smiled in a superior way. "Our orders are to bring him out, so we'll bring him out in one shape or another."

"Go ahead. I'll send somebody for your bodies when the news comes back."

The F.B.I. man proved a little smarter. "Mr. Richardson, how else do we arrest him if we don't go down there?"

S. I. replied, "I can send word you want to see him. He'll be here by sundown."

"Just that easy?"

"Certainly. Most likely the Navajo has already heard from Tuba City by moccasin telegraph that you're after him."

After discussing the situation briefly outside, the F.B.I. agent re-entered the store to say they would try S. I.'s plan. Turning to one of several Nava-jos, S. I. told him to ride down into the canyon and deliver a message. As day began to wane, the officers grew concerned. Much to their surprise, however, the wanted Indian came riding in, got off his horse, and tossed the bridle reins to the messenger. Wordlessly, he got into the officers' car. By that time a large number of Indians had collected at the post; all were dangerously quiet. "There's your man," S. I. told the officers. "One final word of caution: don't put handcuffs on him here. These other Indians might object to the insult and jump you. Your man has surrendered peace-fully, and they expect him to be treated accordingly."

The officers took their prisoner straight to the Tuba City jail. An Indi-an officer manacled him only after they were off the reservation. A Navajo who commits a crime lives with a real sense of guilt. Believing that some-day he will have to pay for it in one way or another, he often confesses in order to end the suspense.

Once more I had to go to war, in the Korean conflict of 1950. Orders came suddenly and no more than six Navajos knew about it. One of them was the second Mrs. Navajo Mountain. She brought a sweet cake made of finely ground, roasted piñon nuts. "I gave all my sons this cake when they went away to war," she said. "This is yours."

Hubert Richardson (Toney's uncle), who spent fifty-nine years on the reservation, with three long-time Navajo friends; *left to right*: Hosteen Yellow Lefthand, 91; Chizzie Yazza en Begay, 79; Hubert Richardson, 76; and Hosteen Sagnitso, 80.

For several years S. I. had known that he had cancer. While I served in Korea in 1951, his condition worsened. He decided to quit the Navajo trading business and sold Inscription House to Stokes Carson. He made arrangements to enter the Mayo Clinic in Rochester, Minnesota. After twenty-five years in business at Inscription House, his leaving was the second time in his life that he knew deepest sorrow; the first had been when Susie passed on in 1948. He told me just before dying in 1959 that had I not been in Korea—even had he thought his time had come to join the Sky People—the trading post would never have been sold.

In later years Inscription House became a small village with two mission stations, a day school, a tribal chapter house, rodeo and fairgrounds, and homes for local residents. Stokes Carson, who operated the post after the sale, was the last old-time trader in Navajo country—he had spent fifty-seven years in the business. Only one other trader lived longer among the tribesmen—my uncle Hubert Richardson, who spent fifty-nine years on the reservation.

The Last Stop

After Inscription House was sold, I never expected to return as a trader to Navajo country, but in 1958 Millie and I took over Two Guns Trading Post from S. I. Following his retirement, he had acquired the place for leasing to others as an investment. Almost at the halfway mark between Winslow and Flagstaff, it perched on the side of aptly named Canyon Diablo. The principal trade was with Navajos off their nearby reservation. Consisting of a store, a beer-and-wine bar, and gasoline pumps, it was the only trading post on deeded land I ever managed. Its three hundred twenty acres stretched for a mile on each side of U.S. Highway 66, in country that was a mass of rocks, with little grass and red-dirt flats.

The bridge over Canyon Diablo marked the snowline, west to Flagstaff, and the fog area, eastward, during winter months. Here skies were not blue all day. The wind—winter and summer—howled over flat-rimmed canyons and sere ranges of the high plateaus with a terrible vengeance. It stirred up ghosts of a pioneer past. And it raced, heedless, over those with no future at all, represented by rows of white crosses along the highway, where automobile fatalities—three, four, five at a whack—were so numerous that no more warning markers were put up after 1959.

Fortunately for me, since I almost immediately became disillusioned about tourists, eighty percent of our business came from Navajo families who had traded with me at Sunrise back in 1932. Most younger Indians worked off the reservation as union men, drawing big wages on construction jobs. They were shovel and bulldozer operators, truck drivers, and craftsmen with unionized operating engineers. One man, unusually skilled as a quad driller, earned thirty to forty dollars per six-hour shift.

It proved a source of constant amazement to tourists that these Indians owned good trucks and cars, and homes filled with new furniture, radios, and TVs. Most refused to believe the Navajos actually earned all this, being convinced a benevolent government provided them with luxurious living. Weekends, when these Indians came home from distant jobs, the store filled with them until midnight—all having a good time. One of them, Frank Nelson, who probably knew a hundred English words, taught himself to play a guitar. Composing his own lyrics in Navajo, he sang and played them to tribal music.

The bull pen wasn't large, and with Frank playing and other Navajos singing, tourists packed it to no standing room, gawking. Some of the best numbers I tape recorded, together with rare chants of medicine men and a few peyote-ceremony songs. One Navajo sang them in the Ute language (which has a faster tempo), even though he didn't understand the words. The peyote ceremony came to the Navajos from the Four-Corners Utes; consequently, they first learned the Ute versions of songs, although many of their prayers were given in Navajo.

There had been a store somewhere in the vicinity of Two Guns since pioneer days—falling stone walls of several were visible from the store's front door. Not until 1923 was the name "Two Guns" given. That year Earl Cundiff bought a homestead relinquishment from a man who had lived there eighteen years and never bothered proving up. Being a World War I veteran, Cundiff was able to take over without delay. What became U.S. Highway 66 was shifted to pass before his first stone trading post, which at that time was the only stop between Flagstaff and Winslow. In wagon days we had crossed the canyon four miles upstream from where the bridge was later built. Later structures were built on the relocation of a still newer road.

Cundiff gave a ten-year lease to Harry "Indian" Miller, part Oklahoma Indian. Miller established a native wild-animal zoo inside walls enclosing a rim point at the old site. The large store at the long-ago-abandoned bridge on this site burned out mysteriously. During the few years Cundiff operated Two Guns, he bought his merchandise from my uncle Hubert Richardson's wholesale house in Winslow. A narrow cave, which entered under the plateau in the point of a side canyon below the old ruins, had been explored for nearly nine miles. Miller engaged Hopi Indians to construct small, pueblo-type buildings on the bench above to attract tourists, who were taken into the cave for so much per head. He also at times employed floaters—and paid them fifty cents a day or nothing at all—who put up more stone buildings on the canyon rim. Frequently, old men stopped at Two Guns to tell me that, as wandering youths, they had once worked for Miller. A man with a considerable past, Miller was running the Cave of the Seven Devils just inside New Mexico, west of Gallup, when he died in 1952.

The range adjacent to Two Guns in early days was all sheep country, but later it was occupied by large cattle outfits. Earlier even than the sheepmen, outlaws often hid out in the vicinity. To the west, under a high bench, stood the walls of a large, stone stockade, probably used as a hideout by a number of gangs. Horses were kept inside the walls at night so they couldn't be run off by Indians. Several outlaw gangs did operate in and through the country, and one March night in 1899 four bandits held up a fast Santa Fe mail train at Canyon Diablo Station, three miles north of Two Guns. It was northern Arizona's most celebrated robbery. The bandits fled north into Utah, were chased back into the Arizona Strip, and were captured by the famous Sheriff Bucky O'Neill. Convicted and sentenced to the hell-hole of Yuma Territorial Prison, one was shortly released on the theory that he would lead lawmen to the stolen goods. Instead of proceeding to the buried loot as expected, however, he went to Los Angeles and died. The express company then got the second thief pardoned; he promptly took himself out of this world in El Paso. The third remained in Arizona; under an alias, he joined the Rough Riders in 1898 with Bucky O'Neill and was killed with him in Cuba. Finally, the fourth gained his freedom, but express company detectives never managed to follow him to any money. Years after they gave up watching, he suddenly owned a large ranch in southern Arizona, stocked with fine cattle.

On the witness stand at Prescott, during the federal court trial, the express company agent had refused to state the exact amount taken in the robbery. Asked if it was ten thousand dollars, he said yes. Forty thousand? Yes. When they got him to seventy thousand, he admitted to that also but refused to divulge anything more. Thus came into being the legend of a buried treasure, claimed to be down in, or along the rim of, Canyon Diablo. Perhaps it is still being sought.

Canyon Diablo enjoyed a reputation as one of the Southwest's toughest towns. It had its dead men every day, and, when Boot Hill (south of the tracks) became filled, victims were buried almost where they fell. The gambling joints, saloons, and bordellos faced each other for a mile along the north side of the tracks. These were temporary affairs of tar paper, tin, and framework. After the railroad moved on, there remained only the trading post, followed by the huge post of stone built by Fred Volz, a couple of warehouses, the railroad section house, and the depot. Today nothing exists; even the grave markers and plot fences of Boot Hill have disappeared—all except that of the one man who died with his boots off, the old German trapper-trader Herman Wolf.

The newest Canyon Diablo trading post, a mile east of the long-vanished railroad station, was built by Joe Stiles in 1934. Indian trader Billy Williams ran it until he was killed in an automobile accident with his wife on

Navajo children were rarely punished, but they were brought up to be courteous and respectful of the rights of others, especially elderly people.

their way home to Winslow. It had a succession of owners after that, but never proved a very valuable business because the nearby highway offered easy access to cheaper merchandise in railroad towns. Indians traded at Two Guns only because they knew me; I spoke their language, took pawn, lent them money, and bought their blankets. Their business and personal association made it possible for me to hold out for three years at Two Guns without letting the tourists drive me nuts.

During the time I was at Two Guns, every day at least one white traveler would ask, "Don't you get awfully lonesome way out here all by yourself?" At least a million people passed Two Guns every year, and a good percentage of them wheeled in off the highway—always to my complete annoyance. On first going there, we had hoped to do well with such tourist trade, but it turned into more trouble than profit. The arrival of tourists always called for increased watchfulness. In the tourist crowds containing children, things always managed to disappear. Sometimes even small children, without restraint from their parents, would pick up "souvenirs." No Navajo child ever stole anything in a trading post or anywhere, that I ever heard of. Navajo children were seldom, if ever, punished, yet they were brought up with utmost respect for property rights and courtesy toward others, especially elderly people. Nor did they ever get noisy or rambunctious.

Professional and organized moochers traveled the highway continually. One, making periodic visits, would replace his ordinary hat and coat with a blue uniform, cap and jacket, before entering the post. He claimed to be accepting donations for his mission. On his second visit, I insisted on knowing where his alleged mission was located, but I never managed to find out. Every year along the scenic stretch of highway between Flagstaff and Winslow there were many crimes, involving petty theft, armed robbery, kidnapping, rape, and murder. Although a few trading posts were burned, and maybe one trader on the average was killed every year, no such steady crime waves ever occurred in the big Indian country.

When we were first married, Millie had entered the Indian country with many misgivings and much trepidation, but she soon realized that the peaceful people were friends, not enemies. At Two Guns, after a few weeks, she understood enough to feel safe from tourists only when Navajos were around. Even drunk Indians could be handled easily and never gave her the least trouble. Indeed, when one got out of line, all she had to say was, "You take a walk." In every instance—and there were times when Indians came around mean with alcohol—they departed immediately. Most returned the next day to apologize to her.

When S. I. took over the property in 1957, he consistently refused to lease or sell it again, even though he was not physically able to look after the business. He stayed at Two Guns, however, while Millie and I ran it. He had lived among Navajos and been engaged in trading too long to dissociate himself completely and be happy elsewhere. Visiting and conversing in the tribesmen's language, which in many ways is more expressive than English, meant something to a man's spiritual life.

As soon as they learned where S. I. was, and that I was there with him, Navajos we had not seen in years began stopping at Two Guns. A misty closeness surrounded those meetings—one of bygone days never to be relived, of incidents we shared, and the realization that some of us would never meet again in this world. Navajo friendships last for life, unshakable and firmly welded; The People never forget the bonds and responsibility of friendship. Despite all the changes coming into the lives of the Navajos, at least one thing remained as in days gone by: they still considered the "old" trader their best friend, father, son, and brother, all combined. He remained the one to go to for help and advice. They were firmly convinced he could and would stand by them.

One day while Millie and I were running Two Guns, we drove over to Sunrise Trading Post, which we had not seen in almost thirty years. Of course, we expected changes, but what had happened to old Sunrise really saddened us. A succession of traders had very nearly destroyed all business. The stone building had cracked apart and seemed ready to fall down. The huge store had been cut to a third of its former space, and bedrooms had been constructed behind a flimsy partition. The former living quarters, which used to have a beautiful Hopi pottery plaque and a paneled fireplace, had been turned into a ready-made clothing room. As we drove on west, neither of us felt like commenting. Along with other old trading posts, the days of Sunrise were numbered. On the plateau to the west, where wind always blows hardest, the government had completed a boarding-school plant. Farther on, a natural gas pumping station had been established on main lines to California, affording employment to twenty-five Navajos, who all lived in company-owned, modern houses with TV sets.

Turning off the Flagstaff road, passing the crumbling walls of old Wolf Post, we went in against the canyon rim of the Little Colorado River. Here a narrow hole that pitched down through solid stone had once given entrance to an aboriginal cliff village hanging high over the river below. At one time the ruins were crowded with people who traveled there to crawl in and investigate them, but a great rock had shifted to block the entrance; no one could now descend into the ruins. Backtracking, we returned to the flat cliff at ancient Wolf Post. Herders, penning sheep inside the standing, bare walls, had nearly destroyed what was left of it. Broken, sun-purpled wine bottles, square nails, and cartridge hulls littered the ground.

Only once more during our stay at Two Guns did we venture to the sites of trading posts that had been established, thriving businesses only a few years before. There was something heartrending and sorrowful about their eternal, wind-whispering silence. It did no good going back, trying to remember the pioneering people who were once happy there and the vanished community life surrounding them. As we looked back, our forty years of involvement with the trading posts seemed short. They were so full, so rich in experience and lessons in living. But they were long enough. Despite pleas of Navajo friends, who begged us to stay, we felt it was time to go. Although we left our last trading post in 1961, the memories of our life in the harsh and beautiful land of the Navajos are as strong as the friendships we made among The People.

Books by
Gladwell Richardson

The books listed below are known to have been published by Gladwell Grady Richardson under the various pen names shown. This list was verified as of the mid-1980s; it may be as long as another decade before a full bibliography of his novels can be authenticated.

Blacksnake, George

Buffalo Head. Frederick Muller, 1956 (see also Richardson, Gladwell, *De Man Met Het Buffelmasker*)
Cross Kady. Frederick Muller, 1957 (see also Richardson, Gladwell, *Harde Leermeesters*)
Riders of the Chaparral. Clerke & Cockeran, 1950
Showdown at Unitaw. Frederick Muller, 1955 (see also No Author Named, *Ein Fremder Mann in Unitaw*)
Sixgun Pass. Frederick Muller, 1956 (see also Warner, Frank, *De Dood Mist Een Kans*)
Squaw Trapper. Frederick Muller, 1955
Wagon Boss. Frederick Muller, 1956

Clarkson, Ormand

Dust on the Sage. Ward Lock, 1938
Gun Thunder. Ward Lock, 1938
Mystery Mountain. No publisher or date listed
River Rogues. Ward Lock, 1938
The Haunted Corral. Ward Lock, 1939
The Kingdom of Mesquite. Ward Lock, 1940
The River of Lost Men. Ward Lock, 1937
The Scorpion. Ward Lock, 1939
Thunder Mountain. No publisher or date listed

Coleman, Buck

Big Tracks. John Lane, 1956

Colson, Laramie

Hardstone Range. Rich & Cowan, no publishing date listed (see also Colson, Laramie, *Raiders of the San Blas*; Warner, Frank, *Treinrovers*)
Marshall from Denver. Rich & Cowan, 1956 (see also Ringo, John Robert, *Holdup at Grizzly Gulch* original title; No Author Named, *Sixgun Marshall*; Warner, Frank, *Morgan Houndt Vol!*)

Raiders of the San Blas. Rich & Cowan, no publishing date listed (see also Colson, Laramie, *Hardstone Range* original title; Warner, Frank, *Trein-rovers*)

Silver Dollar Mine. John Long, 1958

Wild Cowboy. Rich & Cowan, 1956 (see also Warner, Frank, *De Opstandige Cowboy*)

Haines, John S.

Six-Shooter Sheriff. Wright & Brown, 1942

James, Cary

Gunslick Ramrod. Herbert Jenkins, 1955

Revolverkid. Omnia Verlag, 1956 (see also James, Cary, *The .45 Kid*)

The .45 Kid. Herbert Jenkins, 1955 (see also James, Cary, *Revolverkid*)

Jones, Calico

Bugles Before Dawn. Better Pubs., Inc., 1951

Bullet Proof Cowboy. Mills & Boon, 1958

Cattle King. Best Publications, 1950

Dancing Rabbit Creek. Mills & Boon, 1955 (see also No Author Named, *Schurkenstreken*)

Der Raubschatz in den Puma Bergen. Omnia Verlag, 1956 (see also Jones, Calico, *Outlaws Two*)

Fighting Cowboy. Mills & Boon, 1957

Foxfire Creek. T.V. Boardman & Co. Ltd., 1951

Long Riders. United Anglo-American Book Co., no date listed

Outlaws Two. W. Foulsham, 1953 (see also Jones, Calico, *Der Raubschatz in den Puma Bergen*)

Sixshooter Country. Mills & Boon, 1957 (see also Warner, Frank, *Revolvertaal*)

The Fort (A Ranger From Texas). Partridge Pubs., 1952

Vermilion Outlaw. No publisher or date listed

Kent, Pete

Canyon of Hunted Men. Wright & Brown, 1940

Rustler Basin. Arthur Barker, 1956

The Blue Hills. Wright & Brown, 1939

The Chief of Hell's Gap. Wright & Brown, 1938

The Sunset Rider. Wright & Brown, 1938

Kildare, Maurice

Border Raider. Ward Lock, 1950

Cowboy Joe. Ward Lock, 1939

Dude Scanlon. Ward Lock, 1950

Emigrant Gap. Mills & Boon, 1955

Lariat Law. Mills & Boon, 1955 (see also Richardson, Gladwell, *De Wet Van de Strop*)

Mesa Gunmen. No publisher or date listed

Rio Guns. Ward Lock, 1939

Stormy. Mills & Boon, 1954

The Trail to Nowhere. Ward Lock, 1938

Klarkson, Ormand

Arizona Guns. Ward Lock, 1937
The Boothill Kid. Ward Lock, 1937

McAdams, Charles

Rattle Your Spurs. Arthur Barker, 1955

Maxwell, Grant

Action at Timberline. Rich & Cowan, 1957
Texas Trouble. Rich & Cowan, 1957

Meador, Higgs

Stagecoach 'Round the Bend. Arthur Barker, 1956

O'Riley, Warren

Der Grobe Stern. Omnia Verlag, 1956
Forbidding Canyons. W. H. Allen, 1955
Mountain Ambush. W. H. Allen, 1957 (*Mazatal Gun* original title)
The Fireaway Kid. Odhams Press, 1949
Unfenced Meadows. Arthur Barker, 1951
Vigilante Man. No publisher or date listed
Wild Vermilion. W. H. Allen, 1958

Richardson, Gladwell

Arizona Ranger. W. Foulsham, 1949
Bandieten Temmer. De Combinatie, 1957 (see also Richardson, Gladwell, *Bandit Tamer*)
Bandit Tamer. Wright & Brown, 1955 (see also Richardson, Gladwell, *Bandieten Temmer*)
Beyond the Far Hills. W. Foulsham, 1946 (also titled *Kinky Jordan's Trail*; see also Richardson, Gladwell, *Revolverrauch in Pistol*)
Blood Geld. De Combinatie, 1959 (see also Richardson, Gladwell, *Hang the Cowboy High*)
Blood on Muddy Boggy. Wright & Brown, 1947 (also titled *Trigger Fingers*)
Cattle Anny. Wright & Brown, 1958
Cutthroat Trail. Wright & Brown, 1957
De Man Met Het Buffelmasker. De Combinatie, 1958 (see also Blacksnake, George, *Buffalo Head*)
De Wet Van De Strop. De Combinatie, 1957 (see also Kildare, Maurice, *Lariat Law*)
Desert Chariots. W. Foulsham, 1946 (see also Richardson, Gladwell, *Red Moore on the Trail*)
Desert Man. Ward Lock, 1938
Desperados' Range. W. H. Allen, 1955
Dreary River. Ward Lock, 1939
El Vaquero. J. Coker Press, 1949
Greasewood Sink. Mills & Boon, no date listed (see also Richardson, Gladwell, *Nachtruiters*)
Gun Tornado. W. Foulsham, 1946

Guns on the Chugwater. Mills & Boon, 1956 (see also Richardson, Gladwell, *Moordend Lood*)

Hacienda Gold. J. Coker Press, 1949 (see also Richardson, Gladwell, *Hacienda-Goud*)

Hacienda-Goud. De Combinatie, no date listed (see also Richardson, Gladwell, *Hacienda Gold*)

Hang the Cowboy High. Mills & Boon, 1956 (see also Richardson, Gladwell, *Blood Geld*)

Hangman's Bait. J. Coker Press, 1949 (see also No Author Named, *Galgenaas*; Richardson, Gladwell, *Zwei Desperados*)

Harde Leermeesters. De Combinatie, 1958 (see also Blacksnake, George, *Cross Kady*)

Head of the Draw. Frederick Muller, 1959

Heldendad. De Combinatie, 1958 (see also Winslowe, John, *Ride Yonder*)

Het Recht Van Het Western. De Combinatie, 1958 (see also Richardson, Gladwell, *Pards of Far Trail* and *Western Justice*)

Iron Mountain. Arthur Barker, 1955

Killer Outlaw. W. Foulsham, 1951

Land of Men Unhung. Ward Lock, 1937

Lightning Lomax. Mills & Boon, 1955 (*Sudden Slade* original title)

Lobo Country. Frederick Muller, 1958

Mesa Springs. Arthur Barker, 1958

Montana Ruiter. De Combinatie, 1959 (*Hellfire Gulch* original title; see also Richardson, Gladwell, *The Rider of Montana*)

Monument Pass. W. H. Allen, 1958

Moordend Lood. De Combinatie, 1958 (see also Richardson, Gladwell, *Guns on the Chugwater*)

Nachtruiters. De Combinatie, 1959 (see also Richardson, Gladwell, *Greasewood Sink*)

Night Marshall. W. Foulsham, 1955

Night Riders. Ward Lock, 1939

No Name Range. Arthur Barker, 1955

Opejaagd! De Combinatie, 1958 (see also Richardson, Gladwell, *Rider From Rifle Rock*)

Pards of Far Trail. W. H. Allen, 1957 (see also Richardson, Gladwell, *Het Recht Van Het Western* and *Western Justice*)

Ranch Der Verschrikking. De Combinatie, 1957 (see also No Author Named, *Jeopardy Ranch*)

Range Dust. British Empire, 1941

Red Moore on the Trail. W. Foulsham, 1946 (see also Richardson, Gladwell, *Desert Chariots*)

Revolverrauch In Pistol. Omnia Verlag, 1956 (also titled *Kinky Jordan's Trail*; see also Richardson, Gladwell, *Beyond the Far Hills*)

Ride the Last Mile. Wright & Brown, 1958

Rider From Rifle Rock. Wright & Brown, 1957 (see also Richardson, Gladwell, *Opejaagd!*)

Rider of Lost Places. Herbert Jenkins, 1955

Riders of the Long Rope. Ward Lock, 1936

Riders Up. Ward Lock, 1950
Rio Colorado. No publisher or date listed
Roll On Little Doggies. Ward Lock, 1939
Rondo's Man. Mills & Boon, 1959
Rustler Vengeance. Mills & Boon, 1958
Short Rope for Rustlers. J. Coker Press, 1949 (see also No Author Named,
    Rob der Racher and *Voor Veedieven De Strop*)
Silber Im Rio Tuca. Helios (Hilgendorff Verlag), 1952 (see also Richardson,
    Gladwell, *The Gun Drifter*)
Silver Dollar Basin. W. Foulsham, 1946
Sorry Cowtown. Mills & Boon, 1955
Spurs. Ward Lock, 1940
Star Valley. No publisher or date listed
Stoney Butte. Wright & Brown, 1958
Sun in the West. Ward Lock, 1936
The Black Vulture. Ward Lock, 1937
The Border Eagle. Ward Lock, 1950
The Eagles Outlaws. Ward Lock, 1946
The Gun Drifter. J. Coker Press, 1949 (see also Richardson, Gladwell, *Silber
    Im Rio Tuca*)
The Jinglebob. Ward Lock, 1942
The Killers of Strawberry Gap. W. Foulsham, 1945
The Rider of Montana. MacDonald, 1956 (*Hellfire Gulch* original title; see
    also Richardson, Gladwell, *Montana Ruiter*)
The Singing Sands. Wright & Brown, 1948
The Three Mavericks. Ward Lock, 1944
The Train Robber. Arthur Barker, 1958
Thunder on the Range. Ward Lock, 1940
Timberline Grass. No publisher or date listed
Tophand. Wright & Brown, 1954
Two-Bit Puncher. Arthur Barker, 1958
Utah. Ward Lock, 1938
Valley of the Powdre. J. Coker Press, 1949
Wanhoopsdaad. De Combinatie, 1957 (see also Winslow, John, *Dry Gulcher's
    Creek*)
Western Justice. W. H. Allen, 1957 (see also Richardson, Gladwell, *Het Recht
    Van Het Western* and *Pards of Far Trail*)
White Horse Mesa. Ward Lock, 1941
Zwei Desperados. De Combinatie, 1953 (see also Richardson, Gladwell, *Hang-
    man's Bait*; No Author Named, *Galgenaas*)

Ringo, John Robert

Holdup at Grizzly Gulch. No publisher or date listed (see also Colson, Lara-
    mie, *Marshall from Denver*; No Author Named, *Sixgun Marshall*; Warner,
    Frank, *Morgan Houndt Vol!*)
X-Handled Gun. Mills & Boon, 1954

Teton, Don

The Ghost Hills. Panther Books, 1958

Warner, Frank

Arizona Raider. Rich & Cowan, 1955 (see also Warner, Frank, *Cripple Creek Kid* and *Die Geier Von Arizona*)

Bronko. Rich & Cowan, 1956 (also titled *Vengeance at Oak Springs;* see also Warner, Frank, *Wraak Kent Geen Grenzen*)

Cripple Creek Kid. Rich & Cowan, 1955 (see also Warner, Frank, *Arizona Raider* and *Die Geier Von Arizona*)

De Dood Dreight. De Combinatie, 1956 (see also Warner, Frank, *Die Desperados Von Indianola* and *Gunman's Town*)

De Dood Mist Een Kans. De Combinatie, 1958 (see also Blacksnake, George, *Sixgun Pass*)

De Opstandige Cowboy. De Combinatie, 1957 (see also Colson, Laramie, *Wild Cowboy*)

Die Desperados Von Indianola. Omnia Verlag, 1956 (see also Warner, Frank, *De Dood Dreight* and *Gunman's Town*)

Die Geier Von Arizona. Omnia Verlag, 1956 (see also Warner, Frank, *Cripple Creek Kid* and *Arizona Raider*)

Die Marder Vom Jade Creek. Omnia Verlag, 1956 (see also Warner, Frank, *Jade Creek* and *Outlaws of Jade Creek*)

Een Cowboy Neemt Wraak! De Combinatie, 1959 (see also Warner, Frank, *Rustlers of Crooked River*)

Gunman's Town. No publisher listed, 1954 (see also Warner, Frank, *De Dood Dreight* and *Die Desperados Von Indianola*)

Guns at Shadow Creek. Rich & Cowan, 1956 (see also Warner, Frank, *Recht Is Recht*)

Hands Up! De Combinatie, 1958 (see also Warner, Frank, *Reach for Your Guns*)

Jade Creek. Rich & Cowan, no date listed (see also Warner, Frank, *Outlaws of Jade Creek* and *Die Marder Vom Jade Creek*)

Morgan Houndt Vol! De Combinatie, 1958 (see also Colson, Laramie, *Marshall From Denver;* No Author Named, *Sixgun Marshall*; Ringo, John Robert, *Holdup at Grizzly Gulch*)

Mountain Boss. Rich & Cowan, 1954

Outlaws of Jade Creek. Rich & Cowan, 1953 (see also Warner, Frank, *Jade Creek* and *Die Marder Vom Jade Creek*)

Reach for Your Guns. John Long, 1957 (*The Stray* original title; see also Warner, Frank, *Hands Up!*)

Recht Is Recht. De Combinatie, 1958 (see also Warner, Frank, *Guns at Shadow Creek*)

Red River Showdown. John Long, 1959 (*Medicine Man* original title)

Revolvertaal. De Combinatie, 1959 (see also Jones, Calico, *Sixshooter Country*)

Rustlers of Crooked River. Rich & Cowan, 1955 (*Ranahan* original title; see also Warner, Frank, *Een Cowboy Neemt Wraak*)

Books by Gladwell Richardson

Sundown Land. Wright & Brown, 1943
The Branded Maverick. Wright & Brown, 1942
The Outlaw Kid. Wright & Brown, 1942
Treinrovers. De Combinatie, 1958 (see also Colson, Laramie, *Raiders of the San Blas* and *Hardstone Range*)
Wraak Kent Geen Grenzen. De Combinatie, 1958

Winslowe, John

Arizona. Ward Lock, 1939
Bad Man. Ward Lock, 1950 (see also Winslowe, John, *Duivels Kinderen*)
Der Marshall Von Diablo. Omnia Verlag, 1956
Der Todesgambler. Omnia Verlag, 1956 (see also Winslowe, John, *Tinhorn Gambler*)
Dry Gulchers' Creek. Mills & Boon, 1956 (see also Richardson, Gladwell, *Wanhoopsdaad*)
Duivels Kinderen. Vitgeverij De Steenuil Hoorn, 1951 (see also Winslowe, John, *Bad Man*)
Pistol Packer. Ward Lock, 1953
Ranger's Star. Ward Lock, 1951
Red Rock. Ward Lock, 1942 (see also No Author Named, *Red Rock Der Banditenjager*; Winslowe, John, *Red Rock of the YB Ranch*)
Red Rock of the YB Ranch. Omnia Verlag, 1956 (see also No Author Named, *Red Rock Der Banditenjager*; Winslowe, John, *Red Rock*)
Ride Yonder. Mills & Boon, 1957 (see also Richardson, Gladwell, *Heldendad*)
Sundown. Ward Lock, 1939
The Killer of Kamerun. Ward Lock, 1937 (see also No Author Named, *Killer of Shifty Sands*)
The Marshall of Diablo. Ward Lock, 1953 (see also Winslowe, John, *Der Marshall Von Diablo*)
The Rattlesnake Range. Ward Lock, 1938
Thief River. Ward Lock, 1938
Tinhorn Gambler. Mills & Boon, 1955 (see also Winslowe, John, *Der Todesgambler*)
Whispering Mountain. No publisher listed, 1939
Zeb of Rustler Mountain. Ward Lock, 1950
Zero Range. Mills & Boon, 1954

No Author Named

Ein Fremder Mann In Unitaw. Erich Pabel Verlag, 1956 (see also Blacksnake, George, *Showdown at Unitaw*)
Galgenaas. De Combinatie, no date listed (see also Richardson, Gladwell, *Hangman's Bait* and *Zwei Desperados*)
Jeopardy Ranch. W. H. Allen, 1955 (see also Richardson, Gladwell, *Ranch Der Verschrikking*)
Killer of Shifty Sands. No publisher or date listed (see also Winslowe, John, *The Killer of Kamerun*)
Red Rock Der Banditenjager. Omnia Verlag, 1956 (see also Winslowe, John, *Red Rock* and *Red Rock at YB Ranch*)

Rob Der Racher. Helios, 1952 (see also No Author Named, *Voor Veedieven De Strop*; Richardson, Gladwell, *Short Rope for Rustlers*)

Schurkenstreken. De Combinatie, 1957 (see also Jones, Calico, *Dancing Rabbit Creek*)

Sixgun Marshall. No publisher or date listed (see also Colson, Laramie, *Marshall From Denver*; Ringo, John Robert, *Holdup at Grizzly Gulch*; Warner, Frank, *Morgan Houndt Vol!*)

The Thin Gunman. Wright & Brown, 1941 (*Trail Wolves* original title)

Trail Wolves. Wright & Brown, 1941 (see also No Author Named, *The Thin Gunman*)

Voor Veedieven De Strop. De Combinatie, 1954 (see also No Author Named, *Rob Der Racher*; Richardson, Gladwell, *Short Rope for Rustlers*)

Suggested Readings

Articles

Adams, Bruce. "Sketches of a Trading Post." *The Quarterly of the Southwest Association on Indian Affairs, Inc.* (Summer 1975):9–11.

Auerback, Herbert S. "Old Trails, Old Forts, Old Trappers and Traders." *Utah Historical Quarterly* 9 (December 1941):13–68.

Boyce, George A. "Do Navajo Indians Still Need Trading Posts?" *The* (Los Angeles) *Branding Iron* (December 1973):11–12.

Brown, Jo. "Indian Traders of North America." *Arizona Highways* (May 1973):36–39.

DeLauer, Marjel. "A Century of Indian Traders and Trading Posts." *Arizona Highways* (March 1975):6–14.

Dooven, Alice Den, and Gaylord Staveley. "Each One Is a Sandstone Supermarket." *Western Gateways* (Winter 1967):24–27.

Hammond, Al. "The Dirty Brothers. . . ." *The* (Los Angeles) *Branding Iron* (March 1969):10–11.

Hubbell, John Lorenzo. "Fifty Years An Indian Trader," as told to J. E. Hogg. *Touring Topics* (December 1930):24–49, 51.

Locke, Patrice. "The Rise and Fall of the Indian Trader." *The Indian Trader* 12 (December 1984):2–8.

Lowe, Sam. "The Little World of Black Mountain." *Arizona Highways* (August 1979):33–36.

McCoy, Ron. "Navajo Code Talkers of World War II." *American West* 18 (Nov.–Dec. 1981):67–73.

Mott, Dorothy Challis. "Don Lorenzo Hubbell of Ganado." *Arizona Historical Review* 4 (January 1931):45–51.

Richardson, Gladwell. "Bonanza in the Ghost Past." *Desert Magazine* (April 1966):12–15.

Utley, Robert M. "The Reservation Trader in Navajo History." *El Placio* 68 (March 1961):5–27.

Wetherill, Hilda. "The Trading Post, Letters from a Primitive Land." *The Atlantic Monthly* (September 1928):289–300.

Winslowe, John R. "Navajo Traders for Many Moons." *True West* (April 1969):10–14, 63–69.

Suggested Readings

Wright, Kathryn. "Trader Preserves a Piece of History." *The Indian Trader* 10 (November 1979):11, 18, 19, 42, 43.

Books

Aberle, David Friend, and Omer D. Stewart. *Navaho and Ute Peyotism: A Chronological and Distributional Study.* Boulder: University of Colorado Press, 1957.

Adair, John. *The Navajo and Pueblo Silversmiths.* Norman: University of Oklahoma Press, 1944.

Adams, William Y. Shonto. *A Study of the Role of the Trader in a Modern Navajo Community.* Washington D. C.: U.S. Government Printing Office, 1963.

Amsden, Charles Avery. *Navajo Weaving.* Santa Ana, California: Fine Arts Press, 1934.

Boyd, Dennis. "Trading and Weaving: An American-Navajo Symbiosis." M. A. thesis, University of Colorado, 1979.

Chanin, Abe, with Mildred Chanin. *This Land, These Voices: A Different View of Arizona History in the Words of Those Who Lived It.* Flagstaff: North-land Press, 1977.

Counselor, Jim, and Ann Counselor. *Wild, Woolly and Wonderful.* New York: Vantage Press, 1954.

Downs, James F. *The Navajo.* New York: Holt, Rinehart and Winston, 1972.

Dutton, Bertha Pauline. *Navajo Weaving Today,* rev. ed. Santa Fe: Museum of New Mexico Press, 1975.

Hegemann, Elizabeth Compton. *Navajo Trading Days.* Albuquerque: University of New Mexico Press, 1963.

Hollister, U. S. *The Navajo and His Blanket.* Glorieta, New Mexico: Rio Grande Press, 1903.

Iverson, Peter. *The Navajo Nation.* Westport, Connecticut: Greenwood Press, 1981.

James, George Wharton. *Indian Blankets and Their Makers.* New York: Dover Publications, 1974.

James, H. L. *Posts and Rugs: The Story of Navajo Rugs and Their Homes.* Globe, Arizona: Southwest Parks and Monuments Association, 1976.

Kelly, Lawrence C. *The Navajo Indians and Federal Indian Policy, 1900–1935.* Tuscon: University of Arizona Press, 1968.

Kluckhohn, Clyde, and Dorthea Leighton. *The Navajo.* Cambridge: Harvard University Press, 1946.

Lee, Albert Hugh, and Ella Ruth Lee Danoff. *Gaamaliitsoh Indian Trader: An Autobiography of Albert Hugh Lee (1897–1976).* Mesa, Arizona: Lofgreen's, Inc., 1982.

McNitt, Frank. *The Indian Traders.* Oklahoma City: University of Oklahoma Press, 1962.

Newcomb, Franc. *Hosteen Klah: Navajo Medicine Man and Sand Painter.* Norman: University of Oklahoma Press, 1964.

———. *Navajo Folk Tales.* Santa Fe, New Mexico: Museum of Navaho Ceremonial Art, 1967.

———. *Navajo Neighbors.* Norman: University of Oklahoma Press, 1966.

———. *Navajo Omens and Taboos.* Santa Fe: Rydal Press, 1980.

Parman, Donald L. *The Navajos and the New Deal.* New Haven: Yale University Press, 1976.

Reichard, Gladys Amanda. *Spider Woman: A Story of Navajo Weavers and Chanters.* New York: MacMillan, 1934.

———. *Weaving a Navajo Blanket.* New York: Dover Publications, 1974.

Reno, Philip. *Mother Earth, Father Sky, and Economic Development: Navajo Resources and Their Use.* Albuquerque: University of New Mexico Press, 1981.

Rodee, Marion E. *Southwestern Weaving.* Albuquerque: University of New Mexico Press, 1977.

Swanton, John Reed. *Indian Tribes of the American Southwest.* Seattle: Shorey Books, 1968.

U.S. Federal Trade Commission. *The Trading Post System on the Navajo Reservation, June 1973.* Washington D. C.: U. S. Government Printing Office, 1973.

Van Valkenburgh, Richard F. *A Short History of the Navajo People.* Edited by Clyde Kluckhohn. New York: Garland Publications, 1974.

Wetherill, Louisa (Wade), and Frances Gillmor. *Traders to the Navajos: The Story of the Wetherills of Kayenta.* Albuquerque: University of New Mexico Press, 1953.

Young, Robert W. *A Political History of the Navajo Tribe.* Tsaile, Arizona: Navajo Community College Press, 1978.

Yost, Billie (Williams). *Bread Upon the Sands.* Foreword by Merle Armitage. Caldwell, Idaho: Caxton Printers, 1958.

Index

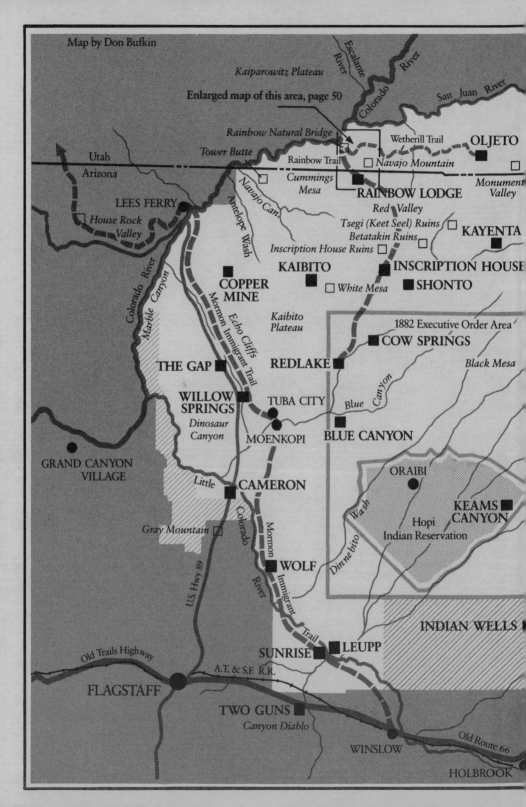

Map by Don Bufkin

Kaiparowitz Plateau

Escalante River

Colorado River

San Juan River

Enlarged map of this area, page 50

Rainbow Natural Bridge

Wetherill Trail

OLJETO

Utah

Arizona

Tower Butte

Rainbow Trail

□ *Navajo Mountain*

Cummings Mesa

RAINBOW LODGE

Monument Valley

LEES FERRY

Navajo Can.

Antelope Wash

Red Valley

Tsegi (Keet Seel) Ruins □

KAYENTA

□ *House Rock Valley*

Inscription House Ruins □

Betatakin Ruins □

COPPER MINE

KAIBITO

□ *White Mesa*

INSCRIPTION HOUSE

■ **SHONTO**

Colorado River

Marble Canyon

Echo Cliffs

Mormon Immigrant Trail

Kaibito Plateau

1882 Executive Order Area

COW SPRINGS

Black Mesa

THE GAP

REDLAKE

Blue Canyon

WILLOW SPRINGS

TUBA CITY

Dinosaur Canyon

MOENKOPI

BLUE CANYON

GRAND CANYON VILLAGE

Little

CAMERON

Colorado

Gray Mountain □

ORAIBI

Wash

KEAMS CANYON ■

Hopi Indian Reservation

Dinne bito

Mormon

WOLF

INDIAN WELLS

US Hwy 89

Immigrant

River

Trail

Old Trails Highway

SUNRISE

LEUPP

FLAGSTAFF

A.T. & S.F. R.R.

TWO GUNS

Canyon Diablo

WINSLOW

Old Route 66

HOLBROOK